T0338105

The Confessions of Odysseus

Other Books of Interest from St. Augustine's Press

Nalin Ranasinghe, *Socrates and the Gods:*
How to read Plato's Euthyphro, Apology and Crito

Nalin Ranasinghe, *Socrates in the Underworld: On Plato's Gorgias*

Nalin Ranasinghe (editor), *Logos and Eros: Essays Honoring Stanley Rosen*

Stanley Rosen, *Plato's Statesman: The Web of Politics*

Stanley Rosen, *The Language of Love: An Interpretation of Plato's Phaedrus*

Stanley Rosen, *Metaphysics in Ordinary Language*

Stanley Rosen, *Platonic Productions: Theme and Variations: The Gilson Lectures*

Stanley Rosen, *Plato's Symposium*

Alexandre Kojève, *The Idea of Determinism*

Gabriel Marcel, *Invisible Threshold: Two Plays by Gabriel Marcel*

Will Morrisey, *Herman Melville's Ship of State*

Daniel J. Mahoney, *The Other Solzhenitsyn:*
Telling the Truth about a Misunderstood Writer and Thinker

Seth Benardete, *The Archaeology of the Soul:*
Platonic Readings in Ancient Poetry and Philosophy

Seth Benardete, *Achilles and Hector: The Homeric Hero*

Seth Benardete, *Herodotean Inquiries*

Aristotle, *De Anima, or about the Soul*

Zbigniew Janowski, *Homo Americanus:*
The Rise of the Totalitarian Democracy in America

D. Q. McInerny, *Being Ethical*

Peter Kreeft, *Ethics for Beginners*

Harvey Flaumenhaft, *Insights and Manipulations: What Classical Geometry*
Looked like at Its Peak, and How It Was Transformed – a Guidebook

Klaus Vondung, *The Pursuit of Unity and Perfection in Human History*

Marvin R. O'Connell, *Telling Stories that Matter: Memoirs and Essays*

The Confessions of Odysseus

by Nalin Ranasinghe

St. Augustine's Press
South Bend, Indiana

Manufactured in the United States of America.

1 2 3 4 5 6   26 25 24 23 22 21

Library of Congress Control Number: 2021934650

∞ The paper used in this publication meets the minimum requirements of the American National Standard for Information Sciences - Permanence of Paper for Printed Materials, ANSI Z39.48-1984.

St. Augustine's Press
www.staugustine.net

Table of Contents

Preface

"We ultimately read Homer not for myths about gods
but for the truth about man and the human state."
—Nalin Ranasinghe

The *Odyssey*, according to Ranasinghe, was the origin of Western Civilization. Not the *Iliad* and the *Odyssey* together, but only the later, less popular but also less understood of Homer's epics. The *Iliad*, in his view, was more like a stage-setting, a prelude for a great drama of the human struggle for glory and triumph, for self-knowledge and life's meaning. It is not that the blind bard did not succeed in making us visualize the shining armor of Achilles and the triumph of his sword. In fact, Homer did it so well that his feat tricked many into imitating the most celebrated warrior of Hellas and prevented us from realizing that the siege and defeat of Troy were a tragic fall that nearly resulted in the undoing of that blossoming civilization. The reflections on Achilles' dazzled even Odysseus, despite his being there to witness the damaged soul of Achilles, as well as the carnage which concluded the irresponsible and greedy adventure to Troy. The central message of the *Iliad*, claims Ranasinghe, is that Achilles and warriors like him—of any war, of all times—need to be pitied, not emulated.

The Confessions of Odysseus is an account of why the great war hero, Odysseus, could not come back to his native Ithaca, so long as he did not resist the temptation of conquest and confront self-deceptions. Instead of rushing triumphantly back, Odysseus returns ten years later, ignobly disguised as an ugly beggar. "The confessions of Odysseus" are the revelations of a lost soul, as well as of a misguided civilization. Odysseus has to reorder his priorities and purify his soul by first renouncing his false heroic identity. Violence and lust are for cowards, asserts Ranasinghe, and Odysseus must win the trust of those he has left behind when he went to chase glory and treasure in a disgraceful war. He has to realize that the greatest battles are not those waged in far-away lands, but those fought at home; not those contested while hiding behind the shining armor but those fought while standing face to face with one's child, spouse, or parent. Before this can happen, Athena sets several tests for Odysseus to prove he has learned from his errors and is ready for the role she has in mind for him. With the help of Athena, not Ares, Odysseus shall first restore his humanity and then recover his homeland from the ills of war. Athena will help Odysseus defeat the external enemies, but he must overcome the enemies lurking within his soul. His courage to undergo this transformation must be born of humility and love, not provided *deus ex machina*.

Disguised as a beggar and calling himself "no-body," upon his eventual return to Ithaca, Odysseus meets his loyal slave Eumaeus. Odysseus soon realizes that this swineherd, once educated by his mother Antikliea (whose name literally means "anti-glory"), is a better ruler than himself. Eumaeus embodies the law of hospitality and traditional moral code, which Odysseus, his war comrades, as well Penelope's suitors abuse continuously. Eumaeus rescues his body; Odysseus will now get a chance to rescue his soul.

Like the prodigal son of the Bible, after years of trials, Odysseus finds his way home. Unlike his biblical counterpart, Odysseus never falls down on his knees and never asks for forgiveness. In the ancient Greek world, the theme was reconciliation, not forgiveness. Greek gods were intimately involved with their heroes in their quests and their adventures, in their deeds and misdeeds. It was these gods who inspired the passions of human protagonists; they led them to rage and ecstasies. But the protagonists should not be seen as the puppets in the theater of the divine amusement. The same gods were willing to guide them toward self-knowledge and transformation, while also gaining much in return. Athena's interventions and revelations guided Odysseus in this process. Despite his relations with his son, his father, and especially his wife, Odysseus was radically incomplete without Athena. She guided him to confess the meaning of many misdeeds he performed, for such confessions do not pertain merely to the facts and a sheer listing of them, but to their meaning and their wider implications.

For Homer, emphasizes Ranasinghe, the relationship between gods and human beings is never one-sided. While it is easier to grasp that Odysseus was incomplete without Athena, Ranasinghe argues that the goddess of war and wisdom herself could not fully exist without Odysseus. Although born from Zeus's head, Athena became animated only through the human being she was guiding. She sometimes appeared as herself, at other times disguised. Through the actions of Odysseus, as well as those of Achilles, Hector, Priam, and other heroes, Athena and other Olympian gods underwent change. Gods could see their images in human beings and transform through them. Human passion and divine order are inextricably connected. As Ranasinghe puts it, "It seems that the very imperfection of a mortal hero serves as the means by which gods gain their more secure self-knowledge; by this, they will then be able to inspire and evoke the fullest potential in our souls."

This epiphany of the double relationship of human beings and gods is extremely important for Ranasinghe's recognition of the *Odyssey's* pivotal role for our civilization. For Homer, neither human beings nor Olympian gods are ever perfect. Nor are they simply fallen. The truth is somewhere in between. Whatever may be in store for the Olympian gods, Homer makes us recognize what this "truth in-between" means for human beings: by rejecting the lure of divine perfection and the trap of human fallenness, human beings can help one another, by friendship and love, and make meaningful and virtuous lives possible for themselves.

Ranasinghe urges us not to see Odysseus as either a "sacker of cities" or a "pathological liar," as he is often one-sidedly regarded to be. First, it is the cunning and courage of Odysseus, more than the rage and violence of Achilles, that brings about the capture of Troy. Even more importantly, like the rest of us, Odysseus is a being divided against himself. He is both a war criminal and a hero, the tortured soul who weeps over his vices while missing them at the same time. Odysseus goes to reconcile with his father, whom he approaches with a sense of deep guilt; nevertheless, he initially disguises his real identity for he could cannot help himself but play a little game first, before he can reveal who he is and why he comes. Once he does so, the bridge between them is reestablished.

In what is perhaps the culminating episode of the *Odyssey*, Odysseus and Penelope test each other to achieve their reconciliation, and they do so on several levels. Twenty years have passed since they last stood face to face, but their lives have unfolded in somewhat parallel, although inverted, fashions. Odysseus departed as the king of Ithaca and returns as a beggar. He left Penelope as the queen and now finds her struggling as an abandoned wife. While Odysseus had to fight the war by invading another country, Penelope has had to fight what Ranasinghe calls "the war's bastard imitation"—the home invasion of the seducers of Odysseus' palace. While Odysseus created the horse that enabled the Achaeans to deceive Troy, Penelope devised a worthy counterpart of her husband's trickery: the tapestry that she wove during the day and secretly unwove at night enabled her to hoodwink the suitors. Despite years of separation, Odysseus and Penelope quickly recognize each other at the most obvious level. But this is only the beginning of their process of reconciliation, for there is a considerable distinction between gross facts and subtle truths. Odysseus is, in fact, finally home, but is he home in truth? Is his heart in the right place? Is his human integrity preserved?

Much more could have been said about the magnificent Penelope, but Ranasinghe does not go in that direction. He recognizes that, like the faithful servant Eumaeus, who preserves the ancient law of hospitality, Penelope also safeguards something of the old: the bow of Odysseus. Ranasinghe comments upon this episode in his characteristic manner: "It is good to know that best resources of civilization were only hidden and not exhausted." But Ranasinghe does not pronounce the *Odyssey* the origin of our civilization on account of preserving the old and not paving the way toward a further development of that civilization.

The full account of this development would take us beyond the *Odyssey*, toward Socrates and Plato, and later toward Jesus. Ranasinghe maintains that Socrates clearly recognized the central messages of the *Odyssey* and its far greater significance than the *Iliad*. Socrates understood Odysseus as a post-heroic archetype who, after years of stumbling, comes to honestly confront the sacred values with all the erotic passion of his soul and with all the power of his quick mind. Odysseus' understanding with Athena, as well as his reconciliations with Telemachus, Penelope, and Laertius, pave the way for a new civilization in which the lyre should be far more important than the bow. It furthermore anticipates a new cosmic order and divine justice, which Ranasinghe believes came to fruition with the arrival of Jesus and the further expansion of Christianity.

This path of development has been anything but easy or straight. Just as many continue to be seduced by the adventures of Achilles, Ranasinghe laments that many have been persuaded by the authorities no lesser than those of Aristotle and Augustine to stray away from the lessons of the alliance of Odysseus-Socrates-Plato-Jesus. Despite these grand "A"-ces—Aristotle and Augustine, as well as Alexander and later Aquinas—Ranasinghe maintains that we should realize that neither human beings nor gods possess wisdom or perfection; nor are gods indifferent and human beings—incorrigible sinners. The *Odyssey* was the origin of Western civilization because it displayed for us a human being who is neither perfect nor impervious. In Ranasinghe's view, Odysseus is both the first recognizable human being and a model of curious and concupiscent human rationality that constantly strives toward the virtues of self-knowledge and moderation. Homer leads us to believe that the cosmos leans toward virtue, although its fundamental truths may be inherently unspeakable. This is the line of thought that Ranasinghe believes was further developed by Socrates, Plato, and Jesus, while being obscured by Aristotle, Augustine, and their followers. Homer's later epic and his central insights are, according to Ranasinghe, the most fertile soil on which a humane civilization can grow and flourish.

Before writing *The Confessions of Odysseus*, Nalin Ranasinghe devoted more than two decades to the studies and Socrates and Plato. They resulted in his Socrates trilogy: *The Soul of Socrates* (Cornell University Press, 2000), *Socrates in the Underworld: On Plato's* Gorgias (St. Augustine's Press, 2009), and *Socrates and the Gods: How to Read Plato's* Euthyphro, Apology, *and* Crito (St. Augustine's Press, 2012). While working on *The Confessions of Odysseus*, Nalin was also preparing a book on Shakespeare who, together with Homer and Plato, was his favorite writer. In a more distant future, he envisioned writing a book on Erasmus, and one on Voegelin as well. Nalin's premature death, on March 13, 2020, prevented him from reaching these goals.

Nalin's life was dedicated to friends and books. I was very fortunate to have been one of them and to have discussed many books with him. Never have I met anyone who read so much, so widely, and with such keenness. Books were more important to him than food or rest. Whatever he gained by reading books—and writing them—he was looking forward to sharing. Nalin's passion for learning and exchanging ideas were unmatched. The book in front of us, *The Confessions of Odyssey*, is testimony to his passionate soul and his powerful mind. As Nalin himself put it in the conclusion of this book, "A positive view of the soul's erotic powers for wondering and wandering can free us from falsely divinized idols of cave, caste, or creed … only when men can trust themselves enough to accept grace, admit to imperfection, and seek friendship will they be freed to echo Laertes' cry, 'There are gods indeed on high Olympus!'"

Predrag Cicovacki

Introduction
The Eternal Return of Achilles?

When I started this book, it was Obama's hour. He hoped to end the Bush wars, fix the economy and bridge our divisions. Homer's epic pointed towards a new Oresteia: a millennial trilogy going from oracular Oprah and orgulous Osama to obsequious Obama. But we fell from tragedy into a satyr play, an infernal Punch & Judy parody of Achilles' divine rage/*menis* at Troy. This internecine strife delights the ruling rich; taking sides like Olympians, they pit puppets against proles. Yes, they can plunder without risk (or even dismantle the state) if we're distracted by rage.

Our masque of *menis* began when a new Clytemnestra enraged the white proletariat; its honest but blind fury soon found a demagogic messiah. Thirsting for hot blood they declared war on the bi-coastal elite, "deep state," Jews, blacks, aliens, science, and the world. While this rebirth of rage thrills the mob, our hidden gods use its innate nihilism to push a crass agenda. As his war against all rages endlessly, their puppet-messiah mocks morality, fakes news, fosters crony capitalism, and gets America high on hatred. My tale ends apocalyptically when his puppeteers emerge to claim power over a bankrupt state and its alienated citizenry. Corporate tyranny, race war, cyber addiction, and debt slavery await if we do not stop this fake Achilles and the real rage he arouses.

That is why we must return to our origins—reading the *Iliad* and studying the blinding power rage exerts over city and soul before seeking Homer's cure for this disease. While the remedy is found in his tale of Odysseus' late return from Troy to save Ithaca, we must first ask our oracle the right question by decoding the *Iliad*. Homer has done most of our work for us; Socrates and Plato only retrieved what was implicit in his texts. They used a way of Midrash finely begun by Attic tragedy. This playful exegetic art was replaced by Aristotle's scholastic science, but it can yet be recovered.

Homer must be read as the wisest Greeks did, not for fantastic tales of the Olympians but because his myths reveal eternal constants of the human state: the soul's ruling passions and the possibility of knowing and educating these false gods. Wrestled with thus the *Iliad* becomes a cautionary tale, not one urging literal reading or mindless mimesis. It may always be that for the few who grasp Homer, many more will obey his gods or imitate his antiheroes; but the *Odyssey* hints that while its poet sees this potential for misuse, he is willing to take a noble risk and hope that eros can listen to and educate thumos. This faith is implicit in his tale of Achilles and the Trojan War. It is vital today that we see how the West's end resembles its angry origins, as depicted in the *Iliad*. This is why Homer is said to be as fresh as the morning newspaper. His wisdom may outlive our literacy.

Even as subservient propagandists try to justify the ways of kings to man as divine providence, genuine inspired poetry continues its subversive struggle to reveal how the true gods see the world in all its fragile beauty; to this extent bards are literally poet/makers or better, savior/refreshers of reality. Thus, the *Iliad* shows how a plague of *menis*, divine or divinized rage, infected our ancestors. But if this tragic poem is not read rightly—but seen as a paean to the glory of Ares/Achilles—this plague will return to punish our perverse piety and violent ignorance. Eris' apple that began the Trojan war thus resembles the forbidden fruit of Eden that brought us the Fall. These very forces, viral strife and toxic knowledge, have joined their baleful powers again today.

The Unlikely Aristeia of Hephaestus

Achilles is the starting point of each generation. Politicians raising new armies to kill each other rekindle his wrath and deploy his ever-alluring archetype for power and profit. He is used today in a way that would make even Agamemnon's gross shade blush. The formless souls of our young are stunted by easy access to infernal weapons; we become self-forgetting, superpowered and superfluous by technology. Hephaestus does not hobble anymore; by his artifice and Hobbes' counsel, the war of all against all has been escalated exponentially. No more Aphrodite's cuckolded spouse, this god now exceeds Ares and Athena in glory and might; he makes angry boys socially inept and economically useless, but able to take pagan vengeance on judgmental Christian culture.

In short, as Max Weber sagely saw, Hephaestus the deformed deity once thrown down from heaven, may now be seen to have restored the Olympians for a secular second sailing. Today it is a truth almost universally acknowledged that the Gods (worship them as Hera, Ares, Aphrodite and Dionysus or call them jealousy, violence, sex and alcohol as any good sociologist would) are more powerful than that Enlightenment paradigm, the educated post-Christian individual, could possibly imagine. The confidence in calculation that led men to abandon the Homeric, Platonic, or Christian soul and replace it with Aristotle's nous or silicon chips is thus proven by experience to be misplaced and unfounded. Even artificial intelligence or the much-anticipated event of the "Singularity" cannot save us from ourselves. Thus, if they have not done so already, the Gods and/or centrifugal forces of postmodernity have chosen to tear soul, city, and cosmos apart. Today technology has created a world where everyone from 8 to 80 strives to be Achilles at 18. Even worse, since our culture has been infantilized by promises of eternal youth and mindless pleasure, we are all concupiscent consumers: selfish suitors as ripe for slaughter as Penelope's wooers.

But the deeper question is if we, like Achilles, his comrades, and the stupid suitors, are trapped by Hephaestus in a Hobbesian Hell, a war of all against all from which there are only apparent armistices but never any true respite or relief. Even Jesus could not bring peace on earth. Then, after Christianity became the exclusive faith of a persecuting empire, St. Augustine rendered unto Caesar the perverse doctrine that due to original sin, life on earth is a dark state of continual deserved punishment; further, as peace is impossible, good Christians must meekly await the apocalypse. In this condition slavery is to be preferred over rule since there are fewer opportunities for sin. Augustine also denied self-knowledge; we only know ourselves as sinners. He asserts, and we must believe, that God/the Church knows us better than we know ourselves. He/it also predetermines whether or not we are good or evil, destined for heavenly bliss or hellish damnation.

Made to choose between undeserved slavery/sin and ostracized outlaw-hood, many men plea-bargained: they accepted the false charges against their soul and picked theocratic authoritarianism over raw anarchy. This craven wish for liberation from freedom trumps self-knowledge's lonely innocence. As Paul told the Romans, if human righteousness is possible then Christ died in vain.

Modern technology offers a way out of this dilemma. It promises the Epicurean earthly pleasure of a suitor's life to those who follow religion merely to enjoy the bliss of Christian heaven. As long as he renounces egalitarian ethics and spurns talk of human rights or justice, a bold man can enroll himself among the ranks of the elect and become a predator on a natural order that is destined to pass away. In time he may also come to enjoy the exquisite pleasure of chastising the natural slaves of creation. Augustinian Christianity, as both Luther and Calvin discovered, even gives a religious justification for this Darwinian distinction between the elect, the few mysteriously and undeservedly favored by God, and the losers left behind, unredeemed and doubly predestined. In short, we can enjoy a glorious life of a predator on earth and do so with a divine mandate. As the allied gods of terror and technology have brought us back to Homeric times, this book will claim that only Odysseus can redeem us from Achilles and set the cycle of civilization in motion again.

The Afterlife of Achilles

But does blind Homer presume to criticize shining Achilles? Is the hero of the *Iliad* truly more like one of Penelope's suitors than Odysseus? Is Achilles' tale but an epic tragedy, and not the West's founding epic of a betrayed hero? Can we hear his cry of rage and not hear Roland's horn in an empty forest? I will argue that instead of trying to emulate him, as Alexander did, we must instead resist the siren song of his splendid vices and opt for the way of life led by Odysseus and Socrates. Achilles and Alexander spelled death to civic friendship, even as their bellicosity seemingly united Hellas. Achilles' rage caused the Dark Ages as surely as Alexander ended Athenian freedom; Augustus then destroyed the Roman Republic and became universal landlord of a pacified empire. Later Augustine solidified this Thousand Year Reich by making a castrated Christianity its creed.

Perhaps only Odysseus and Socrates/Plato deliberately deviated from the brutal order wrought by Achilles' potent afterlife. Achilles, Aristotle, Alexander, and Augustus are ultimately imperial and un-Athenian in that they address *hoi polloi* in the imperative. It is presumed that their divine mandate, tradition or *force majeure* trumps any right of plebs to think, speak, or act for themselves. Silencing dissent is necessary once the "best"

4

lose reverence for the soul, their own included, and deign to rule directly over the huddled many they could have had killed. Statesmanship becomes a technique serving the Hobbesian imperative of keeping the people alive, orderly, and productive.

In short, the natural result of charismatic Caesarism is implicit slavery. And, if Caesarism is the telos of Achilles' immortal desire for glory, his legacy or body is empire. From each of Caesar's wounds grows a tradition, a Roman road or information superhighway, bringing civilization and trade smoothly down to every categorized part of a far-flung empire in time and space. There is no possibility of questioning precedent or going upstream by the liquid medium of dialectic; truth is reified as sacred tradition or even naturalized so that other possibilities cannot be imagined. Happiness is found when men pursue safe commodious pleasures under their landlord's shadow.

Shakespeare saw that while the evil men do out-lives them, the good is interred with their bones.

Even a benign Imperator will use bad epic poetry to elevate his deeds, power, and divine mandate; he does so at the expense of nobles like Glaucus and Sarpedon who looked to tragedy to hallow their heroic rights. Poetry rather than sheer force of arms is the ultimate basis of lasting power over men; it gives their hegemony divine sanction. This is why Homer is greater than Achilles; what is a hero without a poet? While Augustus rather than Aeneas is the hero of Virgil's artificial epic, Homer is dishonored when paid epigones turn his heroic tragedy into pseudo-epic founding poems.

This is why we must continually ponder if Homer sought to elevate Achilles to the unrivaled status he came to enjoy in pagan antiquity and every subsequent classical revival. In short, was Homer's original intent descriptive and cautionary or prescriptive and valorizing? And if his true purpose is the former, could it be that the Iliad's alluring surface serves to preserve its esoteric meaning over time, to survive a barbaric or imperial age when texts had to be memorized and recited? We shall make this argument later when we consider the end of Book 5 of the *Odyssey* where this very possibility seems to be analogically depicted. It is possible that Homer arrived after the Dark Ages and saw the potential for a tragic rendering of much older tales of Achilles and his mad wrath. Even though my reading of the *Odyssey* presupposes the ultimate insufficiency of the *Iliad* and its hero, a vexing matter that has consumed more gallons of ink than the quantity of heroic blood originally shed at Troy, and thus necessarily cannot be irrefutably proved here, I can show plausible grounds emerging from within the *Iliad* to support this outlaw interpretation.

It all began when Achilles lost faith in Zeus. After first rebelling against the selfish ways of Agamemnon, Zeus' mortal counterpart, he then found himself to have been ultimately tricked by the god. But what is he apart from Zeus' favor? Achilles once likened Patroclus to a little girl crying to her mother but is he any different? Further, the toxic deal Achilles has with Zeus leads to the disgrace of the hero as well the discrediting of the *Iliad's* gods. Both Zeus and Achilles, not to mention Agamemnon, are ruled by necessity and care only for their own ascendency, glory, and power. While Zeus undergoes change in the shift from *Iliad* to *Odyssey*, Achilles only sees the emptiness of the deathless glory he cold-bloodedly sought. First, the sad wraith of Patroclus indicates the existence of soul, then Hector's body proves immune to every humiliation Achilles can inflict, and finally Priam reveals that he too is braver than Achilles. Priam humbled himself, before the man who killed so many of his sons, out of love. This fond folly made him risk war for Paris; now it leads him to travel with Hermes, the leader of souls to Hades, to plead with Achilles' Hellish rage. But Priam's action shows us that he is a braver man and better lover than the "Best of the Achaeans." Achilles' guilty secret is that he loves his rage more than Patroclus. It makes him hate himself more than the man clad in his armor whom he slew: Hector. This could be why he protests too much in his humiliation of Hector's body. He is already punishing himself in Hades.

Thetis and the Arms of Ares

As this argument seems to suggest that Achilles is to be pitied and feared but not emulated, let us now pose the Euthyphro question: does heroic virtue ground itself or depend on divine favor? It seems as if the gods fiercely punish the hubris of those who think they excel by their own virtue. Even Achilles gains his unique powers from Thetis and the sea nymph's uncanny ability to protect and nurture Hera, Hephaestus, Dionysus, and even Zeus himself when they were all in danger of being un-deified. While Thetis is closely linked to and even confused with Tethys, a primal "mother" force,

Hera is never hailed by this epithet, and even claims to be going to pay her respects to martially estranged Mother Tethys when she seduces Zeus. This hints that it is not just lust that led Zeus to wish to divert her by sex from this power source beyond his control. Thetis is not only between gods and mortals, she seems also to be from an element that is prior to this distinction; Zeus and Poseidon fought over her until hearing that her son would be greater than his father, hence the conjugation to Peleus. Polymorphous as Proteus and unruly as Fortuna, Thetis fiercely resisted Peleus by changing shape and had to be bound before being married off. Like Fortuna, Thetis ever favors the angry youth over his lawful sire; she nearly made Achilles immortal though even Zeus could not make his human offspring deathless. We follow Thetis when we put children or family before the city and spoil them in defiance of the common good and their true welfare. Olympian Hera by stark contrast jealously resents Zeus' bastards but cares only for her own glory.

Thetis' rehabilitative power could be the true reason behind the myth about Achilles being made almost deathless by being dipped in the waters of Styx. It seems that she has access to the very source of immortality itself. But this uncanny power is limited by her maternal love for her mortal child. The entitlement felt by Achilles seems to come from the Olympians being aware of past or future times when Thetis was/would be desperately needed by them. But, ironically, this entitlement has the effect of spoiling her beloved son; it sets him apart from others, prevents him from empathizing, knowing friendship and/or growing by suffering. In short, his invulnerability becomes Achilles' greatest handicap. It makes him, in Nietzsche's words, an inverted cripple.

By birth Achilles enjoyed an unearned and undeserved access to that liminal area between divine and human that a hero like Diomedes or Odysseus only gains temporarily and mostly by his utmost exertions. Then, by the tragic way of Patroclus' death Achilles passes from psychopathic indifference to godlike fury; his soul's titanic and mortal parts are now no longer separated from each other. This Dionysian aspect reflects the divine spark in every human soul denied just recognition by the arrogant gods, but only Achilles has the power to do something about it. Although he is tricked by Zeus into being made to request a swift death as opposed to what could only be seen as obscure immortality, Zeus also suffers from Achilles' regression into primal Dionysian rage; even the gods must fight each other to prevent Achilles from exceeding the bounds set by necessity. The Zeus of the *Odyssey* is clearly but a mild shadow of what he was in the *Iliad*.

Achilles seems to embody the summits of martial excellence *and* titanic resentment. The *Iliad* also celebrates this second quality, perhaps because all other Homeric mortals secretly felt the same emotion towards the insouciant gods? The very name Achilles means rage/ache of a people/laos. The pain of the unrecognized young is potent. Any antisocial angry youth identifies with Achilles (or Dionysus) and seeks to fulfill a false nature that destroys the city instead of becoming a political animal realized in it. While anger at lack of respect spawns rage, we also see with Achilles that this blind power has long been used by rulers like Agamemnon to gain power and wealth. He now sees his enemy through Thersites' eyes and finds Agamemnon to be the ugliest Greek at Troy. This leads him to have Thetis ask Hephaestus, the ugliest god, to artificially equip his mad rage.

Anger never travels in straight lines; it destroys self-knowledge, is frequently deflected or mediated, often blind and usually expressed indirectly. When Achilles was justly enraged by Agamemnon's refusal to accept a reasonable offer as ransom for Chryseis, he failed to see himself and we share his illusion. Compared to his corrupt warlord, Achilles almost seems human; he even feels the irrationality of the disproportion between the One and the Many. But as he soon reverts to his nature we see that, rather than seeking justice, he wants to replace Agamemnon as the One. We surely do not wish to swap Agamemnon/Zeus for Achilles/Ares! Yet it is only after Patroclus' death that Achilles finds himself to be greedier than Agamemnon and just as two-faced as Ares.

While he has always been powerful, in that a man usually prefers victory an enemy over the truth about his soul, two-faced Ares is hated as himself. Yet, though succeeded by Athena/Odysseus, the Ares/Achilles default ever remains at the origin of politics. This is how Ares is reborn as Mars in the Roman era. While Augustine saw that Rome lusted after eternal glory, Agamemnon saw earlier that Achilles' wish for immortal *kleos* is but a psychopathic blood-lust disguised in divine armor; perhaps he also knew that Zeus his divine alter-ego began the Trojan War to end the heroic age itself? Jealous gods and/or priestly judges of evil often feign outrage at merely incontinent human badness even as they coldly coerce hapless men to obey their far more malevolent will. In short, Ares, Zeus, and Hephaestus (and their human factors) form a trinity or vicious cycle of evil. Even as Achilles represents a badly botched attempt at incarnating divine spirit in human form, the Zeus of the *Odyssey* has fled Hephaestus' rage to become a pre-Christian god of hospitality.

We can see why Hephaestus, who as the ugliest god resembles Thersites, is also a comic Achilles—albeit no longer vulnerable *but wounded* in the heel. What is tragic to the doomed heroes is merely comic to the deathless Olympian gods. It is fitting that Hephaestus' antics end the nasty quarrel between Zeus and Hera over tragic human matters at the end of *Iliad* I; but this also shows how the techne of the armorer replaces a warrior's tragic arete. Later, Hephaestus makes Achilles arms that do not protect his heel; both near-immortals thus come to share a common area of vulnerability. It is also noteworthy that at the time of his virtual apotheosis, upon receipt of his armor, Achilles reveals himself as pure fire. Achilles is far more like Hephaestus, or a product of his art, than we imagine; the swift-footed hero leans on the lame fire god. We even see the god of technology, the slayer of old humanistic civilization, as a zombified/reincarnated lame Achilles. The *Iliad*'s virtue of "all-in" thoughtless spontaneity is ever renewed by Hephaestus. This shows how post-heroic man tries to be fully actualized without an enlightened Promethean mind bearing his fire; only the necessity of techne rules his self-immolating fury. Technically enhanced mindless rage is limitless, apocalyptic, and soul-destroying. Even the armor of the lie cannot save a corrupted soul from itself.

The beauty of efficiency and technique disguises murderous mindless necrophilia. While it was insulting to call a hero a "bowman" in the *Iliad*, the reason Odysseus did not take his bow to Troy, our rulers wage drone warfare; slaying invisibly, they conceal their souls and avoid placing their lame feet on the ground. These cool killers-in-chief are blameless as Hephaestus, they have never seen war and only seek utility; techno-wars are profitable, invisible, and shameless. This is why we look forward to Athena/Odysseus, not back to Ares/Achilles; if we rage against Agamemnon's greed, a new nihilistic necessity will replace his corrupt calculation. Hephaestus promises to make every angry youth into Achilles. But these techno-thugs will be led by a greedier faceless elite and as the war of all against all persists, strife and injustice will be deemed just, natural, and necessary.

Voluntarism and Nihilism

War is easy to declare and almost impossible to conclude. For this reason, unjust relationships are so hard to end. Admission of prior wrongdoing leads to a demand for compensation and discredits illicit authority. This is why Agamemnon readily concedes Achilles' martial superiority but then invokes a qualitative difference he must maintain by force of will; if not, he ceases to be king (or God in the case of Zeus). Even Zeus must maintain this irrational ratio with the other gods. Any true king or god thus *must* exceed logos! This absurd necessity compels masters but rules slaves.

Agamemnon grants that Achilles is a better warrior—but only because he displays a psychopathic indifference to life that his corrupt cynical commander can only feign sometimes. The Lion King creates rough order within but claims that he must always fight the original chaos outside. Yet if this logic is taken to an extreme, Agamemnon fears it will expose its ugly origin in his greedy will. The evil Achilles rages against is not ontological but artificial; it feeds on human selfishness. In short, growth and becoming must not be denied for the sake of being—defined as rigid order. Men need not be herded like unruly animals. Such an attitude denies the fluid quality of a human soul, affirms the cosmic primacy of violence, and denies the goodness and beauty of ultimate reality.

The seemingly craven Greek kings know quite well that if they query Agamemnon's arbitrary will and undeserved hegemony, it is not only the justice and plans of Zeus that will come ultimately under fire, their own lordship will soon be scrutinized by men like Thersites; and so even meritocratic Odysseus cannot voice the resentment he feels towards aristocratic Achilles. The prospects of demagoguery and nihilistic anarchy loom once we have an exploited army united by unjust suffering; the demos must never see that sacred hierarchy ultimately rests on the human soul unknowingly denying itself. As they vainly defy Zeus' will, Hera and Poseidon hint that their brother's claims to total power are not as absolute as he says. This is also mimed in Odysseus' duel with the Cyclopes when the hero claims to act in Zeus' name. Wordy Polyphemus, the hero's own ugly shadow, voices the resentment of the chthonic life forces exploited by Cronos' crooked son. But this craft of cheating craftsman is not a tool to be readily turned against its users; if not used prudently, it can be a potent demagogic/fascist device once the many wrest power from their rulers. Freedmen must not emulate divine power; they should try instead to become fully human. Homeric humanism deftly steers between the Charybdis of greedy kings and the Scylla of the mob.

This is why the potential Achilles stands for must not be ruled by Ares or armed by Hephaestus. While he posthumously serves as an archetype by which angry youth are manipulated, Achilles himself is not courageous; true courage is erotic, it is not born of thumos, rage, or despair. Achilles is as solipsistic as Hamlet, but his rage is indulged by Thetis the ultimate helicopter parent. His guilt for Patroclus reveals all that is left of Achilles' humanity. Patroclus was the last human Achilles had a loving relationship with. His lover's affection was all that could contain Achilles' titanic rage. After his death, many mediocre myths about his quasi-divine rage for glory began to possess/infect other men, even Penelope's wooers. The myths made its victims as blind to results as to causes; they were happy to live in the immediate now, in the presence of the deluding power possessing them. Ares is not in the *Odyssey*; he is replaced by the giant shadow of Achilles. Ares only exists in the past via pre-Homeric bards, or in a caricatured form, in the present, as the suitors.

By reducing Ares to human proportions, both in his comic portrait of the god and by his tragic account of Achilles, Homer makes it possible for the contagious power of rage to be understood and addressed. But as we saw, Ares will be reincarnated as Mars the father of Romulus founder of Rome. Such a resurrection spells death to city and Eros; Roma is Amor spelled backwards. It represents a recipe by which a cold-blooded will to power can be made sacred and eternal; in effect, the so-called Eternal City is actually the death of the city state and the triumph of oligarchic family values. By contrast, Athena stands for the erotic ideal of a polity based on the potential for logos in all. The *Odyssey* may be read in this political way, not as the mother of all revenge tales.

Moving to the *Odyssey*

This political reading can be summed up simply. *While Achilles saw too late that political theology's gods are as unjust as its goals are empty, Odysseus is fated to atone for his sins and order his soul. Only then can he reconcile with Athena and receive a new account of divine justice, Troy's true treasure, that may be brought back to Hellas.* The two Homeric works are two halves of a whole: the first, a tragedy describing the perennial temptations inherited by every generation; and the second, an epic prescribing how these psychic diseases are cured. But while all youth seek to be Achilles, a truth as universal as that attributing mortality to Socrates, few gain the telos of life; Odysseus' self-knowledge is as hard to hold as Socratic wisdom. The *Iliad* attracts the diseased many by its angry allure before a self-selected few are cured by continually re-reading the *Odyssey*.

While Homer is magnificently impartial in his refusal to take sides in the tragic conflict between Greeks and Trojans in the *Iliad*, it is evident in the *Odyssey* that there is a chasm between the two texts that has to be resolved. There is also a most urgent political problem to be addressed. This state of affairs may be seen to stem from the *Iliad* and the Trojan War but is found to derive more immediately from Achilles and Agamemnon. The mimetic attraction exerted by the former and the latter's inability to assert legitimate authority have led to the state of affairs we see at the start of the *Odyssey*. It is not just the anarchy in Ithaca that is troubling. Many of the best heroes have perished and those who survive are but shadows of their great reputations. For all their fine war stories and professed love for his father, neither Nestor nor Menelaus can offer Telemachus even minimal military aid. They can no longer lay claim to Zeus-given authority over their war veterans or their angry orphans. This is why Odysseus is warned not to return home as Agamemnon did.

The losses and disillusionment caused by the war has made the alliance between Greeks forged by Agamemnon disintegrate. Anarchy reigns in many places and there is no longer any stomach for war or respect for rule. While Nestor, the ultimate survivor, is now more priest than king, Menelaus seems to rely on magic potions and money to rule Sparta. The Dark Ages are upon Hellas and they result from the Trojan War's bitter aftereffects. Before it men thought they were divine puppets; too weak for self-rule, they preferred currying favor with gods and kings that licensed them to violate the even weaker. But the war exposed the weakness and folly of kings and even gods. Men who cannot trust their betters often lose the power to believe in their own virtue or that of others.

Hannah Arendt saw that politics, the basis of any human community that fosters true virtue, is the opposite of violence. The *Iliad* and *Odyssey* both reveal this crucial disjunction. In the *Iliad* Ajax and Priam are both braver than Achilles for neither embraced rage. Aristotle teaches that courage involves virtuous but risky acts chosen deliberately despite loving life and hating death. While Ajax is always there for his comrades, Achilles likes to slaughter the fleeing for his greater glory. His psychopathic indifference to other lives is punctured by his lover's death; Patroclus' display of civic courage shows the emptiness of Achilles' entitled excellence; love, courage, humility, and friendship are all erotic and relational virtues. As such, they are alien to Achilles' thumotic soul.

No longer secure in his thumotic identity as the chosen one, Achilles is driven back from his unreflective "heroic" existence between divine and human realms, down to the shallow depths of his soul. It now means little for him to be the spoiled darling of the gods. Even if fools imitate him and envy his great *menis*, Achilles' spirit is already dead. In his lurid tale of the underworld Odysseus hints that like Heracles, the *Iliad's* hero is in two places at once; despite the rage that made his glory immortal in Hellas, Achilles' soul only knows self-hatred in Hades. It is clear that he does not want to be recalled or admired for acts that now torment him eternally. He wishes to be even less than a slave; even a slave is trustworthy within limits. We too realize that Achilles is limitless and untrustworthy. Role models like him make politics—and its basis, trust—impossible.

It follows that Achilles, being incapable of friendship, is inimical to cities and civilization; he must not be seen as the West's founding hero but as the hater of every city and wall—not just Troy's. Walls do not make a city, but a wall of fear is built around the Greek camp after Achilles changes the quality of the comradeship between this band of pirates. Even Troy becomes less of a city by the favor Zeus bestows on Hector at Achilles' request. Though for a while Hector is the besieger of the Greek walls he is but Achilles' factor, even before donning his fatal armor. Is the temporary rout of the Greeks due to Hector, Achilles, or Zeus? Once Zeus withdraws his favor, hubris-hungover Hector elects to fight outside the walls, dooming himself and his city. The loss of Hector cost the Trojans more than Achilles' death weakened the Greeks. It could even be that Achilles had to die before Odysseus takes Troy; glory is exchanged for guile and human intellect seems to matter more than the short-lived gifts of immoral gods. It is as if

Odysseus must bring Achilles down with Heracles' bow for the war to end. Athena's metis has to defeat Ares' raging *menis*.

The reader of the *Iliad* has knowledge that neither Greeks nor Trojans were privy to. Intelligence of Thetis's successful request that Zeus help her son by humbling Agamemnon's forces helps us see through the brazen "armor of the lie" worn by Achilles; he is not one who hates more than the gates of Hades someone who says one thing and means another. While Nestor shrewdly suspects that Achilles has a secret deal with Zeus, a deal never disclosed even to Patroclus, but which serves as the basis for his confident expectation that Agamemnon will come begging to him, we see that Achilles is not just a spoilt glory-hound but a real traitor. This pledge explains Achilles' belated promise to arm when his own ships were attacked. But, as with most divine bargains, he is fooled when Patroclus is killed. Then, as Phoenix warned, an ugly thumotic necessity, born of rage, shame, and self-hatred makes Achilles take up arms but at the cost of the immortal glory he madly desired.

Achilles stands for the disillusionment of the young with corrupt leaders and the rigged community norms sustaining them. Like him they return to their tents or Hobbesian suburbs and commodious booty. While Achilles' earlier immediate and unreflective "all-in" state is like Heidegger's fatalistic rejection of self-knowledge, for it lets us be at the disposal of Zeus or Hitler, his deep grief is proof of a soul's existence. But this sorrow must be led from the tent/cave and clad decently—not left in the brazen armor of the lie. Achilles was first ruled by false value-markers that disordered his soul; those were norms of virtue set by corrupt Agamemnon. These honors he rejects with fitting disgust. But nihilism is not the answer. Neither is a long obscure life. We turn to the *Odyssey*. It is Odysseus who must "transition" from Ares/Achilles into himself: he must be more than a Hephaestus who captures the Achilles-miming suitors of Aphrodite/Helen's cousin in his web of lies and trickery.

How a City Should Read the *Iliad*

Achilles' tale is tragic, not epic. The *Iliad* is cautionary and not foundational. After losing his quasi-divine self-sufficiency, realizing that he too needs the political goods of love and comradeship, Achilles sees that his peers could no longer give him respect or friendship. Since he is favored by gods and not truly fighting beside them, he is merely a tool for victory: like Philoctetes' bow. So even killing Hector is empty; it cannot remove the disgrace or negative kleos he sustained by allowing Patroclus to be killed in his place. Achilles reveals the extent of his knowledge when he rigs the games for Patroclus. Earlier he rejected the glory gained from a rigged war and the cheating Olympians. Next believing there is nothing more and, playing the role of Zeus as he presides over the funeral games, he offered a less violent glory for those like Antilochus who belong to the next generation. Then, as noted, he meets a braver man than himself: Priam. Priam's futile love for his dead son penetrated Achilles' arms and did what Hector could not. The *Iliad* teaches that there is no glory without courage; but this quality is born of love, not from mad despair or tragic thumos.

Tragedy exposes the deeper rules undergirding the beauty of the cosmos and the tragic hero is happy to see this sublime vision, even in death, although he gains no profit from this insight and lacks the ability to take it back to the cave. Achilles is not truly the best; what he has is the unfair favor of the gods, compounded further by the treacherous deal he makes with Zeus. This inequity is imaged in Patroclus' funeral games. It is also so with Ajax; it is ultimately the favor of Athena who gives Odysseus Achilles' arms. Yet this very apotheosis as Achilles/Ares destroys Odysseus; he cannot educate his own soul. As Heraclitus said, "it is difficult to fight thumos, it buys what it wishes at the cost of psyche." Odysseus must learn to renounce this rough magic, become invulnerable in the heel and spike the landing or return to common humanity in a way that truly redeems the ache/rage of his laos/people. *This is how he truly surpasses Achilles!* The hero of the *Iliad* merely stands beside the people's pain but does not mitigate or represent it. Homeric tragedy becomes true epic in the *Odyssey*. Here, instead of living off his thumos, Odysseus uses his psychic and erotic ability to see all souls and cities. He thus gives fine expression in both speech and deed to what Aristotle would describe much later as a soul's power to be all things. The soul is also the basis for the axiomatic assertion of human equality, a lofty ideal first explored in the *Odyssey*.

The Greeks came to see that human souls were best cultivated in a polis. And, as Aristotle tells us in his Ethics, a polity finds its origin in the extension of friendship. The *Iliad* shows how even the gifts and favors of the gods were not sufficient to actualize Achilles' soul. While interactions among the Greeks provide fine examples of comradeship, their union does not on final analysis exist to foster a good life for all; despite providing us many pregnant pre-political instances of ad hoc deliberation among pirate kings, their discussions pertain to tactics rather than the common good. It is only after the war's bitter pyrrhic end that the true interests of the many become visible.

But Troy does not serve as an example of a polis either. Priam's city is but the oikos or household of a wealthy family; the Trojans do not argue over strategy or discuss whether or not Helen should be returned to Menelaus. It is hard to imagine the besieged men of Troy putting Paris' marital bliss before their bodily safety and fighting ten long years just for Helen. While men like Priam and Hector were pious, and duly offered fine sacrifices to the gods, there is something lacking in merely ritual virtue— although failing to honor the Olympians in this way will certainly incur their ill favor. Trojan piety is stagnant and there is no mutually beneficial interaction with the gods; Troy's god-built walls are too thick. The towering city of Ilium is but a royal citadel held together by its great wealth. His gold lets Priam indulge Paris, buy allies, and withstand a long siege. It is vital to see that Odysseus' household is like Troy. Here too, great wealth is feasted away and not replenished.

But the *Iliad* also gives many reminders that Olympus itself is like a rich household. The gods seem to lead an Epicurean existence that is only relieved by the excitement of the war. But even the gods are not truly self-sufficient since they crave honor and a self-knowledge they cannot give themselves; it seems that happiness or eudaimonia is closely related to divine activity beside heroic mortals; the deathless gods can only revel in their power when they use it meaningfully. This involves human tragedy and not divine comedy. Left to themselves the gods are like the idle playful Phaiakians, and Athena is no better than lovesick princess Nausicaa; it seems that even gods must go "slumming" like Paris to find beauty and meaning beyond their perfect essentiality. Even the gods are political animals; they can best be groomed, known, or seen by us in a just city.

The converse of this ironic situation is seen in the *Odyssey*'s second half; now we find that the heroes whom the gods need do not hold virtue apart from the gods or their fellow men. This is the essence of tragedy; the case of Achilles is paradigmatic and not exceptional. As much as we admire

16

towering Ajax, he is not self-sufficiently clad in virtue. Sophocles will have jealous Athena break Ajax: first by seducing him with glory, then manipulating his rage, and finally leading him to see his comrades through divine eyes: as cattle. While Ajax never manifested this fury when he took on Hector and was most himself when he fought fearless foes threatening these comrades, he seems no better than an angry ox once Athena champions Odysseus, his rival for the arms of Achilles.

Upon final analysis the *Iliad* could be read as a duel between a god and man: Zeus and Achilles. Both seek to remain in unrivalled unchanged superiority and yet, by the tragedy's end, both have lost. While Achilles' fall is more overtly imminent, the seeming victor—following a pattern seen with Patroclus, Hector, and even Achilles himself—is warned of his own swift approaching death. Even as Zeus and Apollo will unite to bring about the end of Achilles, seemingly the greatest threat to the limits between gods and men, the doomed mortal's disillusioned rage has exposed the "two-faced double-dealing" ways of Zeus and himself. While these most ignominious epithets were hurled at Ares, careful readers/hearers of the *Iliad* know that the god and man to whom they best apply are Zeus and Achilles. They are as badly exposed as Patroclus was before Hector slew him.

But how then do we deal with the problem of Achilles? His angry ghost appears before each new generation of disillusioned youth, and his siren song lures them towards short brief lives of rage and destruction. As noted before, the issue is most acute in our time; surely it is not by chance that a zombie-resurrection of the Greek gods occurs before us. Hobbes' mad "war of all against all" has reached a crescendo today with a loss of faith in Christian logos and a recognition that our technocratic elites are as shamelessly corrupt as they are ignorant. We must find a better way of interaction between gods and men before Achilles' rage gives us up to scavenging birds and dogs. In short, the corruption of Agamemnon/Hillary does not prove Thersites/Trump to be our savior.

I will conclude by saying that Homer's solution to the problem of Achilles is to be found in his *Odyssey*. While the *Iliad* describes it with unmatched eloquence, the problem would have existed whether not Homer would have given it expression; but his tragic poem provides an account of *menis* and its causes that makes it possible for us to discern the outlines of a response. We need to conceive of a relation between gods and men in terms that are less adversarial and fatalistic. Homer helps to us view Achilles skeptically, to not allow his blazing anger and mimetic attraction to blind our capacity for prudent action. Odysseus exemplifies this human power when he successfully prevents Achilles from leading the army against Troy before it was fed. Homer likewise provides intellectual nourishment that protects his careful readers from the heady intoxication of the *menis* he describes so well; he makes it possible for us to not be stampeded into seeing Troy through Achilles' bloodshot eyes; as noted, Agamemnon's corruption does not make Achilles infallible or even right. The armor of glory given him by Hephaestus make Achilles' soul hard to see. It is only by studying his afterlife, in Hades and Hellas, that the tragic truth of Achilles becomes visible. As we shall see, even Odysseus must overcome Achilles' blinding charisma if he is to return home.

While Bruno Snell brilliantly describes Homeric divinities as puppeteers manipulating men through strings attached to their various emotions and vital organs, Vico is more faithful to the esoteric intent of Homer. He depicts heroes wrestling with their gods, much as Jacob did with the Angel of the Lord, gaining meaning and identity from this nightlong struggle. I suggest that a similar agon is undertaken in the *Odyssey* by its hero, himself a peerless wrestler as Book 23 of the *Iliad* recounts. But Odysseus must not only strive against the gods, he has to also contend with two other equally slippery opponents: his own soul and the *Iliad* itself. For this ultimate trial he must descend into the psychic underworld and reconstitute the collective consciousness of Hellas. His tale gives posterity a mythic account of a higher justice, a subtle erotic power that guides souls better than anointed king or jealous god could. The humanistic arc of civilization itself originates from Odysseus' bow and Homer's lyre. The following book seeks to describe this epic beginning.

Chapter 1
The First Human Being: Books 1–4

A skeptical reading of the events and meaning of the *Iliad*, emphasizing the horrendous consequences of the quasi-divine *menis* or rage of Achilles, makes it possible for the *Odyssey* to be approached in a vastly different manner. While never forgetting that the *metis* or divine cunning of Odysseus is just as uncanny and potentially destructive as the rage of his predecessor, we shall see that this new quality is capable of a longer and more satisfactory incarnation in the human clay. Bluntly, *menis* is to the short, glorious, and destructive career of Achilles what *metis* is to Odysseus' longer and ultimately more constructive—albeit picaresque—lifespan.

While it seemed initially that the absence of Achilles' celebrated *menis* caused the near destruction of the Greek forces at the hands of Hector, in retrospect it is clear that it was the intervention of Zeus that tilted the scales in favor of the Trojans and their allies. It was Zeus' hardly disingenuous acquiescence to Achilles' treasonous desire for glory at any cost that diminished the valiant qualities of the other Greek warriors that were displayed in Achilles' absence. The unassisted but superhuman courage of Ajax, the ability of young Diomedes to even smite and defeat Ares the god of war, and the proto-Christian and truly courageous sacrificial love of Patroclus, all suggest that this quality of *menis* is far more likely to destroy the unity of the virtues and shatter the integrity of the soul. The shift from destructive divine rage to human strategy also reflects a basic turn from the law of the gods to the rights of man.

This is why the word that is *not* used to begin the *Odyssey, metis,* is just as important as *menis,* the opening word of the *Iliad*. The "absence of mind" turns out to be as significant as the lack of an *aner,* the first word and exiled ruler of passion in the *Odyssey*. Lacking both divine reason and confidence in our own powers, we now turn to daimonic revelation and beseech the

Muse to tell us about this man of many ways, whilst yet recalling that he is as much a figure of myth as a man of reason.

Odysseus' fabulous journey —from the sacred heights of Troy to the obscure depths of concealed non-existence—remind us of Eros as described in Plato's *Symposium*. Here too the subject of our song is a daimonic figure, a motley combination of divine plenitude and demotic need, simultaneously prince and pauper, who must perform a feat that the aching heels of Achilles were unequal to. While many Homeric heroes can ascend to divine heights and sack sacred citadels, they prove themselves quite incapable of "spiking their landing" to use the familiar idiom of contemporary Olympian heroes and heroines and returning to live and walk among other eaters and breakers of bread; in other words, the real challenge is to not be destroyed by the hubris that can consume one who has successfully wrestled with, and wrested superhuman honors from, the gods. While the essence of tragedy consists in not being dissatisfied with a short but glorious career that results in immortal fame, the consequences of feats of this kind can be more than deleterious to *hoi polloi* who must dwell laboriously alongside the shadows cast by these larger-than-life egos. Such a Hades-like existence condemns the rest of mankind to a perpetual state of "unhappy consciousness." As Hegel saw, this bitterly alienated state is bad for both master and slave; the real task for the real man or *aner* must be in redeeming the normal human existence that even he must resume. Otherwise the "rich eyes and empty hands" of the tragic spectator will only behold that the sublime deeds of heroism culminate in the gimpy-legged senescence of a blind beggar like Oedipus. Hubristic heads and swollen heels must be overcome by Odysseus' divine capacities of endurance; for better or worse, he is only invulnerable in the heel!

It is also vital that we see that Homer's voice is not yet elevated at the time of his invocation; this means that he is asking the Muse for an inspired account of a story that is already known by *everybody*—as opposed to nobody a.k.a. *outis*/Odysseus! In other words, although nobody knows who or where he is (even perhaps after his return home) everybody already knows that Odysseus has sacked Troy and has seen many cities and the minds of many men. It is likewise well known to common sense that Odysseus struggled mightily to save his men, the several hundred members of the Ithacan contingent to the Trojan War, from the inevitable results of their folly and indiscipline. It is said that they were destroyed by their wild recklessness in consuming the cattle of the sun god. As was the case with another noble group of six hundred, while "someone had blundered," nobody took the responsibility for this disaster. Everybody does not know that by then only one of the original twelve ships that Odysseus had left Ithaca with, and that too only manned by a skeleton crew, remained. Also, little mention is made of the insatiable curiosity of their captain, a vicious quality that often far exceeded the bodily lusts of his crew.

For these reasons also, we should regard with a jaundiced eye the earlier claim that Odysseus saw many cities and minds of men. If the account of his travels that the Muse provides is correct, the only cities he visited were Ismarus and Scheria. None of his other ports of call qualify as human communities. Even his contacts with men, fellow eaters of bread, after the murderous raid on the Ciconians and before his shipwreck on the isle of the Phaiakians are very limited and qualified. All of this suggests that we must distinguish sharply between what is commonly said of Achilles and Odysseus on the one hand and the mythical or poetic revelations that are provided by two great Homeric poems. We shall also see grounds for believing that the truth is distinct from both the common opinions held by the many and the inspired poetic accounts given about or by the hero. Here we follow Socrates' justly celebrated claim in his *Apology* that while the poets were indeed divinely inspired, they were the worst exegetes of their own winged words. While Odysseus may have seen many cities and minds, these encounters occurred outside the epic account of his heroic wonderings. Paradoxically he is most truthful when he impersonates a liar.

Our final observation regarding the proem has to do with the fact that it explicitly points out that this tale of Odysseus the *aner* is for us; as Fagles puts it, the muse is asked to "sing for our time too." Homer in other words is writing, just like Hesiod, for the sake of his own Dark Ages. His timeless intentions and immortal yearnings may thus be expected to be of some relevance to *our* own time also. Just as Telemachus wished mightily to be delivered from the alienating Age of Antinous, we too yearn to be redeemed from our age of technological enslavement by a real man: a true king who will establish a city of gentlemen who both will rule and also will be ruled by the just and the beautiful. Even though our first truly human hero Odysseus will be seen to often fall quite short of this lofty standard, there is no doubt that he yet embodies the very virtues that make it possible. Just as the *Iliad* takes a last, lingering, backward look at an age of divinely assisted heroes and irrational gods, the *Odyssey* lights the way towards a still unrealized future marked by mutually complementary interactions between the gods and men.

Book 1

The epic proper begins after a short description of Odysseus' plight, trapped on an inaccessible isle by a lovesick sea-goddess, until the time for his return has come. He seems to be uniquely singled out by being placed in a not physically uncomfortable but psychically unbearable state of suspended animation like Schrödinger's cat until Hermes appears as a *deus ex machina* to deliver him from his place of concealment. This uncanny condition suggests to us that Odysseus cannot be defeated but only humiliatingly stalemated; while he cannot escape the cave or cavern of Calypso, his mighty adversary the sea god Poseidon is somehow unable to break down his sheer physical resilience and wound our odious hero in his invulnerable heel.

Why is Odysseus being punished in this absurd manner? While the official reason has to do with his boastful blinding of Poseidon's son, the Cyclopes Polyphemus, a feat that seems to have been predestined—since the inhospitable giant was warned of it by a prophet from among his own people—the deeper causes may turn out to be more psychic than physical. Angry Poseidon may be but a symbolic representation of deeper limits that Odysseus has violated for reasons that may have as much to do with concupiscence as hubris. This conduct has placed him outside the protection of Athena and beyond the human realm of speech and artifice that is his very element.

While these claims will be addressed and defended later, it is vital to entertain the possibility that the *Odyssey* is structured dialectically; it could be the case that the reader learns alongside Odysseus and his son. Of course, this means that our hero is not a finished product at all but one whose very essence may consist in restlessly striving towards truth as he wrestles with gods and even challenges the elemental powers. If Odysseus is Ur-Faust, the Telemachus is just as surely Ur-Hamlet. It seems that by choosing to begin the *Odyssey* with Telemachus, Homer is signaling what his final verdict on Achilles is. Devotees of the *Iliad* and its heroes must be reeducated.

Just after we are told of Odysseus' plight, a sad circumstance that has come about despite the pity of all but one of the gods, the story starts with an Olympian feast where only Poseidon is absent. With the recent slaying of Aegisthus by Orestes in mind, Zeus muses on the tendency of mankind to blame the gods for the evil results of their own foul misdeeds. These actions only bring sorrow to men "beyond what is allotted them." Zeus points out that Aegisthus was warned by the gods not to kill Agamemnon or court his wife for fear of the nemesis that would inevitably be visited on him when Orestes came of age. The suggestion seems to be that the gods do not directly intervene to punish mortal evil but rather allow our evil actions to produce their natural punishment. While all of this is far removed from his activist role in the Trojan War, we must also note that Zeus was defending his hegemony. Yet we cannot forget another source of woe; the penalties for evil actions are often borne by the progeny of the original sinner; but in the case of a man like Aegisthus, born into a harsh allotment of pain and fury, is it not natural to defy these limits? Further, was not Agamemnon also accountable for his injustices? While the gods punish impiety, don't human crimes also demand retribution? It could well be the case that the *Odyssey* reflects this shift from sins against gods to crimes against men.

Her father's rueful remarks provide Athena with an opportunity to rhetorically ask Zeus why Odysseus—whose name means "odious"—is so distasteful to him. Zeus denies this charge; after truthfully or conveniently blaming the absent Poseidon for this sad state of affairs he calls upon all the other gods to work together and bring about Odysseus' homecoming. Athena herself delegates the lesser task of securing the hero's release to Hermes, the very party who had earlier unsuccessfully warned Aegisthus, and sets off to Ithaca in search of Orestes' counterpart in this analogy: Odysseus' son Telemachus. It seems that she is anxious to make sure that the awful circumstances of Agamemnon's return are not repeated in the case of Odysseus. She realizes that while it is easy to secure Odysseus' release from Calypso, and even possible to persuade Poseidon to relent in his rage, all will be to naught if Odysseus returns but is unable to gain a secure footing in his own house and homeland. In other words, divine powers cannot simply override human ties and chthonic bonds.

Athena reports that Odysseus' palace is overrun with dissolute young men. They are shamelessly engaged in courting his wife, corrupting his servants, and depleting his estate. It seems that the goddess has been aware of this scandalous state of affairs for quite a while but has either chosen to or is unable to act until now. While she plans to educate Telemachus, his very name means "far from strife," and prepare him to receive his strife-bringing sire, Athena also sets about giving Odysseus ample grounds for massacring those who violated his home by making the suitors manifest the evil lurking within their souls. Much of what the grey-eyed goddess of intellect and strategic war does is indirect; while she thinks many moves ahead of those she intends to destroy, her salvific efforts are exerted with equal acuity.

When Athena arrives at the house of Odysseus, disguised as a iron trader called Mentes, she finds Telemachus engrossed in revenge fantasies as he sits among the suitors; he is imagining how his father would come home and scatter the shameless wooers of his wife. However, further questioning elicits his deeply conflicted feelings towards Odysseus. After first wishing that he had been born to a man fortunate enough to have died either gloriously at Troy or gently in old age at home among his possessions, Telemachus suggests that his father's strange disappearance has only brought him an inheritance of disgrace and sorrow. Like many children of divorced parents, he seems to blame himself for his father's absence, and even calls into question his own descent from Odysseus. These doubts are compounded even further by the strange behavior of Penelope his mother. He is shamed and angered by her refusal to dismiss her suitors, even as they ridicule his impotence and eat him out of house and home. All of this suggests clearly that Telemachus is in no state of readiness to offer his father any material or moral support upon his return to Ithaca.

Athena's response to the angry and dispirited young prince shows her focus on and mastery of the big picture. She sets about rebuilding Telemachus' confidence and also gives him excellent strategic advice that, while seemingly setting him up for further humiliation and a dangerous wild goose chase, actually provides him with much needed confidence and experience for the critical days that lie ahead. She first puts in Telemachus' mind a picture of his father standing armed in the threshold of his own house and cunningly introduces the idea of poisoned arrows, the very best means by which one could slay many enemies. He is also told to summon an Ithacan assembly (with a view to expelling the suitors) and then go off on a voyage to Pylos and Sparta so as to find out what has become of Odysseus. Although both of these excellent plans are foredoomed to failure, as she well knows, for reasons that have to do with human character rather than divine destiny, Athena's real purposes have to do with advancing the corruption of the suitors (along with the justification for their liquidation) and the concomitant maturation of Telemachus. She makes it very clear that he should leave his childhood behind him and seek to emulate his glorious contemporary Orestes. He must do so by dedicating his thoughts and efforts towards slaying, whether by fair means or foul, those who would disgrace his name by seducing his mother, squandering his fortune, and dissolving his kingdom.

After Athena departs, flying away like a bird and convincing Telemachus that his visitor was a god in disguise, he is filled with courage and returns to take his seat among the suitors feeling like a real man for the first time in his life. This leads the son of Odysseus to assert his personal authority over his mother and house when she attempts to prevent Phemius the bard from singing about how much the Greeks suffered from the wrath of Athena as they limped home from Troy. While we are surely expected to wonder *en passant* whether it is Athena or Poseidon who is most to blame for Odysseus' troubles and tribulations, it should also be clear that naïve Telemachus has no idea as to the specific identity of his presumably divine visitor.

The young prince boldly tells Penelope that she should not blame the bard for being "inspired" to sing this latest sad song about the sorry conclusion of the terrible war. Now attributing all sorrows to the will of Zeus, and thus echoing the very outlook that the king of the gods had found fault with earlier, Telemachus urges his mother to harden her heart and listen; he pointedly reminds her that Odysseus was not the person who failed to return from the war. This is important because many of the suitors had fathers or brother who fell into this category. The suggestion is also that as a grown man Telemachus can endure listening to the song without succumbing to emotion. Conversely, by behaving hysterically, Penelope has only provided further evidence to her greedier suitors that a woman cannot rule over the wealthy estate of Odysseus. Telemachus orders his mother back to her quarters and womanly duties, asking her to leave the talking to him since he is the master of the house. He is brave enough to raise and confront matters than she can only helplessly weep over.

Yet, typically, after this moment of mastery, Telemachus goes on to overplay his hand. Ordering the drunken suitors out, he rashly informs them of his plan to summon an assembly and goes on to say that he desires nothing short of their death as vengeance for the dishonoring of his house. These brash words naturally cause the drunken rabble to coalesce around their leaders in opposition to the angry young man when otherwise many could have been led to abandon their courtship. Antinous now counters Telemachus' prayer to Zeus with a counter-request to the Olympian that the young man never be made king of Ithaca. When Telemachus clarifies that although kingship is attractive, his main interest is to retain ownership of the household and property his father won by force, Eurymachus—the other leading suitor—smoothly assures him that nobody had designs on his property. Then, shrewdly suspecting that Telemachus' mysterious guest had something to do with his sudden assertion of authority, he asks who this stranger was and whether he brought news of Odysseus. Although the prince parries these questions just as smoothly, telling Eurymachus that his visitor was Mentes from Taphos, he now feels in his heart that it was none other than Athena. We follow him now to his bedroom where he spends the night pondering the many things he was told by the goddess.

It is also worth noting that like "Mentes" Athena too is replacing bronze with iron. The brittle heroism of the Bronze Age was as gloriously short-lived as Achilles the one who epitomized its values. Odysseus, who is often said to have a heart of iron, is the newer and better kind of hero, less flashy but far more resilient and effective.

Book 2

Here we see Telemachus leave the fleece-like comfort of his household and attempt to display in the agora the very mastery of words that he had laid claim to in his loud admonishment of Penelope. While following the advice of Athena, who had advised him to address the assembly of Ithacans, Telemachus soon reveals that he lacks any appreciation of the purpose behind such a gathering. This will underscore the truly radical break with the past and tradition brought about by the Trojan War. Old men like Laertes clearly no longer possesses the authority they once had and the young men of Telemachus' class and generation, the best of whom seem to be among Penelope's suitors, seem to be both fascinated and corrupted by the ethos of war. The result is of this "greatest of motions" is an endemic shameless-ness on the part of the young that is only matched by the resigned apathy of the older generation. But justice surely has no meaning if the human soul is unable to bear its idea or mark?

Although the assembly, the first called since Odysseus left for Troy twenty years ago, begins well for Telemachus he soon loses control of his audience. The Ithacans are impressed by his noble appearance, but it soon becomes clear that his grievances are entirely personal and economic. Telemachus openly admits that it is not a public matter that he wishes to discuss; the crisis is his own. It also has as much to do with pride as with economic loss; we find out that the storerooms of the palace are still over-flowing with treasure. There is not even the pretense of concern in his speech for the common good or for the far poorer folk who have lost fa-thers, sons, or even children in the war. Under the heady influence of self–pity Telemachus soon forgets the very flaw he was quick to discern in his mother's conduct as he selfishly laments *his* misfortunes. He demands the assistance of the Ithacans and angrily blames *their* inactivity and disloyalty for his misfortune. He speaks as if they, not the suitors, are his chief perse-cutors. In his distress Telemachus forgets that the king or strongman is sup-posed to protect his subjects and dependants; it is for this that he is granted wealth and honor. It is significant that Telemachus all but accuses the Itha-cans of allowing his house to suffer because of unvoiced resentments they feel towards King Odysseus and the men he did not bring back from the war. He even says that it would have been preferable for them to directly rob his flocks in compensation for their losses. Telemachus' speech ends as angrily and petulantly as Achilles' when the latter separated himself from the Greek host in the *Iliad*. He too throws down the speaker's scepter, gen-erally acting as if this quarrel over a woman is all about him.

The initial response of the Ithacans was sympathetic, and none had the heart to "match anger with anger"—perhaps in the sense of pointing out how misguided his words were. It is left for Antinous to reply and he does so by blaming the Queen for promising to marry one of them and refusing to make up her mind. It seems strange that he singles out Penelope for this state of affairs in a situation that was clearly forced upon her until we realize that he is playing out a Trojan War scenario that has the Queen standing in for her cousin Helen. Just as Aphrodite's gifts made Helen irresistible to Paris, and made it impossible for the Greeks or Trojans to give her up, so too do Athena's endowments of weaving and cunning intellect make Helen's cousin Penelope unmatched in the eyes of her suitors. Thus, they too will not give up on their siege or home invasion and cannot be expected to; they find these qualities—coupled with her wealth of course—to be irresistible. Could the Trojan War have been in vain? It is also worth noting that Agamemnon's wife and Helen's sister, the majestic and jealous Clytemnestra, is the representative of Hera, the third contender for the golden apple of Eris.

Even though Antinous' disingenuous explanation can hardly be taken at face value, we must recognize that Penelope has been playing a very skill-ful and dangerous game, one that she cannot discuss with its beneficiaries: her absent spouse and loose-lipped son. Just as Telemachus was wildly im-prudent in telling the suitors over and over again that he intended to kill them all, thus undoing all of Penelope's efforts to keep him eponymously "far from strife" by infantilizing him and make him seem less of a threat, his mother was deftly albeit desperately playing the 108 suitors off against each other and preventing them from killing her son and simply dividing up Odysseus' estate collectively. The hope of winning Penelope and becom-ing King of Ithaca kept the household intact until she made up her mind. The shroud of Laertes, that she wove by day and undid by night, was just one of the ways by which she warded off the worst consequences of a home invasion that had already happened; by flirting with everyone, she surren-dered her chastity (and household) to no body!

Telemachus responds to Antinous by pointing out that he could and would not send his mother away against her will; he repeats his request that the suitors leave and threatens to pray to the gods for their destruction if they refuse. But yet when two eagles come down as a sign from Zeus that is interpreted to mean that Odysseus will return soon and bring bloody death to his enemies, Eurymachus violently threatens the prophet, along with anyone else who stirs up Telemachus' anger, with a heavy fine. For Eu-rymachus, ambiguous divine signs are well replaced by clear threats of direct violence. The suitors are now seen to have moved, perhaps by implacable Athena herself, from the seductive power of Aphrodite to the brutal *ananke* of Ares. Their lust is now violent and shameless as they go from being tyrannized to becoming godless predators. For himself, Eurymachus is more interested in rule over Ithaca than marriage to Penelope. His overt sexual involvement with her maid is clear evidence of this priority. He is more cold-blooded and manipulative than Antinous.

Still obeying Mentes/Athena Telemachus then requests a ship, that he may go in search of his father and either wait another year or honor him in death before giving his mother in marriage. When his father's old friend Mentor speaks in support of this proposal, chiding the Ithacans for their silence and apathy before the heavily outnumbered suitors, we must see what is at stake is the passive acquiescence of the "decent people" in the events of the last three or four years. By boldly exploiting both the silent resentment of the Ithacans over the loss of their war contingent along with the moral confusion caused by the absence of their king, the suitors turned the previous guilty silence and involuntary hospitality of Penelope and Telemachus into an implicit acceptance of their hegemony over the palace and estate of Odysseus. This no longer impartial moral middle ground had been occupied in bad faith by the silent majority of Ithacans for too long for them to remain free to pick sides or resist the new status quo without much exertion of mind and muscle. Yet as they more or less honestly felt that they had not either approved or disapproved of the suitors' actions, these good men were now outraged by Mentor's charge of passive treason. Now that the lines had been redrawn, they found too late that their dead weight now supported the suitors and threatened the continued existence of the family and house of Odysseus. But it is now far too dangerous to oppose the suitors' hegemony.

Mentor is answered by Leocritus, a hitherto silent and obscure suitor, and told that they would even kill Odysseus himself if he were to return to his own palace. Thus, he suggests that even the beleaguered queen would not want her husband to return to his certain death. In a sense Leocritus is exonerating the guilty apathy of the Ithacans against Mentor's accusation. According to him the situation is absurd and as public virtue is both meaningless and impossible; they may as well stay in overt internal exile. The professed lovers of Penelope have now gone from being invaders of her home to potential murderers of her husband and son. It is in this spirit that they later maliciously speculate about various possible accidents that could befall Telemachus were he to go to Pylos or Sparta in search of allies and intelligence. If he would be Orestes, they believe that his mother could become Clytemnestra.

This quest for external assistance has become necessary now that the young prince has shown his hand and only succeeded in forcing his enemies to make their shameless intentions public. Just as Achilles involuntarily advanced the plan of Zeus, Athena has pushed Telemachus out of his infantilized comfort zone into what is pretty much a battle to the death against the suitors. Even though Telemachus was very foolish to publicly blurt out his desire to slay the suitors, this was consistent with, and probably even a part of, Athena's master plan to school his naïve potential.

Once the rift between the son of Odysseus and his mother's suitors has been made public and reconciliation is no longer possible, a bloody outcome is inevitable. It is clear that Telemachus must leave Ithaca. The suitors will be equally anxious to prevent his departure for fear than he will return with armed support from Pylos or Sparta. The situation Telemachus faces is quite dire; no sense of public-spiritedness exists in Ithaca, not even in the young prince himself, and neither is there any belief in justice or the soul's capacity to bear it. All Telemachus can do is pray to Athena for the help that his countrymen failed to provide. She responds in the form of Mentor, providing a ship and assuring him that he has courage and cunning sufficient to his task. Athena tells Telemachus that while not yet his father's equal, his voyage cannot end in defeat or failure as long as Odysseus' spirit lives in his blood. Both he and his countrymen must learn much about true virtue and a real man/*aner* who embodies it. By going on this voyage Telemachus will prove to the Ithacans and himself that he is no longer a spoilt child incapable of living away from the protection of his mother or nurse. At the end of Book 2 he tries to cast off his sheep-like covering and claim his inheritance as the grandson of Autolycus, the wolf itself! True to his sire's nature he sets sail on the high seas of fortune; no longer for him the stifling banality of the townsfolk that has left them totally impotent and even artlessly acquiescent in the suitors' shameless hubris. He must learn for himself that true virtue is neither defenseless against nor only quantitatively different from evil and immoral despair.

It would seem as if Telemachus could blame Mentes or even Athena for the bad advice he has received. Now that the opinion, or weakness, of the townspeople has been ascertained, again something like Schrödinger's Cat that doesn't really exist until it is measured, the young prince's situation has now been rendered untenable. Yet the craven banality of the Ithacans serves to insulate and normalize the elsewise insufferable hubris of the suitors from its natural punishment. The more peace is sought by appeasement, the greater the chance that these very accommodations will lead to the overthrow of the state of stability they desired. Yet now that Telemachus and Mentor have spoken and acted bravely, it is possible for Athena to act through or even as them. It even seems as if her grace is only made impotent by our despair.

The *Odyssey* will point us towards a new paradigm of how divine grace may interact with human virtue. Both passive piety and angry atheism fall short of this high mark. *Pace* Zeus' words, resilient men are not doomed to fester and rage within the sorrow allotted them. What passes for pious resignation can well be the outer aspect of god-killing and soul-corroding despair; as the *Iliad* shows, even the gods quail when this maddened fury erupts. For this reason, both men and gods are best served when the middle path between despair and hubris is bravely probed by heroes like Odysseus. While the will of the gods needs to be acted on by men to be as effectual on earth as it is on Olympus, and is as such open to being scorned or defied by evil men like the suitors, the person who follows the mandate of heaven is assured of divine support.

Book 3

Telemachus left Ithaca under the ambiguous sign of the two battling eagles, an omen that the seer Halitherses took as a warning for the suitors. But viewed in the light of Homer's own simile, used later in the *Odyssey*, we may see these royal birds as truly representing Odysseus and his son. The barely concealed hostility that Telemachus has towards his father, sometimes taking the form of a love/hate ambivalence and at others shown in a desire for certain knowledge of his lost father's death, needs to be resolved before Odysseus can be said to have truly returned home. What Halitherses saw as a sign that Odysseus was bringing evil to many other Ithacans—as he planned the death of the suitors—could also be seen as a private warning to the young prince. Telemachus cannot grow up in Ithaca. His maturity depends on his learning certain things about gods and heroes that cannot be revealed while he's "far from strife." The youth must renounce this safe identity to learn what it is to be the son of Odysseus.

When Telemachus and his crew safely reach the shores of sandy Pylos he finds the aged king and his people participating in a great sacrificial feast honoring Poseidon. Nestor's name means "returner" and this is appropriate for a very old man who has successfully returned from both the epic expedition of the Argonauts and the Trojan War. Nestor's people are arranged in nine tribes of five hundred men. This detail is in obvious reference to the ninety ships of fifty men that accompanied Nestor to Troy. The suggestion is that the kingdom's population has finally been restored to something close to its pre-war levels. The fact that they are offering only 81 bulls rather than the full hundred needed for a hecatomb reinforces this inference. Nestor has clearly dedicated Pylos to peace and piety rather than honor-seeking warfare. In a sense, Nestor's longevity suggest that his skill is found in returning from action, not necessarily in attaining the hubristic heights of glory or excellence; his piety may be seen to result from his fear of the gods. Nestor does not challenge the gods. This is why it is fitting that Telemachus and Athena are beseeching the favor of Odysseus' greatest enemy at the very time when the man himself is struggling home over the angry waves of the sea. It is significant that neither of them mentions his name; Athena merely requests that Poseidon help them to succeed in their mission.

The first question Nestor asks of these strangers should make us pause. He wants to know if they are traders or pirates. His non-judgmental tone is startling; there is clearly no shame in making a living from piracy in these times. Indeed, it was much in the same way that the suitors came to Ithaca; even the heroic Greek expedition to Troy was a barely rationalized act of piracy. An age where law ends at the threshold of the king's home must rediscover what is right. Nestor is little better than a priest; it seems that political authority must bridge the divide between piety and violence.

Telemachus says that he came to Nestor seeking news about his father. While Athena fully intends for him to inquire after the present whereabouts and—eternal essence—of Odysseus, Telemachus himself seems to be seeking little more than confirmation of his sire's death. His ambiguous feelings towards his father coupled with his rough experience at the assembly of the

Ithacans doubtless contributed to this attitude. He does not seem to realize that news of such an event will almost assuredly lead to his losing his house, his mother, and even his life. He is both angry and impatient; it is as if he seeks bad news to confirm and justify his foul mood.

Nestor's reply gives very little information concerning Odysseus' whereabouts. They were last together almost ten years ago following the sack of Troy. What is most remarkable about this tale, which recounts how Nestor became separated from both Menelaus and Odysseus at critical points on his eponymous "return" home, is its account of how Menelaus reaches home just after Orestes has avenged his father. The clear suggestion seems to be that the gods had it in for Agamemnon, so much so that they even allowed Aegisthus, his killer, to be properly buried beside his mother by Orestes; Menelaus would never have allowed Aegisthus this courtesy. It is also noteworthy that when the storm hit Menelaus' ships, just before they rounded Cape Maleia, it split into two groups of five ships. This is all that remained of the eighty ships Menelaus took to Troy. The others also probably sustained similar attrition.

Telemachus had earlier sought news of Orestes' fine feat with a clear intention of emulating him and clearing the house of his mother's would-be seducers. However, three things stand in his way. First, Penelope unlike Clytemnestra, is very much alive and is actively struggling against her would-be lovers; second, Telemachus is badly outnumbered in Ithaca and is offered no material assistance at all by pious Nestor; and third, Telemachus himself is overwhelmed by feelings of his own insignificance.

Concerning the last of these, we should note that Athena seems to intend that this voyage should educate Telemachus about the truth concerning the Trojan War. Since popular tales of this heroic enterprise have spread all over Hellas, mitigating or overshadowing the terrible material cost of the ten-year struggle, a great gap has opened up between the generation of those who fought at Troy and their children; the already bleak realities faced by those living in post-war Greece are only made more humiliating by hyperbolic tales of the heroic virtues possessed by those who fought on the plain of Troy. Telemachus, for instance, is overawed by the fabled wisdom of Nestor and must see for himself that the old man is little better than a garrulous blowhard. Likewise, he must also gain a true sense of his father's virtues and begin to believe in his own capacity to support and stand by, if not surpass, Odysseus.

Most importantly, Athena wants him to realize that both Odysseus and he are loved and favored by the gods; this preference dramatically tilts the odds towards him. Yet first she must explain why Odysseus, said by Nestor to be more openly divinely favored than any other man at Troy, has been unable to return. Otherwise any sign or promise of divine favor will not make very much sense; either the gods cannot bring him back or they are too fickle to maintain a consistent relationship with a mere mortal. This basic question of theodicy resides at the very heart of the *Odyssey*; Athena must show both suspicious father and skeptical son that while her affection for them is both constant and strong, there are limits to divine unilateral powers.

In this specific context (as Mentor) she tells him that while a god can easily protect a man from death, even at a distance, once he has died not even a god can save him. This seems to suggest that while it is possible for a god to keep a favored mortal away from physically deadly circumstances, such as the ambush Aegisthus arranged for Agamemnon, if he loses this favor or fails to heed their advice and is delivered to the hands of death then nothing can save him from his fate. But what does it mean to lose the favor of a god? Is it possible to lose the qualities that make one attractive to the deity in question, to break the link between divine grace and human agency? Or differently put, while a god can quite easily destroy one who is odious, often by the means of another person under his power, is it possible for a god to help a mortal who is unwilling or ill-disposed towards the essential attribute he holds in common with the god? This may be the first instance of the *Euthyphro* question: is something holy because it is loved by the gods or is whatever the gods loved holy? In this case Athena seems to be saying that the gods cannot love what falls short of being lovable (or admirable). While we shall address another aspect of the *Euthyphro* question later, the problem of how different gods may disagree in their love or estimation of the same mortal, a question that often becomes moot because of the incapacity of the frail human soul to bear the weight of Olympian favor for too long, it is striking here that a shift away from the arbitrary divine volition of the *Iliad* has taken place.

While pious Nestor has tried to show Telemachus that the gods act with a deliberate speed and timing that humans cannot understand, rational Athena has stressed the complementary truth that the gods are (as Einstein doggedly maintained) subtle but not irrational. It is amusing to note that Athena is all but invisible to wise old Nestor; his self-proclaimed wisdom in counsel amounts to little more than the scriptural tag that the beginning of wisdom is fear of the Lord. While his reduction of wisdom to fearful sacrificial piety is hardly likely to mark him out for Athena's favor, it can yet mark him as a philosopher to the extent that he is at least aware of his ignorance. Yet the erotic quality of Odysseus' burning desire for knowledge is quite alien to his pedestrian Epimethean intellect. It is clear that in believing that only sacrificial punctiliousness can gain the favor, or at least forestall the wrath, of the all-powerful Olympians, Nestor is clearly on Euthyphro's side of the argument with Socrates. His kind of piety seems to be directed towards the older irrational gods like Poseidon.

Once Athena has revealed who she is, in the symbolic guise of a vulture (rather than an eagle) for Nestor's benefit, she can no longer sail beside and protect Telemachus as his Mentor. This could well be why she advises him to travel by land and chariot rather than via the turbulent element of the sea, Poseidon's domain. In the interim, he is well advised to reflect on what he has learned from Athena and Nestor. He has learned both that the gods are taking an interest in him and that their ways are not ours, for reasons that have as much to do with the human soul as with divine power. These revelations, which have come from Athena herself, certified by Nestor, must be taken very seriously. He must also dwell on the one positive item of information concerning his father that Nestor has imparted, how Odysseus surpassed all men in strategy and cunning. This is surely the quality that connects him to mighty Athena. But Nestor has also told us that the disasters sustained by the Greeks had everything to do with the wrath of Athena; this means that the bond between Odysseus and his goddess must somehow be restored. It would seem that while Athena is more than willing, Odysseus is somehow in a place where he cannot or will not respond to her.

Book 4

Telemachus has yet to learn very much about his father or his whereabouts. This lesson lies ahead in Sparta, where he will also meet the two surviving principals of the Trojan War and be taught a good deal about that epic event itself. Just as he was overly intimidated by the renowned wisdom of Nestor prior to his arrival in Pylos, he is now faced with the objectively impressive fabulous wealth of the recently returned Menelaus. Furthermore, this naïve, probably virginal, teenager will now make the acquaintance of his legendary aunt, Helen of Troy.

While Nestor's court was preoccupied with religious ritual, Menelaus' establishment seems to have very little piety in public. Telemachus and Pisistratus encounter bards and jugglers amidst the wedding festivities taking place as they arrive. Yet the Spartan King's mood is curiously somber; he warns his awestruck visitors against comparing his wealth with that of the gods and, pointing out that his brother was murdered through the cunning of his treacherous queen while he was away out East amassing his fortune, goes on to volunteer that he would gladly give up two-thirds of the wealth he has accumulated in exchange for the lives of those lost fighting at Troy. Menelaus' words even carry the suggestion that it would have been better had he remained home and not destroyed his household by leaving to bring back Helen. Should Odysseus return, it will be to a loving wife, a matured son, and a cleansed household; Telemachus must see the advantages of playing Athena's long game.

Menelaus confesses to the young men that he often gives himself over to these lonely gloomy lamentations, allowing the inference that he would be happier in Hades with his dead comrades than be alive as the richest king in Hellas, before going on to speak of the one man he misses and laments more than any other: Odysseus. This is not merely because he labored harder and achieved more for the Greek cause, but also on account of his long absence and unknown fate. He suggests that the obscurity surrounding Odysseus is worse than death itself. In this sense, Odysseus is already in Hades. Menelaus associates himself with the grief Laertes, Penelope, and Telemachus must all feel for their loved one. These words, consonant with Telemachus' own feelings of guilt and uncertainty, cause him to weep for the first time for his father, and not merely for himself. This action identifies him to Menelaus who is uncertain how to proceed until Helen, who as we shall see is famed for her ability to see things for what they are, enters—looking like chaste Artemis—and immediately proceeds to claim that Telemachus resembles the son of Odysseus.

This remarkable perception, seeing that the young man is both different from and yet clearly the son of his father, is somehow not the same as

Menelaus' later claim that Telemachus' hands, feet, eyes, head, and hair all remind him of Odysseus. While Menelaus' belated recognition was sparked by the youth's weeping at the mention of his father's name, Helen—arriving after these concealed tears—sees something about Telemachus, or perhaps in his reaction to her, that immediately reveals his identity. Even though it is possible to suggest that Helen was also struck by his likeness to her cousin Penelope, it is more probable that it was Telemachus' untypical reaction to her presence that reminded Helen of his father and marked him as himself.

Helen's identification of Telemachus is made in the context of a ritual denunciation of her own shameless conduct in causing the Achaians to wage reckless war against Troy. Even as Menelaus has expressed regret that he left home for her, she too has stated that the Trojan War was a worthless endeavor, with regard to both cost and goal. Menelaus now makes an even stronger if subtler statement of his love for his wife, stating his willingness to depopulate one of his own cities—almost a second Troy—so that nothing could separate him from a relationship of friendship and pleasure with Odysseus. This implicit preference for his long lost comrade over his dearly recovered wife reduces them all to tears and it is left for Helen to change the mood of the party by drugging the wine with an Egyptian potion supposed to make men forget all sorrows but having the actual power to make it impossible to weep.

Because she cannot hope to recount or even number all his exploits, Helen now proposes to tell them all a plausible tale about Odysseus—in other words, poetry that possesses in power to reveal universal truth what it lacks in factual accuracy—during the Trojan War. She offers a story of what transpired between them when Odysseus disguised himself to go on a dangerous spying mission within Troy itself. The whipping that the King of Ithaca inflicted upon his own body, along with his degrading dress, apparently made him unrecognizable to all but Helen. The brazen queen, whose uncanny ability to see through any kind of disguise is only equaled apparently by her insatiable need for attention and recognition, is naturally drawn to the "iron heart" or pre-Socratic "withstanding power" of Odysseus. While he can deftly become nobody, Helen can identify any body anywhere, even within a horse.

Helen claims that although Odysseus initially eluded her questioning, he eventually told her all the goals of the Greeks after had she bathed and anointed him. She then provided this most polymorphous of men with a new disguise so he could leave laden with much information. She goes on to blame the madness of Aphrodite that led her to forsake country, daughter, bedchamber, and a husband second to none. While it could be convenient to infer that Odysseus told Helen of the Trojan Horse, thus explaining her mysterious awareness of the warriors concealed within its belly, this story fails to do Odysseus justice. Even if he had succumbed to her enticing blandishments, Odysseus certainly would never have expected that fickle Helen would have been true to her vow of silence. It is worth noting that she only pledged to keep his identity a secret until he got back to the Greek camp. The purposes of the Greeks that he shared with her would have been more strategic than tactical; they would largely have had to do with the plans Menelaus had for her. Ever the smooth diplomat, Odysseus would surely have told her what she wanted to hear; if it suited the interests of his side, he may even have told her the simple truth. Whatever his real feelings towards her were, there is no doubt that the cuckolded Menelaus needed to come back home with his wife as a tangible sign of his success and virility.

Even though she is now closer to fifty than forty, Helen is still anxious to prove her irresistibility. Well aware that this quality consists more in reputation than in substance, she would doubtless even prefer Menelaus and Telemachus to believe that Odysseus disclosed the secret of the Trojan Horse to her over the more probable truth that his heart of iron withstood her wiles; the not unjustified charge of treason is only a small price to pay for having her renowned power over all men re-confirmed. Such an admission also undercuts Menelaus' publicly expressed preference for Odysseus' company over hers. We may also infer that Helen now sees in Telemachus the same strong aversion towards her treacherous nature that she once saw in Odysseus; from this it follows that the aging queen is willing to say anything that will convince her nephew that he must emulate his father and madly desire her beauty. While this siren is quite willing to describe Odysseus' virtues and resilience, these admirable qualities are all finally subject to her beauty; she is the true *telos* of the Trojan War.

After ironically praising her well-crafted tale, Menelaus now goes on to tell a story about Odysseus that seems to refute Helen's claims. Throwing back in her face Helen's famous excuse that "some god made her do it," he recollects how Odysseus nobly defeated his queen's treacherous wiles at the most critical moment of the war. Menelaus tells of how when the pick of the Greeks, Diomedes and himself included, were hidden in the wooden horse in Troy, Helen walked around it with her latest husband and perfectly imitating the voices of the Greeks' wives, enticed them to come out of the horse and thereby lose the war. Only Odysseus manifested the presence of mind to both withstand her voice and prevent his lovesick comrades from giving their presence away. The danger only passed when Athena finally lured Helen off from this murderous seduction. Although upon hearing this Telemachus can only gloomily remark that even his father's iron heart did not save him from destruction, Helen's moment has passed and Menelaus has successfully defended his friend's honor. Most importantly, Telemachus has learned a very important lesson about the polymorphous ingenuity and "enduring strength" of his heroic father. We may also hope he will recognize that Penelope is also a practitioner of these virtues.

When Telemachus finally has a *tete-a-tete* with Menelaus and is asked whether he came if he came on private or public business, he does not answer this directly but describes the state of his home and asks for news of his father. By not emphasizing his private interests as crassly he did earlier, Telemachus shows new signs of public-spiritedness; his own desire for closure or revenge must also be informed by a better appreciation of the Trojan War and its ruinous cost. Helen is clearly not worth the cost of her recovery. It is just as clear that Menelaus, who left with eighty ships and returned with five, is not able to offer Ithaca any meaningful military aid.

Menelaus' intelligence concerning Odysseus is contained in a very long and magical story about Proteus, the old man of the sea. This is the only part of the Telemachy that resembles the fantastic tale of his wanderings that Odysseus performed before the court of Alcinous. Menelaus tells Telemachus how, when becalmed in Egypt, he captured Proteus and found out, among other things, the fate of the three victorious Greek heroes who had not made it back from Troy. While Telemachus finally hears that his father was last seen being held captive on the island of Calypso, without men or ships to bring him home, it seems that the story of how Proteus was caught is just as important to the successful completion of his Athena-directed mission. We must also note the name "Eidothea"—this may be another of the goddess's disguises.

The six forms assumed by Proteus, before he finally reverts to his own identity and speaks the truth, may be seen to correspond to several of the many situations or shapes taken on by deceptive Odysseus before his triumph over the suitors and delayed final reunion with Penelope. Proteus' first disguise, as a lion, is in keeping with Odysseus' becoming a part of the Mycenaean Lion King Agamemnon's Trojan expedition. The serpent must surely represent Odysseus' legendary cunning and skill with words and his sinuous or polytropic ways. The third metamorphosis into a panther or leopard may have to do with Odysseus' new identity as a privateer or pirate at the end of the war; this hybrid beast seems to combine qualities of both lion and serpent. Alternatively, the feminine gender of the word *pardalis* could refer to Circe, who held him in her arms for over a year during his wanderings; Circe had the power to turn men into large beasts like lions and wolves. While the first three shapes of Proteus describe Odysseus' past, and he will shortly disclose the literal truth about the hero's present humbled and concealed location, the last three forms correspond to the circumstances under which Odysseus will make his way home.

Proteus' final animal metamorphosis into a great wild boar matches well with what is most elemental about Protean Odysseus; this aspect of him resists the offers of effortless pleasure Circe and Calypso made. While we will hear later about the great boar he killed as a youth, the primal darkness of this beast's leafy lair resembles the deep pile of leaves from which he emerges like a mountain lion on Scheria. Neither can we forget that Circe had earlier turned all Odysseus' shipmates into swine; could this also reflect the condition Circe's niece reduced him to? Or is there something about Odysseus that always resists stagnation or mindless bliss? Next, the running water corresponds to the river god who saved his life when he was shipwrecked as well as the cleansing or spiritual rebirth he undergoes by this abysmal experience. Lastly, the great tree represents the living olive tree around which Odysseus builds his marriage bed and house on Ithaca. While this bed is the sign by which he proves himself to justly skeptical Penelope at journey's end, the tree's towering branches symbolizes the renewed dynasty to be set up when the king returns home at last.

Proteus also told Menelaus that on account of his being married to the daughter of Zeus, both Helen and he are destined for the Elysian Fields where the climate is always temperate and life is always easiest for humans.

Even if it seems that such a life is perfect, further reflection leads one to conclude that being bound to Helen forever is hardly a pleasing prospect. Indeed, it may well be the case that Odysseus' plight as Calypso's unwilling consort, neither alive nor dead, is very similar to Menelaus' future. It seems that neither son of Atreus has found joy in his marriage.

Much of what Menelaus has recounted is of direct relevance to Telemachus' present predicament and the young man proves that he has not listened unreflectively when he goes on to decline the offer of three fine stallions and a chariot, pointing out that such a gift would be useless in Ithaca. In a like manner we see that Helen, the erotic daughter of Zeus, is poorly suited to life on the plains of Lacedaemon. Telemachus' education is all but complete. He must decline Menelaus' offer of further hospitality and return home, accompanied by a mixing bowl in which he can blend all the many lessons he has gained. Meanwhile, as if in recognition of his new heroic status, the wanton suitors are preparing a bloody welcome for a man they now fear greatly.

Although he swears by Zeus upon hearing belatedly of Telemachus' voyage from the aptly named Noeman son of Phronius, Antinous is quite oblivious to the fairly clear sign that the gods had a hand in this matter. Ignoring Noeman's observation that since Mentor could not be in two places at the same time, the man who borrowed the ship from him was a god in disguise, Antinous defies both prudence and thought. He hotly convinces the other suitors to equip another ship and plan an ambush for Telemachus that he will lead. It is also quite noteworthy to find that Eurymachus, the other leading suitor who was present at the time Antinous finds out, neither speaks nor joins the twenty "best" suitors who make up the crew of the ambushing ship. We see once more a distinction between Antinous' hot-blooded intemperance and the more cold-blooded ways of his rival Eurymachus. Even though the suitors seem to find out about Telemachus' voyage by accident, it is clear to the attentive reader that Athena, who initially borrowed the ship, wants the suitors to become increasingly complicit in the consequences of their originally mindless criminality.

The Telemachy ends with Penelope's discovery that her son has been gone from Ithaca for many days. Originally supposing that he has been with Eumaeus the swineherd, a surrogate father who is mentioned here for the first time but will soon play a crucial role in Odysseus' return, the Queen is devastated by the news. She finds little comfort in being reassured by Eurycleia that the gods have not entirely abandoned the house of Arceisius, but Penelope does take her advice to petition Athena. For all her tearful grief, the noble Queen is compared to a lion hemmed in by hunters as she asks Athena, in the name of Odysseus, to save her son from her vile suitors. We must also take note of Eurycleia's treachery. Surely her first loyalty is to her mistress?

Athena's response is as swift as it is subtle. Having first put Penelope to sleep and silenced her tormented ponderings, the goddess sends down a phantasm of her distant sister Iphthime to offer comfort. Penelope is told that the gods do not wish her to weep and be troubled. The dream further promises that her son will return for he has not sinned in the sight of the gods. Penelope responds with her typical circumspection. She explicitly bemoans her lot, going from the case of her famous lion-hearted husband to that of her innocent son, while yet alertly heeding the voice of the phantasm and seeking further information and specific reassurance. When told that she should take courage since Athena herself is escorting Telemachus, and informed further that the message itself is from the goddess, the long-enduring Queen pounces and tries to get news of Odysseus himself. Never once mentioning her husband by name, she asks the dream to prove its veracity by telling her whether the other one unfortunate lives and looks on the sun or is already in Hades.

Athena's oracular response is well worth pondering. The phantasm says that it since it is bad to engage in empty talk, it will not tell her whether that other one is dead or alive. Since—for the first time in this epic—we are dealing with an exchange between two almost evenly matched masterminds, it is significant that neither alternative that Penelope provides is correct. Odysseus seems to dwell in a state of suspended animation on Calypso's literally concealed island; physically comfortable but yet spiritually hyperconscious and inactive, his infinitely restless and resourceful mind is trapped in non-being and forced to go deeper and deeper within itself and achieve a kind of self-knowledge unprecedented in either the epic age or that of the Homeric bards. This is the very opposite of Hades. There the soul has literally "no idea" at all of who it is or what it has done and suffers for. But we cannot forget the straight meaning of these words either. While Athena can almost guarantee that blameless Telemachus will make his way home, she does not know whether Odysseus can brave the wrath of

Poseidon and overcome the furious aspects of his own psyche that have caused him to be in as uncanny an ontological situation as Achilles himself.

We must also see that the Telemachy is Homer's contribution to a tale of Odysseus he inherited from the past. He now confronts the daunting task of singing about a hero well known to his audience. This means that while he cannot deviate too far from what they know about Odysseus, the bard must also reveal unknown things about their hero that better explain his mysterious absences and actions. Like divine Hermes, he too must visit Odysseus to deliver him from a Hades-like state of exile or irrelevance in the land of myth and memory, into their own lives of quiet despair. Odysseus turns out to be more than an old legend. His audience, like my readers and Telemachus, has to be readied for what is both truly needed and wholly unexpected. This union of novelty and necessity will reveal the truth of Homer's revelations; it will propel our hero from the cloud palaces of poetry into a fallen everyday reality made all the more bleak by its invisible but invidious indebtedness to the *Iliad*.

Chapter 2
Re-Entering Reality: Books 5–8

Book 5

Book 5 of the Odyssey, having made us almost as impatient as Penelope and Telemachus, finally takes us to Odysseus. After a second scene in Olympus, where Athena rehashes her complaint that the gods have dealt especially harshly with long-suffering Odysseus, Homer is dispatched to the island of Calypso with specific instructions to the goddess about the prompt liberation and sending off of our long-languishing hero. Out of ostensive respect for Poseidon or perhaps in accordance with our hero's pre-determined destiny, Calypso is told that he must not receive aid from gods or men but has to leave Ogygia on a raft and suffer many woes en route.

It is noteworthy that this long-deferred account of Odysseus' departure from Ogygia strangely parallels his son's almost simultaneous journey from Ithaca in search of him. A god instigates the trip off an island in each case; furthermore, the traveler-to-be is found in a state of deep frustration. He is immobilized and/or infantilized by a powerful and possessive older woman who claims, not without some justice, to have his best interests in mind. While youthful Telemachus makes a journey into manhood as a result of his expedition, his father is symbolically reborn as he leaves a place of changelessness and prepares to reenter human history. Just as Odysseus eponymously is thrown into trouble, Telemachus is equally appropriately taken far from strife; he will only return when it is time to receive his father. All we said earlier about the importance of the tragic hero being able to "stick" his landing in the human world is crucially important here; the vital connection between the divine and human realms depends entirely on his exertions.

We must also be mindful that the reader or hearer of the *Odyssey* does not know who Odysseus is. We know his popular reputation, whether as hero-king or trickster-strategist, and we have also found out with Telemachus—from Menelaus and Helen—that he was admired for by his peers for self-possession and resilience. Further, through Proteus, we have been made aware of certain forms ruling his past and future metamorphoses. But we still do not know what drives our hero, the ruling passion making this anti-Achilles in Nietzsche's memorable expression "invulnerable only in the heel." To really know who Odysseus is, we must somehow find out why this man who had suffered so much could resist the lure of immortality and renounce a life of effortless comfort in order to return home to his aging wife, angry son, and rebellious kingdom. We saw Achilles as a botched conception of divine incarnation, godly power that could not be contained within mortal and political limits; now we see his rival Odysseus freely "fall" down from paradise to reclaim his humanity. All these choices make Odysseus even more mysterious than the son of Thetis; his absurd preference for a life of eternal striving over a state of unconditional pleasure is of the utmost interest to us as we await the imminent death or redundancy of man.

In a sense these questions about *who* Odysseus is are redundant because he is being reborn at this point in the story. This means that we can make a distinction between something in him, a drive that demands to live—in time and challenged by adversity—as opposed to a fixed identity that this man of many turns can never be bound to. This is the Protean aspect of Odysseus that co-exists with an "iron heart" or sense of personal integrity that even divine Calypso must love although, or precisely because, she cannot overcome it. Yet the question of who Odysseus is lies at the very heart of this work. It is even more important because, as we have argued earlier, this *aner* is the first recognizable civilized human hero. His integrity amounts to an ability to be true to himself and keep promises. This quality must be seen to be higher and more admirable than the schizoid dilemmas and perplexities of other archetypal figures like Hamlet and Bloom who fascinate us and ultimately demand our sympathy only because they lack the psychic power and erotic energy of Odysseus or Socrates. While it is customary to ridicule the primitive simplicity of these ancient heroes, it may be worthwhile to examine the counter-possibility that they were more honest about confronting certain sacred values that our modern heroes and postmodern realists willy-nilly lack the moral courage and deep self-knowledge to stare down.

Our first clue concerning Odysseus' identity comes from Zeus' choice of messenger. Hermes, quite apart from being the ancestor of Odysseus' grandfather Autolycus, is also the emissary between this world and the Underworld. This suggests to us that Ogygia is not so much a physical location as a psychic realm between worlds that Odysseus must be reborn from. Calypso is literally a place of concealment, and it is where our hero must take and hide his terrible traumatizing memories of the Trojan War. But Hermes, the father of Autolycus, is also the patron of tricksters and interpretation, as opposed to Apollo who deals with inspiration. Homer tells us that Hermes' wand has the power to both enchant and awaken the eyes of men; this means that the rare ability to see things for what they are is a gift of the gods. Men who live huddled in the Hades-like caverns and hollows of the Earth cohabit amidst many comfortable rationalizations and false representations of events otherwise too shameful to ponder in common. In this sense, Homer is Hermes in claiming the myth of his hero from its hiding place. We must also remember that disguised Odysseus will very often claim to have come from Crete, renowned as the birthplace of liars.

Seen in purely physical terms, Odysseus' condition on Calypso's island is far from miserable. His every material need is instantly met and the lovesick goddess is necessarily qualitatively superior to aging Penelope in looks or power to please; it is as if Calypso has sought to accomplish what Circe did to Odysseus' crew. She has tried to change Odysseus into a happy untroubled animal. Such a post-human being could even forget the Trojan War and contemplate the end of history with ease and equanimity. Yet Odysseus seems to remain trapped in his miseries; he has too much mind or consciousness to forget himself, and enjoy the pleasures of a pig that Circe, Calypso's aunt, effortlessly seduced his doomed shipmates with. His exile in this sad place of self-concealment may have as much to do with his bad memories and guilty conscience as with the powers of Calypso or the implacable hatred of Poseidon. Like the shades he met in Hades, he tortures himself by endlessly reliving his misdeeds. He must surely yearn for death as he eternally repeats these cycles of recollection and sleep—he can only be compared to heroes of Hades like Sisyphus or Tantalus. Such an ingenious self-punishment must surely gratify his old enemy Poseidon. The very absence of physical pain would only make his psychic guilt all the more acute.

Although Calypso, as she bitterly denounces the Olympian's double standards when it comes to dealing with those whom female goddesses love, says she promised Odysseus immortality, there is every reason to doubt this possibility. While someone cute like Dawn's beloved Tithonus can be given physical immortality, and perhaps even be preserved cosmetically, it seems that no human *soul* can bear this burden. This is why Menelaus' reward for starting the Trojan War is being bound to Helen for all eternity, without being allowed to forget who exactly she is or just how much suffering the Greek allies endured for her sake; it follows *a fortiori* that the immortal restlessness of Odysseus' soul can never be reductively fashioned into a beautiful object for the lovesick goddess to toy with. This much subjectivity cannot be reified.

Hermes, who initially brought a gift of the gods to Odysseus just before he met Circe, will now demand that our hero use this divine power to reinterpret his experiences and deliver himself from a Charybdis-like black hole of depression and solipsism. At a more literal level of our text, the gods require that Odysseus must leave his place of concealment and resume his proper position in Ithaca and the human world. This task of being re-born, which is comparable to being shipwrecked, alone and naked in a strange land, sees Odysseus achieve an uncanny separation of soul and body before he rebuilds his story around the enduring elements of his enigmatic essence. Likewise, Homer himself must abstract the essence of Odysseus from the tall stories told of his exploits and somehow justify his transformation from a figure of myth into an all too human hero. In this sense he works alongside Odysseus himself, to the extent that his hero longs to leave his concealed state, however well this secures his eternal fame, and resume his human destiny. Why do they both reject perfection?

Zeus' seemingly stern rule that Odysseus could not receive aid from either mortals or gods simply amounts to saying that he can only return as himself. Odysseus may only be reborn by being stripped of all other alien influences. If he were to return in any other form it would only negate the purpose that only he can fulfill. In his own way, Odysseus is as unique as, and even more novel than, Achilles. But this requires that he leaves Calypso's Eden-like state with rich eyes and empty hands; he must reach the human world as sinner and suppliant. All ideas of self-sufficiency or pride in his own arms, toxic aspects of his old Machiavellian persona, even the piggish elements of his body that were seduced by Circe and Calypso, must be purged from his soul. Yet Zeus also ordains that Odysseus will finally come home with prizes well exceeding his booty from Troy. Once cleansed of sin, what he earns or creates by his own confessional poetry is seen to be worth far more than the rewards of piracy.

This cleansing takes places quite literally when wrathful Poseidon sees him on the high seas and assembles the winds and thunderclouds for a terrible onslaught. The very sight leaves Odysseus echoing his son's sullen wish that he had died a noble death before the walls of Troy. Although this is not the first time that he has yearned for death, his reasons now have nothing to do with wounded pride or bitter sorrow. But nevertheless, the moment the storm actually hits him Odysseus faces up to it with his characteristic resilience. Violently thrown out of his little craft by the first massive wave, he somehow scrambles back aboard. He only accepts an offer from a sea goddess of a magical veil that keeps him afloat after his boat is totally destroyed. In a sense, this is yet another suggestion that the real story of his arrival is hidden from us. Now the choice is simply between humiliating death and reaching out; he can no longer remain in his former, almost comatose, state of suspended animation.

At this point we hear that Poseidon leaves off tormenting Odysseus and left him to swim for his life, many hours and days away from the shore. Although Athena is said to intervene at this point by sending a busy north wind that sends him towards Scheria, it is only on the third day that he finally sees land. Over this time, when we are told that our hero foresaw his death over and over again, it is remarkable how his body and spirit display a ferocious will to live even when his tired mind seems to despair of surviving. Homer quite strikingly compares Odysseus' joy to that felt by the children of a sick man when they see their father, long ravaged by an evil illness, amazingly recover his health through the gods. This gives us some sense of how Odysseus is able to detach his resilient spirit from his exhausted and despairing mind and somehow command his enduring body. Perhaps these is also a sense of the relief that the children feel about the matter having being resolved one way or another; by alluding to Nietzsche's very Homeric image of an inverted Achilles we suggested that knowledge of one's strength or sheer physical resilience is almost not always a comfort to one whose mental resources are depleted past the point of care. In other words, awareness of one's power to bear suffering is not always a blessing.

But Odysseus' ordeal is not yet over. The exhausted man now faces the prospect of being dashed by the sea's powerful waves against the smooth slippery rocks and jagged reefs lining the coast of Scheria. But yet, by going out into the open sea again, he could easily reach the limits of his physical endurance and be drowned or worse. Once again, addressing his fighting spirit, our hero bemoans his predicament; he fears that he's yet again facing the false choices that the gods tormented him with in the past. It is noteworthy that while Hermes' gift of interpretation helps one to see real meaningful choices in the face of seemingly overwhelming necessity, these options were not available during the nightmarish final stages of his voyage from Circe's isle. But at this point, now that Athena can and will assist him, Odysseus is not helpless.

This freedom of indifference is taken away from him when a huge wave dashes him against a rock that he clings to before he is hurled out to sea by its backwash. Here he is both less and more fortunate than the lesser Ajax, who successfully clung to a cliff only to be killed by Poseidon, after vainly boasting that he had defeated the gods. This is how, by placing him outside the scope of his own powers, Athena forces wary Odysseus to trust in the gods again and ask their help. Though he only prays after he escapes from deep under the waves and sees how to reach land safely, this escape from the self-verifying skepticism of internal exile is at the heart of our story.

We are told that if Odysseus had drowned, it would have been against the will of fate. This means that while destiny defines the outer limits of a man's power, its realization is ultimately up to him. But this freedom does not exclude the powers to seek grace and place trust in the gods. Human erotic striving and divine grace are not mutually exclusive. Odysseus's first prayer in years is a spontaneous ejaculation that emerges out of his deep desire to live when he finds himself in peril. This real physical danger is quite different from the more insidious risks he ran on Calypso's island where his self-pity was his own worst enemy. His cry for help is made to the god of the river that can provide him refuge from the sea into its womb-like delta. This plea must have been answered since Odysseus finally finds himself on land. Still amidst the deep reeds of the riverbank he kisses the earth, as if to acknowledge that he is back home in the real world at last. The risk was that he could have drowned in his own despair, never having left the deadly gravity of his own solipsistic self-pity.

But even after returning to reality, his troubles are far from over. Odysseus must address his fighting spirit yet again and decide where to take the sleep he so desperately needs at this point. Once again, as in the case of the reef and the rock, the choice is between the rough and the smooth. Odysseus must choose between sleeping out in the open, where the cold and damp could cause him to die from exposure—this would be death in its gentlest form, from the sea—and sheltering in the dark woods where he could be attacked by wild beasts. Prudent as always, the wily Odysseus here opts for the overt and rough over the insidious and smooth. He is surely reasoning that while his aforementioned fighting spirit or thumotic animal powers will be roused and set in motion by strife, the unopposed wish of his body to fall into a dreamless sleep could animate an inner thanatos drive and lead to a banal death. There are no clocks in the forest. Odysseus needs danger to awaken—himself.

Stripped down to what is most elemental in his psyche, Odysseus is very much like the great wild boar we observed in the metamorphoses of old Proteus. As he finds shelter beneath two entwined olive trees amidst a deep pile of dead leaves, Homer compares him to a fire that a farmer in a remote area will try to protect from the elements since he lacks the means to kindle a new flame. Likewise, our hero fears to douse his own light fearing that it will never be lit again; while his own body yearns for the nirvana of nothingness, he knows full well that his life and experiences will never be repeated again in the post-war Dark Age of Homer. Our story of a true *aner* must be seen in this light; what seems to be the mother of all revenge tales is really a subtle confessional story, artfully concealed from, and involuntarily passed on by, those who can't read past the deceptively pretty pictures on its pages/ leaves. While there are many more mysteries about Odysseus to ponder, their answers will only emerge from our wrestling dialectically with this protean man of tricks and turns.

Book 6

While Odysseus is left asleep in his bed of leaves, Athena goes about arranging for his speedy return into human society. His hosts-to-be have divinely guided ships that can traverse even the greatest distance in the course of a day; they are almost as swift as Hermes himself. It is fitting that the

Phaiakians should be his conveyors as they are closely related to the monstrous race of Cyclopes with whom Odysseus's adventures outside normal human reality commenced. Yet the Phaiakians are completely the opposite of their savage cousins; this is why the Cyclopes seem to have harried them away from the neighboring isle of Hyperia just two generations ago. Now that the gods have relocated the Phaiakians in far-off Scheria, they follow a hyper-civilized lifestyle that seems both idyllic and unreal. We find that while Ithaca cannot really have heroes because exaggerated accounts of the Trojan warriors' fabulous feats has made their imitation impossible, the subjects of Alcinous cannot really understand the gods because of their unnatural closeness or literal familiarity with the Olympians. Furthermore, the gods can no longer envy these mortals or take joy in seeing their form reflected in human flesh; this is because without the pathos of distance, the subtly formed Olympians cannot inspire mighty passions or great virtues in their mortal favorites. Their bard's comic story about Ares and Aphrodite seems to capture the essence of this somewhat prelapsarian take on divinity. In a strange way it is Odysseus who will initiate them into the ways of Zeus; this poetic palinode atones for the far more cynical manner in which he once claimed to be investigating the Cyclopes' devotion to Zeus, the god of hospitality, whilst pursuing his own selfish purposes. Yet, in this case too, we must see how his clearly self-interested actions inadvertently served the ultimate ends of the Father of the Gods.

Acting with characteristic indirection, Athena slyly places Nausikaa, the unmarried princess of Phaiakia, at the disposal of Odysseus by promising her through a dream something better or more ideal than the Disney-like reality of the happy kingdom of Alcinous and Arête can provide. When the nubile princess is courted by all the eligible youth of her kingdom, she is clearly dissatisfied with what they have to offer. While she is easily led by Athena to desire something more beautiful than the smug self-sufficiency of her own kin, Odysseus has to teach her the bitter-sweet lesson that heroism is both uglier and harder than the effortless transcendence the bards have taught her to admire. This marriage between Ares and Aphrodite can never be.

The scene that is set before Odysseus' abrupt emergence from the bushes is more suitable for one where a beautiful mortal is seduced by a god; preparatory dreams and omens are followed by a divine epiphany; one could imagine Apollo and Cassandra meeting under divinely arranged circumstances of this kind. Yet we find out that Athena's agenda is distinctly different; sexual mingling is not what the subtle virgin goddess has in mind. Instead, as Nietzsche understood, Odysseus will take his leave of Nausikaa as one should say adieu to life: with lasting gratitude rather than a still clinging desire that comes from the lovers' despairing knowledge that the beloved will be forgotten as soon as they are physically separated. Seeing Nausikaa gives him joy but Odysseus does not desire her; he merely wishes her well.

Nausikaa, whose name literally means "burner of ships," is compared repeatedly to the Olympian goddess Artemis. The comparison is first made by the poet then later by Odysseus. Its implications are quite interesting. Artemis vehemently opposed the Trojan War, demanding that its promoter, Agamemnon, sacrifice his virgin daughter Iphigenia to her before she will let the winds blow his armada to Troy. This command was probably made at her shrine at Delos, just across from Aulis where the Greek ships were becalmed. Odysseus' reference to Delos and the mission he undertook "on behalf of a mighty army before beginning a war that brought much suffering to him" suggests that he travelled to Delos, in his accustomed role as Agamemnon's ambassador, to verify the truth of Calchas' claim that Artemis had to be appeased. Only Delos offered the mother of Apollo and Artemis sanctuary from the rage of Hera, and the famous palm stalk Odysseus mentions was reputedly clung to by Leto as she gave birth to her twins. Though he compares her to Artemis, Odysseus is actually comparing the Phiaeakian princess to Iphigenia, some of whose blood stains his hands if Euripides' play *Iphigenia at Aulis* is to be believed. He is now asking sanctuary from someone who greatly resembles the former princess he once helped sacrifice. He is surely praying to Artemis and promising that he will not become complicit in another atrocious betrayal. Perhaps Artemis' demand that Agamemnon sacrifice his daughter was framed in Delphic terms? Could it have been the case, as Euripides claims, that Odysseus forced reluctant Agamemnon's hand? We recall that when Palamedes forced him to join the Trojan War by placing Telemachus before his plough when his sire feigned madness, Odysseus revenged himself by framing Palamedes for treason. Could Odysseus have exacted an equally hard penalty on Agamemnon also? If Nausikaa resembles or reminds Odysseus of Iphigenia, could it be the case that this sometime war criminal thinks he is being given a second chance, to hit the reset button and redeem himself? But what would this redemption amount to? Does the beautiful princess stand for virtue or temptation in this case?

Unlike Helen, whose face famously "launched a thousand ships," Nausikaa's name surely means that her beauty leads voyagers to *burn* their ships and abide by her: in this sense she is more like Penelope than the notorious daughter of Zeus and Leda. This interesting name for the princess of a seafaring people takes on a deep meaning when we understand the strong temptation that she poses to wandering Odysseus. She is the third in a series of women, all of divine ancestry, who are strongly attracted to him. In the first case, that of Circe, Odysseus will claim that a god, Hermes, commanded him to make love to her. Hermes delivered him from the clutches of the second woman, Calypso; in this case too he could claim with no little truth, if Homer's words can be believed, that this goddess made him sleep with her.

In this third case, however, while the attraction Nausikaa feels towards this exotic and handsome stranger is just as strong as that felt by a man who has not been with a member of his own species in seven years, Odysseus is in a position to make a truly meaningful—albeit difficult— choice. Nausikaa will offer him youth, an easily gained kingdom, and fabulous wealth, as well as an easy life that will save him from the task of having to undertake a bitter struggle for his home, lost reputation, and aging wife that Circe, Calypso, and Tiresias himself all warned him about. But is it possible for the famously protean Odysseus to simply reinvent himself by casting aside name, reputation, and character? Isn't this daunting challenge well within the capabilities of the only man who twice resisted the blandishments of Helen herself, the iron-hearted hero who even managed to successfully listen to the enchanting voices of the Sirens? There is also another possibility that surely must have crossed Odysseus' lightning-swift mind soon after discovering Nausikaa's identity. Though he first merely requested safe passage home, the recovery of his kingdom would be greatly eased if Odysseus were to forge a marital bond with a rich nautical power.

But we have far outshot our place in the text. When Odysseus first set eyes on lovely Nausikaa he does not know that she is a princess; the striking and nubile beauty is simply the only person left standing before him while her maids have left screaming in horror before his fearful presence. While she is filled with courage by Athena to hold her ground before this human predator, Odysseus for all of his physical desperation has already fast debated whether or not to clasp Nausikaa's knees when making his plea. Having decided to plead at a distance, he will now humbly, albeit in the most flattering terms, simply beg for a rag to cover his nudity and directions to town. Having been symbolically reborn from the sea, it is entirely appropriate that this nameless stranger is placed in a situation where he is washed and clothed in accordance with the divine laws of hospitality that apply in all parts of the world.

As usual, Odysseus' words falling like snowflakes to cover his terrifying physical appearance, reveal far more about the man than his unprepossessing appearance; after first placing himself at her mercy and asking the regal maiden whether or not she is a goddess, he goes on to declare that he has never seen anything as beautiful in all his life. Now comparing her to Leto's famous palm-tree at Delos, he declares that only humble awe stops him from grasping her knees in the traditionally abject manner of a suppliant. Then, after making his minimal request, Odysseus slyly raises the ante along with his own status. He promises to pray to the gods that she receives what every woman most wishes, and the greatest claim to glory: "the finest gift in the world: a home shared with a spouse with whom she can be united as one in both heart and mind." His timeless words, reminding another generation of Bob Marley's reggae song, both reveal and conceal a great deal. They show her that he has quite transcended his own desperate plight and grasped at first sight what Nausikaa's deepest desire is. To this extent he has deftly altered the asymmetrical terms of their initial relationship and shown that beyond being cultured and widely travelled, he is also fully attentive to the nature and *telos* of the beauty standing before him.

Nausikaa's careful and courteous response shows us that she has understood the meaning of his words well, and upgraded his status accordingly. After according due respect to Zeus, the source of all good and ill fortune, she promises him clothing and every benefit in her land. Now identifying herself as a Phaiakian and the daughter of King Alcinous, the basis of all power in the land, she calls sharply on her maids to return and provide her new friend with food and drink before bathing him in the river at a sheltered location. Nausikaa then proudly says that the gods love the Phaiakians too much to allow any enemy to reach their soil; she proclaims the law of hospitality: every stranger and beggar should be treated as a guest sent by Zeus.

While Odysseus has already quite fascinated Nausikaa, both by his dramatic entry into her life and through his captivating speech, it is only after he has bathed, oiled, and dressed himself that the princess is physically attracted to him. We are told that Athena, for the first but not the last time on his long journey home, augments Odysseus' beauty by making him seem taller, broader of build, thicker of hair, and overall handsomer than this middle-aged man would have been in reality, whatever that means. It is now that Nausikaa gazes on him in wonder and, comparing him to an Olympian god, openly shares with her maids the wish that a man like Odysseus could be called her husband and stay with her forever. The princess desires her frog.

It is after this explicit admission that she conveys these sentiments in an indirect form to Odysseus himself, as part of the directions to her father's palace that he had originally requested. Explaining why he could not travel with her to their common destination, Nausikaa tells him that it would be deemed highly inappropriate by the common Phaiakians if she were to bring a tall handsome stranger to her home. She goes on to suggest that they would be swift to draw the legitimate inference that their princess, despite being courted by all the most eligible young men among her own people, has brought an unknown alien lover home with her. While it is quite noteworthy that she has taken the opportunity to both compliment him on his looks and inform him of her availability for marriage under the proper circumstances, we will soon come to see that even more is going on here—under our very eyes. Like our hero, we must await aid from Athena to discern the pattern she is weaving.

The first indication that something important is taking place here comes from close study of Nausikaa's directions to Odysseus. She tells him that rather than lingering about the ships while she and her maids make their way home, he must wait for her *in a grove sacred to Athena*. Although the redoubtable daughter of Zeus has been helping Odysseus all this while, this is the first explicit reference to her that our hero has heard over the course of his journey. Odysseus will soon take this opportunity to pray to his goddess once he has followed Nausikaa and her maids to this sanctuary. But we must see that this prayer to her is not optional but actually required by his benefactor! Nausikaa tips Odysseus off when she tells him that once in the palace of Alcinous he must address his request not to the king *but to his queen* as she weaves by his side. Only the queen, Nausikaa tells him, can guarantee his journey home if she will take him to her heart. As we shall soon see, these words will assume a profound meaning when we discover in the next book from a disguised Athena herself that Alcinous' queen is also his brother's child. In other words, although we are clearly still in Poseidon's territory, *it is his niece Athena* who will ensure that Odysseus will make his journey home if she is properly approached! It follows also that while Odysseus has prayed to Artemis, and not inappropriately so since Nausikaa looked like Iphigenia, she is but the signifier, not the signified; the real power behind the scenes here is Athena. We can see how this entire episode with Nausikaa can be seen as a test of Odysseus' virtue. Athena could very well be as jealous as any other goddess concerning her favorite mortal Odysseus. If he were to plead necessity as he did with Circe and Calypso and dally with Nausikaa in bad faith, then green-eyed Athena cannot or will not be in a position to help her once-beloved come back home.

Our narrator confirms this interesting—albeit esoteric—point after Odysseus finally prays to Athena; after we listen to him tell his goddess that he had not done so since she refused to hear him when Poseidon shattered his ship, we discover that though Athena hears him, she could not reveal herself directly out of respect for her angry uncle! Yet this deference clearly does not prevent her from coming directly and lovingly to his aid, albeit in a highly suggestive disguise that he later sees through, just after he has finally invoked her name in prayer. While we see that Nestor spoke truly of the virgin goddess Athena's exceptional love for brilliant and wily Odysseus, the true history and exact terms of their "special relationship" remain to be seen.

Book 7

One of the most interesting things we find out from the description of Nausikaa's return home, seemingly drawn out so that Odysseus can make his own far slower progress to the same place, is the discovery that her old nursemaid was brought to Scheria by Phaiakian piracy. In this she is unlike her opposite number, Eurycleia of Ithaca, who was merely purchased from pirates by Laertes. This is consistent with the disguised Athena's stern warning that Odysseus should not have anything to do with persons that he would meet on his way to the palace; she adds a second degree of menace to Nausikaa's less emphatic comment about the rudeness of her father's subjects. The people of Phaiakia are not as pleasant as their almost divine habitat. While it is clear that the conventions of hospitality do not come naturally to them, their true nature is never fully revealed to us at any point in the story Odysseus tells. His reasons may well have to do with the huge debt he owes to their princess. She is very conspicuously absent when Odysseus makes his dramatic entry into her home.

While we shall later examine evidence suggesting that the entire transit via Scheria did not happen as Homer recounts it, it should be seen that something akin to this occurred before Calypso rather than after her; this story does depict our hero in the act of throwing himself at the mercy of a ruler with great maritime power. It is also clearly the case that he wins their favor by a blend of storytelling and flirtation. Like Othello, he will provide those who merely profit from piracy with glorious tales of heroism and monsters that their own seafarers could not supply. In one sense, the court of Alcinous may also be seen to resemble the Olympian regime of Zeus himself. The Gods too are thrilled by human deeds they could never themselves experience. This parasitic relation between gods and heroes must be seen to also have an erotic aspect; Homer's anthropomorphic deities cannot live without human intercourse.

This explains why Athena serves as our hero's escort to the palace. In fulfillment of Nausikaa's assertion that even an innocent child could show him the way, she now appears as a young girl holding a pitcher. Responding to his invitation to escort him, a total stranger, to the palace Athena addresses him as old father, bids him to stay silent, and covers him in mist that makes Odysseus invisible to any rude Phaiakian. Upon reaching their destination the disguised goddess, who has already warned him that the natives do not like to receive visitors, now proceeds to give him additional sage advice that is manifestly inconsistent with her chosen maidenly appearance.

Before telling him about Nausikaa's endogamous family and urging him to gain the favor of the queen, who can settle all quarrels if she well disposed, Athena advises Odysseus to be bold and fear nothing. This earliest use of the maxim that fortune favors the bold seems necessary because Odysseus is awestruck by the splendor of his surroundings, possibly as impressed as his son was by Menelaus' home. We may perhaps infer from this that his prior travels had not taken him to places as luxurious as the palace of Alcinous. Whatever the houses of Circe and Calypso were like, they do not seem to have been as impressive as this almost Olympian residence. Yet this may not be the main reason for Athena's odd insistence that her favorite's actions should not be limited by the relatively demotic rules of safety and prudence.

While the significance of Odysseus, that most Machiavellian of heroes, paying humble obeisance to what's prayed for/arête rather than might of mind/Alcinous is quite noteworthy, it pales in significance before the stunned silence with which Odysseus' request for hospitality and repatriation is greeted. The king behaves as if he has never found himself in such a situation and it is left to Echeneus, the oldest lord of Phaiacia, to instruct his king in the proper protocol to be observed. All but accusing Alcinous for this indecent state of affairs, this survivor from their previous home near the island of Polyphemus shames his ruler into belatedly acting along with the neglected code of hospitality that Zeus had reiterated at the start of our epic. When the king finally responds, he does little more than echo the exact words Echeneus had used. It seems as if Alcinous has been compelled by observing the boldness of his suppliant to act on a principle that he had previous honored by its never openly being breached. He would never emulate his not-so-distant kin the Cyclopes Polyphemus and deny the principle of hospitality, and by extension the sovereignty of Zeus himself, by virtue of his close relationship to mighty Poseidon. Indeed, we could even say that Odysseus will go on to force the issue by making explicit reference to the battering at sea he had received from the Earth-Shaker.

By smuggling Odysseus into the court of Alcinous, his two patrons, Nausikaa and Athena, provided our hero with an opportunity to display his true mettle and *earn* his trip back home. By disguising him as a handsome potential husband, Athena made Odysseus irresistible to Nausikaa, who in turn dressed him as a Phaiakian and provided the chance to gain favor with the king and queen by his own merit. Soon, by re-dressing himself in his own words, Odysseus will reap far more than he could have had he returned from Troy with his fair share of its spoils and glory. In another sense of course Nausikaa is but the mortal shadow of Athena. We have just seen how the princess ordered Odysseus to tarry in the grove dedicated to her divine aspect.

A lasting perplexity posed by Book 7 has to do with Alcinous' swift willingness to marry his only daughter to a complete stranger. Even if the Phaiakians judge men by appearances, and are led by Odysseus' persuasive speech, glorified presence, and familiar clothing to accept him as one of their own kind, isn't this haste unseemly? Could it be the case that the gods are testing their respect for Zeus and his laws of hospitality? It is also possible that they took him for Hermes, to whom sacrifices were being made when Odysseus made his mysterious or godlike appearance out of nowhere. Despite all of Odysseus' protestations, Alcinous has to suspect, not falsely, that some deeper divine design is being fulfilled through his arrival. The divine dimension of this story makes it easier to swallow; Zeus is naturally charmed by the human correlate of Athena; he sees that Odysseus and his daughter belong together. But before her father blesses their union, it is necessary that the cleansed and all but rehabilitated Odysseus confess to his previous infidelities and ask for forgiveness; as we shall see, this did not happen in the court of Aeolus or with the Laestrygonians, a place where the cannibal king's daughter herself led Odysseus' men to the trap. We cannot fail to see that by this tale Odysseus would subtly accuse Athena of treachery.

Meanwhile the vain Phaiakians will be forced to see, first in wonder and then in awe, what had eluded their prior, falsely divine, take on tragic human reality as a comedy staged for their entertainment. Priding themselves on their easy sheltered existence and kinship to the gods, which led them to see other men as vile Yahoos or quasi- anthropic animals, the Phaiakians had become oddly alienated from their need for piety and potential for virtue. The designer of the Trojan Horse will be the device by which Athena will tear down their walls and drag the spoiled kin of Poseidon into the world order ruled by Zeus, the god of hospitality and protector of strangers. In an oddly comic twist, Poseidon himself will demand that Zeus punish his offspring. The mores of piracy will be defeated by the emergent values of the god of hospitality.

Because of their closeness to the gods, both the Cyclopes and Phaiakians were often allowed to deviate farther from civilized behavior than other less favored mortals; the Cyclopes sought to be free of all restraint and the Phaiakians chose snobbery. Both ways of life turned out to offend Zeus, the god of hospitality and protector of all strangers: Odysseus is destined to be both his educator and his agent of justice. Although, in each case, dark prophetic warnings were given long before the arrival of Odysseus, both groups are far too set in their insular and/or inhospitable ways to imagine how an ordinary looking human being would dramatically change their old entitled way of seeing the world and dealing with inferiors. In due time the old nobility of Odysseus' own island will be taught an equally hard lesson. Furthermore, we see here how the gods themselves are forced to relearn the lesson Achilles had taught them at Troy. The relationship between gods and men, and indeed the very self-perception of the gods themselves, is fundamentally changed by heroic deeds; this, the lesson of the *Iliad* is being reiterated in the *Odyssey* by its unlikely hero. Put bluntly, while the matter of Odysseus' tall tales—the polished perfection of ancient myths about the war that Homer inherited—is served up to the gods and those who live like them; the content of his confessions is for men who will supplant them. It is to this Promethean division of the spoils that we should later give close attention.

Book 8

Athena summons the Phaiakians to their place of assembly to behold something that they have never seen before. Although they have been spoiled by the gods and are well familiar, thanks to Demodokus, with all that popular opinion or conventional wisdom has to say about gods and men, Athena somehow suggests that the godlike stranger is something quite novel and extraordinary in ways they cannot even imagine. While the Phaiakians judge men by appearances, and are entertained by stories recounted by their blind bard to whom nothing can ever appear physically, they have never met a hero in the flesh and lack the power to see the inner essence of Odysseus. Someone unique even among heroes by his interior qualities of mind, eloquence, and endurance can only reveal himself to his naïve hosts in a way that shatters the easy clichés that they make of their bard's sublime words. Odysseus, playing his part in the dark plan of Zeus, will prime the smug Phaiakians for their fall into the fullness of a human reality. For all its limitations, the *Odyssey* seems to say that the potential of the human condition must yet be chosen over and against the beginning and end of history that the Cyclopes and Phaiakians represent. Otherwise put, human striving has to be picked over the pseudo-divine kind of perfection that is enjoyed by those beings who live without toil or turmoil at the end of the horizon.

The Phaiakians see just as the gods and bestial Cyclopes do; for them appearance is reality. This is why the gods depend on man; to the extent that they can only see themselves in the effects they produce in the world, the fates of gods and mortals are inextricably tied. Of course, the Phaiakians do not suffer under this subtle limitation. Yet their physical existence, by its very perfection and uncomplicated character, has left them with shallow souls and very limited capacity for growth. They are much more like the monocular Cyclopes than one would normally suppose. The eruption of Odysseus into their worlds makes them aware of a whole other dimension of reality lurking within the undisturbed depths of their shallow souls.

The songs of Demodokus can also be viewed in a similar manner. While they sit quite well at the surface level of appearances, giving his audience an easy pleasure that seems to confirm their sense of entitled superiority over other mortals, these songs have a deeper significance that may even elude the inspired performer himself. We recall from Plato's *Apology* that when Socrates, over the course of his search for wisdom, questioned the poets, he discovered that their verses were wiser than their makers; they turned out to be very incompetent judges of the quality and meaning of their own poems. This suggested to him that while and when the best poets were indeed inspired, they were not truly poets in the sense of *making* their own finest works of art. We should also observe that even the famous blindness of Demodokus could be Homer's way of telling us that he's equally blind to the deeper significance of his own words; otherwise put, it is for humans to impute meaning to the divine and heroic exploits he describes. To the extent that they are unaffected by fear, disease, hunger, pain or mortality, the actions of the gods simply are what they are. Likewise, the *Iliad*'s heroes pursued their short-lived glorious careers by living fully in the moment; to the extent that they reflect on the forces that nevertheless overwhelm their power for deliberation, both Achilles and Hector also anticipate the new age of the thinking *aner* that will be ushered in by the *Odyssey* and its new hero.

The first song of blind Demodokus is clearly aimed by his muse at the one thoughtful person among the many unreflective shades in the audience. The inspired bard does not merely sing about Odysseus, he sings about the fundamental cause of the great turmoil in his life and soul. Furthermore, the angry argument between Achilles and Odysseus, although unremarked upon in the other synopses we possess of the heroic cycle, epitomizes both the relation between the *Iliad* and the *Odyssey*, and the transition to the beginning of Western civilization that the two works depict when read together. Even as the Golden Age of Pericles dedicated itself to the short and glorious career of beautiful Achilles, and saw ugly Odysseus as merely a proto-Machiavellian schemer and pirate, Plato's ironic Socrates would come to take full possession of the meaning of the *Odyssey*'s anti- or post-heroic archetype and allow Christian virtue to take its stand upon the impregnable soul of the once and future King of Ithaca. Socrates' ignorance has its root in Odysseus' disguise as no-body.

When Demodokus sings to his audience of one and many about the quarrel between the two great heroes, the survivor Odysseus weeps. While we are told that their leader Agamemnon was greatly delighted in this dispute, seeing in it the fulfillment of a prophecy given by Apollo, the obtuse king probably failed to discern the fullest meaning of the Delphic Oracle's words. It is as though he was told, what Croesus would be told many centuries later, that a mighty empire would fall. He little knew that this was a sign of great evil that would be visited on both the Greeks and the Trojans in fulfillment of the plans of Zeus. We could even see Alcinous as being just as oblivious to the stern punishment that Zeus is about to mete out to his people, even as he delights in listening to stories about the terrible and bloody siege of Troy.

It should also be noted that even though Achilles and Odysseus clearly represent brawn and brains respectively, the desired end is identical: the utter destruction of Troy. Although Achilles follows the bloody warpath of Ares in a way which made even greedy Agamemnon single him out as being the only hero who delighted in violence for its own sake, surely the mark of Ares, we find that Athena and her hero Odysseus are just as single-mindedly bent on sacking Ilium. It is as though violence is an end itself to Achilles and only a perfectly acceptable means to a far from benevolent end for Odysseus. Further, Odysseus who is only referred to as the sacker of cities for the first time here, seems to learn many things about cities and souls through violence; he discerns the natures of things by and for destroying and/or taking possession of them. His shining intellect is only a predator's tool.

Such a reading clearly suggests that Ares has seduced not merely Aphrodite but also Odysseus; the values of the *Iliad* have corrupted the protagonists of the *Odyssey*, at least at this point in the story being recounted by the inspired bard. As a result ruin came down on both the Greeks and Trojans; though we have said that this was in fulfillment of the plan of Zeus, it is clear that this outcome is a triumph for Ares, well depicted as "the god facing both sides" as he eggs them on to mutually assured destruction. He is like the arms dealer or "merchant of death" who profits by selling weapons to both sides and creating an arms race where he is the only winner. If the *Iliad* describes the ruinous consequences of the quarrel between Agamemnon and Achilles, the first part of the *Odyssey* silently depicts the terrible results of the rivalry between Achilles and Odysseus. In this case too, Ares' power has driven a hero mad.

While this bitter recognition is surely sufficient to make the rehabilitated and soon to be repatriated Odysseus weep as sadly as he did by the waters of Ogygia, it is swiftly followed by another episode that reminds us that the past of Odysseus is never really past but remains undigested in his psychic belly, the most shameless part of a man that leads him to forget his sorrow and strive continually to serve it. When Alcinous, the sole witness to his guest's hidden grief, kindly or embarrassedly decides to adjourn the bard's performance and leads Odysseus to watch the young Phaiakians compete in athletic events, we are allowed our first glimpse into the true inner essence of our long-suffering hero. Even as Odysseus successfully resumes his persona as an urbane and perfect guest, he is rudely jarred from this pose by an unexpected invitation that soon assumes the unmistakable proportions of an insult.

After the well-born Phaiakian youth, all designated unmistakably with nautical names, have wrestled, run, boxed, jumped and thrown the discus with what we will subsequently find to be greater grace than excellence, the unaccustomed heat of competition and the thrill of victory seems to lead the Kings's favorite son Laodamas and his godlike comrade, the wrestler Euryalos, to invite Odysseus to join them. They are suitably impressed by his powerful arms and legs to believe him to be well capable, despite age and the wear and tear of nautical travel, of taking part in their contests. However, when Odysseus, who characteristically has his mind set on the goal of returning home, politely declines, Euryalos taunts him using winged words that inadvertently find a very dangerous mark. He scratches scars left by Achilles.

It is as if Athena, who previously enhanced the physical appearance of Odysseus, now allows the brash young man to see an entirely different aspect of this most many-sided of individuals. Accordingly Euryalos, after having won an easy victory over other callow amateurs, who best resemble Penelope's suitors or frat boys of our own time, condescendingly informs Odysseus that he did not look like an athlete at all but seemed most like a cautiously coast-hugging merchant sailor, the kind of man who cared only for profit and was too much of a coward to practice piracy. The spoilt pretty favorite of the gods is showing contempt for the ill-favored hick from Ithaca. This is a scenario that Odysseus has been in before, with wounds to prove it.

Accusing Euryalos of hubris, Odysseus warns him of the difference between comely external appearance and the internal psychic qualities of wit and eloquence. We are reminded of Trojan Antenor's astute observation in the *Iliad* that Odysseus, though short, seemingly sullen and unimpressive in appearance, carried all before him when he began to speak. There is an important difference between seemingly divine perfection, which can only be flawed by exposure to experience, and the very human capacity to learn from mistakes, something that makes sweet use of adverse events.

In the context of the bard's song, Euryalos is playing bold Achilles and despising the prudent strategy of Odysseus. He hates more than the gates of Hades a man who ever calculates and dissembles in his words and actions. We suddenly find ourselves back before the doomed walls of Troy, and Odysseus is once again the man he was then. The grief-bringing grandson of Autolycus, the wolf itself, flashes forth. Now he grabs an over-sized discus and hurls it far beyond the marks set by the previous competitors, as easily as the blinded Polyphemus hurled rocks the size of mountain peaks at his swiftly retreating ship. As Athena cried out that even a blind man could distinguish his mark from the others, Odysseus glares at the timid Phaiakians as the Cyclopes once terrified their forebears and challenges them to beat him at any sport. While prudently refusing to compare himself to the immortal gods, and courteously forbearing from challenging Laodamas his host, he all but identifies himself as the greatest surviving warrior of the generation of heroes that fought and died at Troy.

Alcinous now intervenes with great tact and after apologizing to Odysseus, sends for Demodokus to soothe the savage unappeased rage that lingered deep within the temperate soul governing the polymorphous exterior of our hero. Now the dancing feet of the Phaiakian youth prepare the way for the bard, but even his music will be eclipsed by the voice of the great indomitable will of the hero, like the dark blind will of Schopenhauer, as it cries out in sorrow and begs for redemption. Here, yet again, we must observe how the clichéd stories of the war are displaced, first by the true poets and then by a critical account that can barely be put in words, but yet will try to leap over space and time until it resonates in the depths of a sympathetic soul.

The second song of Demodokus goes right to the very heart of the human condition itself. While the song about the quarrel between Achilles and Odysseus has well described the problem of the transition from Ares to Athena and also hints how Odysseus himself is infected by rage as he strives to prove himself to be better than the divinely favored Achilles, this second song depicts the timeless interaction between the forces personified as Ares and Aphrodite that drive human history Even though both deities behave reprehensibly, to the extent that they defy the old sacred bonds of marriage, sexual desire and rage are eternally recurrent principles that give grounds for hope out of despair and threaten all unjust claims to power. This means also that there are no final victories for men. Though Hephaestus claims that he won or bought Aphrodite fairly, fortune's fundamental fickleness will not change; Odysseus may temporarily be Ares but he must eventually be Hephaestus. We also see these gods resolve their differences more amicably than their alter egos in the *Iliad* or their equally implacable short-lived human devotees and equivalents.

Even though we could be perplexed by the strange transformation of the unlovable blustering Ares of the *Iliad* into someone more like Paris, whom wanton Aphrodite finds irresistibly attractive, this myth of Ares and Aphrodite could very well be the earliest rendering of Machiavelli's bawdy insight into the ways of fortune. In other words, this song seems to be saying: "who can teach a lover any law," and warning that even sanctified human institutions often cannot prevail against the eternal and irrepressible power of sexual desire. Yet, instead of just saying "fortune favors the bold," advice that we have seen disguised Athena give to Odysseus, the teacher of evil called personified fortune a whore, and told us that she is often strongly, albeit temporarily, attracted to those young men who can make the most violent love to her. While this connection between sex, violent desire, and the fickle ways of fortune remains to be clarified further by the bard's last song, we can surely see that while angry Odysseus resembles Hephaestus, bold Ares is likened to Euryalos. Ultimately, just as Odysseus will go on to humiliate the brash youth, Aphrodite will ever return to Hephaestus, since his enduring power and art exceed the unskilled energy of her beautiful but boastful suitors. Technique and strength of mind will make better use of fickle Fortune than the youthful promise she wantonly smiles upon and gives beginner's luck to. Although yet again, Odysseus beats Achilles, he's reminded that his victories comes by ceaseless activity rather than from nature. But this also means that he can only win but never fully possess what he has won. Like resentful Hephaestus, he is always denied final victories over fortune, or the recklessly vain presumption of youth, which is incapable of holding what it boldly grasps. While nature/Poseidon will eventually compensate Odysseus, *he* will never be able to own either fortune's unquestioning love or nature's ready compliance, as by divine right. Over and over again, he can only triumph by some new, angry, display of virtuosity. While, like Hephaestus, he often rues the day he was born, this very rage will be the bellows of the fiery unnatural creativity that brings much benefit to his posterity. In other words, Hephaestus needs the dalliances of Ares and Aphrodite to be himself.

After Demodokus has sung, and only this once does not reduce Odysseus to tears, the company is treated to an impressive exhibition of dance. After his guest has praised them to the heavens, and Alcinous has responded by gathering gifts of gold and clothing from the other Phaiakian lords, Euryalos completes their reconciliation by offering Odysseus his own beautiful sword. While the Ithacan's double-edged but smooth response "may you never have need of this yourself" passes unremarked, there is no doubt that he is highly satisfied with the gifts that arrive to be spread before him, and the fine warm bath that the household maids now provide. The gifts and honors, strikingly given by a man whose name Eury-alos literally means "broad-sea" hints that just as Hephaestus was duly compensated by Poseidon, Odysseus has also received recompense from the sea itself for his loss of name, time, and spoils. He no longer needs to conceal his name for fear of awful retribution from Poseidon.

Now that the requirements of hospitality have been fully satisfied, and the favored Phaiakians have, to this extent, been received into the world order of Zeus, Odysseus says a humble and heartfelt goodbye to Nausikaa before he goes out to sit by her father at the feast in his great hall. Here, after first honoring Demodokus with a fine piece of meat cut by his own hands, Odysseus asks the harper, after first proclaiming that he prizes him before all other mortals for his divine gifts, to sing the tale of the wooden horse "which Epeios made with Athena helping, the cunning device that Odysseus filled with men and brought within the citadel of Troy." The bard has told them of the sufferings of the Greeks as if he was there himself or heard it from one who was; now he must sing the song of their ultimate triumph. If Demodokus can do this, Odysseus swears to bear witness to all mankind of the harper's divine talents.

The bard tells us that the Trojans, like the surface-skimming Phaiakians, judged the Trojan Horse by its fine appearance, little suspecting the evil contents that its belly would spawn. The Phaiakians had to choose between killing Athena-embellished Odysseus, throwing him back into the water, and receiving him within their walls. Likewise the Trojans debated whether to destroy the horse, pushing it out into the sea, or taking it in. We hear that Troy was doomed to fall once it took the horse within its walls; can't we say the same of the Phaiakians and deep-souled Odysseus? What effect will the tales tumbling off his tongue have on their subsequent history?

Demodokus now sings of how, while the Trojans feasted and celebrated, the Greeks poured out of the deep-bellied horse and took the citadel by storm. He singles out particularly the exploit of Odysseus who, accompanied by Menelaus and "looking like Ares himself" entered the house of Deiphobus, presumably where Helen had received him earlier. Here he "fought the deadliest battle of his life" and, aided by Athena, emerged victorious. While the name "Deiphobus," meaning god-fearing, is significant, even more attention should be paid to Odysseus' resemblance to Ares.

This odd likeliness is our key to understanding why, at the very moment when his greatest exploit is being recounted and celebrated, Odysseus breaks down and is seen by all to weep like one of the victims of his own craft. He's memorably being compared to someone as unfortunate as Andromache: a woman dragged off to slavery while she clings weeping to her dying husband who has fallen in battle.

But if Odysseus, despite all contrary appearances, is Andromache, then whose body is he figuratively clinging to? What does he suddenly see? What is this uncanny recognition that reduces him to pitiful tears amidst this tale of his literal apotheosis? Just as the Greeks bearing sorrows poured out of the seemingly beautiful horse, so too do the stories provided by De-modokus, despite their apparent beauty, turn out to contain accounts of the many evils and sorrows that great Odysseus has suffered. To the gods, the tale of the Trojan War is as comic as the tale of the affair between Ares and Aphrodite or boastful Paris and Helen! Once the two lovers are trapped together, in the webs of Hephaestus (or Odysseus), a great chain of events is set in motion and Troy is doomed to fall. This is a divine comedy and a human tragedy.

Just as the first of Demodokus' songs helped us to interpret the next, the key to the third song is contained in the preceding two. His first song draws attention to the likelihood that the long struggle to surpass Achilles could pollute the high values of Athena and/in the soul of Odysseus. Once the last song reveals that Odysseus has become Ares-like, we see an image of what he had become during his soon to be recounted wonderings when we look again at the song of the lusty affair between Ares and Aphrodite. Despite the victory over Deiphobos that was granted by Athena, it now appears that Odysseus is a new Ares, madly drawn towards many equally false images of Aphrodite or Helen. This implies that despite her inability to coax Odysseus out of the horse, Helen had the last laugh after Troy fell. In this context, the continual dalliance between Ares and Aphrodite reveals more than the cliché about every girl loving a soldier; we have to see that men traumatized by battle seek to return to the womb; regardless of whether their goal is sexual reaffirmation or psychic rebirth, this divinely enacted cycle of destruction and desire is an essential aspect of the tragic human condition. In Odysseus' case the effects of becoming Ares are tragic; in defeating "Deiphobos" he has literally overcome/lost his fear of the gods. He is necessarily alienated from his patroness, Athena. As a result, she regresses too; maybe, *pace* Nietzsche, she cannot forgive him for what his absence has done to her! This matches how Eris, Ares' sister, corrupted Athena and Hera at the judgment of Paris. Their rage led to the Trojan War and caused the human tragedy of the *Iliad*. By this psychic rift, Odysseus is split in two; both *outis* and the Cyclopes are one-eyed monsters. Our hero must be seen to be weeping over himself. In books 9-12 we go on to see the career of this wretched man, no-body, Odysseus' alter-ego. This persona must be repudiated or left behind in Hades before he can return home.

There is a strong connection between the seeming opposed forces of angry aversive rage and raw sexual desire. As we saw, the power of Ares, the war god, infects all who comes into contact with it; while the wounded warrior's soul loses self-control, it gains a great deal of destructive power. As a result, he defies and exceeds all of the civilizing limits established by convention or sanctified by tradition. These seem to be the very qualities drawing Odysseus and making him attractive to fortune or even to life itself; Ares is about bullying, pursuit, and fear. The Greeks saw Poseidon's realm, Gaia, as Machiavelli regarded fortune: a chaotic force, which continually first desires and then rebels against mastery or order. While the cowardice felt in battle leads to lust, true courage is tied to love. Love is not an indiscriminate passion; it can also be the basis for genuine deliberate action. This may be the key to separating Athena from Ares. The fear felt when Athena lifts her aegis has to do with a thuggish coward's reaction to genuine courage. Achilles reacted thus to Priam's courage born of love. Athena is linked to strategy, prudence, and seeing the ultimate particular.

It is also noteworthy that Zeus does not appear in any of the songs of Demodokus. In the first song it is Agamemnon who takes the place Zeus occupied in the *Iliad*, just as it is Odysseus who replaces Agamemnon in the quarrel with Achilles. Next, in the song of the affair between Ares and Aphrodite, we see Poseidon replace Zeus; it is he who assures Hephaestus that compensation will be made for his loss. Lastly, when we are told of Odysseus' taking of Troy, we hear that he slays Deiphobus; this very name means fear of Zeus. So in other words, just as Achilles' semi-apotheosis serves to change the relation between gods and men, the Trojan War itself has somehow led to the eclipse of Zeus, the god of hospitality and justice. Scheria has the favor of Poseidon, like the Cyclopes. The Phaiakians do not know of, or need, Zeus because they are favored by his brother; or alternately, they are like Zeus being entertained by the other gods as they act out a human comedy. It is Odysseus who must bring this new gospel of hospitality to Gods, Greeks, and barbarians. The delayed justice of Zeus must ultimately be shown to rule over the various divine forces that make men unequal. Or we may even claim that, since the power-based hegemony of Zeus was overthrown by the apocalyptic rage of Achilles, until Odysseus returns, a new view of the gods, one based on Zeus the god of hospitality, cannot be inaugurated.

Chapter 3
A Reprobate's Recollections: Books 9–12

Demodokus has seen Odysseus' soul. Yet as with the poets of the *Apology*, the blind bard is not the best exegete of what he has grasped. It is now up to Odysseus to interpret the meaning of these seminal insights into his soul. He will give a visual account of himself, clothed in spatial-temporal terms, that seems to explain what befell him since the Trojan War. In other words, Odysseus will tell us who he is by a vivid series of lies. They will be seen to make up a false virtual reality, a veritable Charybdis of poetry, we must steer clear of if we wish to see into its tragic core.

We must thus endure and suffer the perplexities of an Odyssey within the *Odyssey*; otherwise put we must, as readers, endure the disorientation amidst whirling chaos our hero underwent. Books 9-12 are often taken along with Book 22 as the whole of the *Odyssey*; as a result this part of the work is best known and least understood. Admitting we are the progeny of the Lotus-eaters, we must struggle to recall what was once greedily consumed, only making it easier to be denied and repressed. In a sense our narrator is Antinous confessing his own misdeeds to his mighty mind—or Alcinous; this interior voyage, like Augustine's *Confessions*, cannot be seen as a literal narrative of an epic voyage over land and sea. Also, our narrator is not a liar *simpliciter*; he is also divided against himself. The gloating sacker of Troy cannot be easily separated from the man who weeps over but misses his own vices. Further, Homer, like Plato, loves to test his listeners by making the unjust speech of the siren stronger than justice's voice. It takes much for Odysseus to confess his crimes; it is even harder for him to physically detach himself from his old identity. Readers prefer picaresque tales to gloomy self-flagellation; we eagerly seek out shameless liars, but avoid them when they become ugly beggars. In a like way the exoteric tales of Odysseus are preferred to their allegorical meaning. Both pirate and smuggler, he is trading in false stories but really sneaking

71

in human wisdom. We ultimately read Homer not for myths about gods but for the truth about man and the human state.

Odysseus, the famed prince of liars, provides this account of his great wanderings in response to a request made by King Alcinous that his yet anonymous guest divulge his name and explain the bitter tears he shed upon hearing familiar stories about the recent war. For Alcinous and for the Phaiakians, as for the Olympian gods, the great Trojan War was the ultimate source of entertainment. What is tragic for mortal man is but a comedy for his immortal gods. Alcinous has just told Odysseus that these sad historical events that make up our days are the work of the gods; many dark threads of death are woven through the fabric of history to make the overall pattern all the more beautiful for posterity. After Alcinous—his name means mighty mind—speaks with smug assurance of a song by which all suffering is redeemed, once it is properly contemplated by gods and Phaiakians, Odysseus takes the lyre from Demodokus. He does this as unexpectedly as he will act in his great hall when he takes possession of another stringed instrument. In this case also, he implies that Apollo's gift is justly his. Only he knows all the misery that the Trojan War visited on the Greeks, and only the tale of this man of sorrows can serve as the basis for the best, most beautiful song about the greatest moment in human history. In this sense the knowledge of the gods is limited; they see all that interests them but cannot imagine what happens in the souls of those men who suffer and strive in silence. The Blues must replace Bach.

Although exiled Thucydides claimed that the Peloponnesian War, and the rather pessimistic lessons gleaned from its godforsaken carnage, supplanted the tale of Troy and the wisdom of Homer that animated Pericles' celebrated School of Hellas; I will argue that a proper reading of the *Odyssey* restores the poetic laurels to Homer. It also follows that the result of the battle between the two Athenians, Thucydides and Plato, over the conclusion to be drawn from the Peloponnesian War could very well depend on a Socratic reading of the *Odyssey*; Pericles' reading of Homer is based on the *Iliad* and the Athenian emulation of the short angry career of glorious Achilles. Socrates' lifelong role model, especially when he understands that he must obey Apollo and cultivate the muses, is Odysseus. Otherwise put, unlike Achilles who paradoxically fulfilled his fate by cooperating with the plan *and* frustrating the intentions of Zeus, Odysseus will stand among the serene

Phaiakians, as Socrates did before the angry Athenians, and discover the truest meaning of his troubled filled life. As with Achilles, the very gods will be surprised by human revelations that point towards a higher current of destiny that deprives them of foreknowledge of the future. Also, by entering the Underworld where, like Tiresias, he retains his wits, Odysseus gives birth to human reflective consciousness. Like Augustine, he walks through the vast fields, or many mansions, of memory as he fashions his memoirs.

Odysseus begins by implicitly contesting "the crown of life." He will dispute the claim that the highest pleasure is experienced by those who hear a bard sing like a god. Presumably this divine passivity, which anticipates the hushed unity of a tragic chorus and audience, enables the rapt spectators to see the sufferings of a hero through the eyes of a god. By this they participate vicariously in his *aristeia* and overcome the order of rank, and feeling of *ressentiment,* that separates them from their betters. They no longer feel envy towards one who is far better than the rabble. Yet Odysseus prepares to do something far more audacious. He will overcome the easy opposition between hero and *hoi polloi*, that which enables us to cheaply exult in the excellence of Achilles while remaining numb to the sorrows of his numberless victims, and force us to share in the trials of a man who could claim to have endured longer humiliations, if not greater sorrows than Priam himself. He will vindicate the human condition itself; in doing so he'll confound and amaze gods and mortals alike. He thus surpasses Achilles, who only sees and wallows in the meaningless of it all.

My point is that the wisdom that comes from suffering, rather than the boundless indignation or vainglorious boasting of a hero, forms the matter of Odysseus' tale. Unlike the reflected but unreflective glory of one sprung of divine stock, this sorrow will double back upon itself and relive—once more with understanding—what really happened, serving as a second punishment for what was first experienced only as humbling loss or defeat. Yet, nevertheless, this suffering will be vindicated and not merely offered up as suffering for the crime of being born of sin or seen as penalty for being delivered from the long misery of human life. Just as Circe will salute Odysseus for having *already* entered Hades twice, when other men only die once, a curious suggestion that he's a worthy mortal counterpart to Athena *tritogenia*, his career will testify to the workings of a mysterious power in the depths of the human psyche that is able to endure, understand,

and even overcome the very forces that blithely disregard the furious demands for justice made by those who had gone before him. Odysseus will dispel any belief that he is a disguised god; he demands admiration from the Phaiakians, and even from the Olympians themselves, by his unmatched power to be equal to any adversity his destiny would serve up to him. While it is true that many of his adversaries had the power to kill him many times over, they—like the villain in any James Bond movie—were compelled to preserve him out of a desire to gain the submission of the mighty hero's heart that proved stronger than any all too human desire to die that his puny human body voiced. It is in this power to be thrice born that Odysseus must be seen to be different from Camus' famous Sisyphus. Boundless indignation may be sufficient to keep one alive but this furious preservative is surely its own punishment, one which far exceeds the power of death itself; Odysseus may only be resurrected in his full humanity.

The stranger now proclaims his name and identity. But Odysseus of Ithaca, son of Laertes, does not mention Penelope. Perhaps he does this out of courtesy, to avoid embarrassing Nausikaa? He reminds us that he is famed above all men for his crafts and strategy. Odysseus goes on to describe his kingdom, paying tribute to towering Mount Neriton, a landmark that reaches to the heavens like Ithaca's most famous son. His Ithaca is described as a good place to raise children; could it be that he still desires to keep his options open? Yet he entrusts himself to the muse, the winds of inspiration, while praying all the while to return home; nothing he says is sweeter than one's country and parents. We only hear of his dead mother and living wife after he has won over his audience; they are safely embedded in his web of lies.

Odysseus' description of his homeward voyage does not refer to the initial swift departure for home that he undertook with Nestor that the old king spoke of. While Nestor said that Odysseus, after having initially left Troy with Menelaus and himself, went back to Agamemnon, who had engaged in a drunken spat over his brother's wish to leave Troy before appeasing Athena, Odysseus only recalls an act of piracy that ends badly. It may have been that he returned for reasons more predatory than pious. This motif of separation and reunion is used as a device to falsely separate two accounts of the same event from each other; as we shall see, the sharply drawn disjunctive distinctions between such parties as Scylla and Charybdis, the Cyclopes and Laestrygonians, Zeus and Aeolus, or Circe and

Calypso exist only in speech. But we must also recall that while Nestor's yarns are literal, Odysseus sells us true lies.

Thus in a vital sense the tale told by Odysseus is a reworking of the *Iliad*, at least as the tale was told by Demodokus and understood by impressionable young men like Telemachus. While these songs of Troy highlighted the glory and ignored the guts, the reality of the war, and most of the years spent fighting it, it may very well have consisted of highly profitable raids that also had the strategic purpose of isolating the otherwise impregnable citadel and walls of Priam. We recall Achilles angrily recounting the several highly profitable raids, twelve over land and eleven by sea, that he led against cities allied with Troy. It is hard to believe that Odysseus, the well renowned "sacker of cities" who saw the son of Thetis as his great rival, had not led other such raids or fought alongside Achilles. They probably worked in tandem for Agamemnon, the one as coldblooded planner and the other as murderous pursuer. It is this uneven relationship that Demodokus seems to recall in his first song of Troy.

The end result of these raids was also clear. We have seen Odysseus dissolve into tears and momentarily assume the persona of one of his victims: a long-forgotten woman being led off to slavery who has just seen her husband die before her eyes. Even if his listeners lacked Homer's art of simile, Odysseus' own stark account of this raid suffices to enlighten an audience used only to glorious tales of monumental history; he tells of citizens slain, women taken into slavery, looted possessions, and a city burnt. We see that Homer is now having Odysseus recall the very events that made his hero weep earlier, as though he was one of his own victims; while we do not know how he came about this ability to reverse perspective on his own deeds, it must be seen how his tales of his wanderings can be taken in two different ways. We can either focus on the spectacular images or their miserable human reality. It is as if Demodokus reminded him of who he was; Odysseus works this knowledge into an account of where he had been, in psychic space, in response to Alcinous' questions.

Book 9

Odysseus tells us that the raid on Ismaros turned out badly; despite initial success, his men succumbed to hubris and overstayed their good fortune.

This ugly pattern of behavior—involving drink, physical excess, and disobedience—results in disaster over and over again. Just as the angry gods punished eventually Agamemnon's vainglorious army, so too did the Kikonians gain reinforcements from inland and eventually inflict heavy casualties on Odysseus' outnumbered and unready troops. They ended up losing a tenth of their force, six men from each of their twelve ships. The details of this raid are important; they recur in several of Odysseus' Cretan lies. But this defeat is also important for another reason. It is a sign that they have lost Athena's favor. Yet, like a bad gambler, Odysseus refuses to learn from this check.

The defeated raiders only leave after three shouts of defiance honoring their fallen dead that prepare us for the other times when six lives will be lost. We shall find this to be one of many triads that subtly pervade and structure the meandering course of Odysseus; it could be the case that these repetitions are but different ways of reliving the same ugly event. The fleets' mood of shameless pride is somehow connected to a terrible storm from the north that will shred their sails and force them into shelter for two days. Finally, when they are about to round Port Maleia and enter home waters, a combination of currents and the same baleful North Wind drives them for nine days, far off course to strange lands. After this, apart from one fleeting, perhaps illusory glimpse of smoke from Ithaca, Odysseus and his crew are blown back to the past, doomed to be lost in inconsistent images and invidious illusions; his men never return and their king fights to earn his passage to human reality even as he speaks to Alcinous' court. Yet he can only do so by enchanting them with truth-giving lies.

This is why it is appropriate that Odysseus' next misadventure occurs in the land of the Lotus-eaters. Somewhat like Scheria, this is a place where literally nothing happens. The inhabitants feed on the sweet fruit of the Lotus. Odysseus recounts that the three crewmembers he sent ashore with instructions to scout out the land preferred staying with the natives to rejoining their shipmates. Although it is customary to assume that the Lotus had soporific and or narcotic properties, this information is not found in our text. In other words, with these captivating stories Odysseus will seduce his hosts and readers by relying a great deal on our all too willing suspension of disbelief before his seductive speech. It is reasonable to suppose that men exposed to ten years of brutal combat would prefer to spend a good period of time recovering from these ordeals before rejoining their pirate king on the seas. But this also means that his tales cannot be seen as literal accounts of events that took place in real space and time. Odysseus is like Socrates making his *Republic*; he is recalling the dystopic desires of a formerly diseased soul rather than rendering a report of things that should ideally exist. Further, unlike his crew who want to forget the war and resume their former identities, their king is reluctant to pass up further opportunities to gain recognition and acclaim for glorious deeds performed under the aegis of Ares. Or otherwise put, Odysseus could not be drugged or enchanted as he was already under an evil influence strong enough to overpower his iron will and matchless mind. Although pride is often stronger than rationality, our intemperate reason can override *thumos* or even the very *thanatos* drive itself.

This means that we must remain firmly anchored in reality and not allow our greedy imaginations to overwhelm the little rational capacity that remains part of man's lot. It is possible and consistent with his character for us to assume that Odysseus had his scouts tied and probably gagged only because their news, that the Lotus-eaters' land had nothing to pillage and no enemies, did not suit his trouble-seeking nature. All the more cause for us to listen to his siren songs, voluntarily tied to the mast, but never forgetting the distinction between poetic and literal truth; like Glaucon, we are entering a domain where the darkest temptations of rationality itself will be revealed in all their seductiveness. Odysseus is far from free of them. We must not become complicit in his sins but learn from them, as they are shown in full allure.

The winds that blew Odysseus back from his home also seem to have pushed him back in time; while his men prefer to eat of the Lotus and forget their sinful past exploits, Odysseus chooses not to; neither does he seem to regret any of the actions he performed when he looked like Ares himself. As a result, he is driven back by fate to revisit a primal scene, the cave of the Cyclopes; this where the terrible truth about the war and its monstrous effects on his psyche are revealed in a context quite as deceptive as its most famous imitation: the infamous cave image of Plato's *Republic*. The subterranean structure described by Socrates to Glaucon is not only ruled by poetry, it also represents a false self-knowledge that the soul has or makes of itself. In choosing to deceive others, he ended up believing his own glittering untruths. His brutal realism has literally brutalized him; Odysseus no longer has self-knowledge.

Thus, upon entering the dark cave of the Cyclopes, we ourselves must listen closely and cautiously to what Odysseus will tell us. Considering our subject matter, and the several physical impossibilities that we are obliged to swallow before breakfast, it is best to wink at what is literally absurd and focus on the real meaning undergirding this fantastic tale. However this must not be done too hastily; we must not forget to distinguish carefully between three discrete elements in play here: the folk story Homer has inherited, Odysseus' story, which is equivalent to its surface meaning, how it would appear to a Cyclopean, Phaiakian or literal reader without any depth perception—and the deep meaning or logos that our bard shapes out of this mythos. Even though the gigantic figure reflected on the walls of his (or Plato's) cave took on a life of its own, escaping and going far beyond the limits of the tale while making it all but impossible to interpret the meaning of the *Odyssey*, this hardly means that his origins are unworthy of interest. This is why it is best to start with the most literal level of this myth before allowing it to raise questions that will inevitably require us to ask deeper questions of poet and poem. We must place our trust in the dialectic. Like Penelope's shroud, this fabric of lies must be continually woven and unwoven.

We must also recall that even while implicitly confessing that this exploit led to the loss of six of his best men and delayed his return to Ithaca by ten years, our hero took much pride in recalling and recounting his pyrrhic defeat of Polyphemus the inhospitable Cyclopes. This may only be justified when we see that the truth behind the Cyclopes episode takes us further back in time, before the raid on the Kikones, to the Trojan War itself. While this suggests that this story may represent a past event or perhaps even a symbolic depiction of the meaning of Odysseus' past, it is vital that we study this episode on its own terms before going on to speculate as to what it reveals about our wily hero's lack, loss, and eventual dearly bought gaining of, self-knowledge, either at the time of the event or when the story was told at last; what is depicted here is the first descent made by a man into the depths of his soul. It seems that the first entry of the truth into his mind's eye only blinds our intellectual giant.

While we were first content to be unabashed partisans of brave Odysseus, blithely ignoring moral considerations and eagerly sharing in his daring adventures, this cold-blooded account of the raid on Ismaros has ended all doubt as to whether he was pirate or trader (we recall that Polyphemus also asks Nestor's cynical question) and made clear that his only regrets were tactical rather than moral. His conduct upon visiting the land of the Cyclopes now reveals that his acts of piracy were not motivated by hunger or need. We also see that his men were not of the same mind. While wily Odysseus comes up with many pious pretexts to justify his eponymous and insatiable appetite for trouble, his followers prefer to abandon themselves to drink and lethargy. Although such conduct is attractive to his hearers, who to the extent that they have no skin in the game, participate in his exploits in a vicarious or disembodied way, his battle-wearied men would surely be far less likely to share his concern for whether the Cyclopes were god-fearing or unjust and inhospitable. We observed earlier that their divine ships placed his hosts above the reciprocal code of hospitality. We must now wonder if Odysseus is testing their own sense of justice by his tales. Just as a Platonic dialogue reveals far more about the souls of his interlocutors than it does of the enigmatic nature of Socrates, how we listen to this siren has a disconcerting ability to disclose our own natures, less because of the content of his song but owing to how our response to his speech becomes our deed. Differently put, Odysseus turns his piracy into a kind of trade that panders to and arouses our worst appetites. We must ask ourselves if we are better and more just than his war-wearied crew and unsuspecting victims; have his tales seduced us? Are we just as prone as his discredited discarded crew to prefer entertainment to truth?

Odysseus has recently twice seen the Achaeans, the whole army on one occasion and his own troops on another, succumb to wine; indeed it is possible that the very wine he received from Apollo's priest was used to dissipate his men at Ismaros. This time he plans to use wine to put the Cyclopes to the test. Again, it is worth asking ourselves whether he is again, at this moment, intoxicating the imaginations of his listeners, both those at Scheria and ourselves; could it be the case that, like Helen, he is drugging us in such a way as to make us immune to the moral implications of the tales that he recounts? Just as Helen's Egyptian drug ensured that sorrows would not be recollected, regardless of how terrible they were, Homer's Odysseus could well be testing our own moral imagination and its ability to withstand temptation.

Nevertheless, the suggestion is provided that Odysseus' arrival at the land of the Cyclopes was predestined. Again we're reminded of Helen's claim that some god made her do it when Odysseus tells us that his ships entered the island's natural harbor without effort or intent on his part. Polyphemus will seem to confirm this attribution of fate when he recalls the prophecy that Odysseus would blind him. Yet this seems to be at variance with the claim that all of Odysseus' misfortunes are the result of this vaunting deed; the Cyclopes could hardly curse Odysseus for what was long foreseen. If this blinding is a punishment for violating the laws of hospitality, the gods would surely not condemn their chosen instrument of justice for this deed; even Odysseus' proud boast that Poseidon could not heal his son could be seen as part of this fated pattern. Furthermore, since Polyphemus would inevitably have deduced that his blindness could only have been brought about through Odysseus, our hero's angry disclosure of his real name cannot have been so reckless a deed. It could be the case that the "how" matters more than the predestined in this case; we must also recall that Homer himself is operating within the parameters of a well-known story. In other words, our bard's contribution to the Odyssey must also occur at the level of providing an inner narrative behind already famous mythic events.

While Polyphemus is justly cut down to size by Odysseus, the relation between the two is reciprocal; while Odysseus blinds the Cyclopes for his crimes, we find that he is too is blinded by an arrogance that does not take others in account. The Cyclopes exploit does not reflect well on our hero; the Ithacans abuse the laws of hospitality about as wantonly as Penelope's suitors. We are also reminded of Agamemnon's equally flimsy pretext for besieging Troy. The Greeks invaded a well-ordered *oikos* that resembles civilized Ilium. These parallels are intended, but what do they imply?

Is Polyphemus to be blamed for desiring to trap and kill his unwelcome visitors, any more than Odysseus must be found culpable for his, nearly identical, murderous treatment of his home invaders? The only difference between the cases seems to be the massive boulder that prevented the Ithacans from leaving the cave, but this detail turns out to make Odysseus' story even more difficult to swallow. Even if we blithely accept this giant's existence, something that no ancient audience could dismiss a priori, there is still the sheer impossibility of a giant, able to move a rock twenty-two four-wheeled wagons could not have hauled away, being able to gain sustenance from—and have the delicacy to milk—normally proportioned sheep and goats. Nor can we see how this boulder could then be used by the Cyclopes to shut the cave off from outside without leaving ample room for men little bigger than his hands to escape. The inconsistencies add up: how could Odysseus seriously expect to kill a sleeping Cyclopes with his sword when he was too big to be attacked by ten armed war veterans? If the men are so puny and small, why is it so easy for the Cyclopes to see and catch them in a cave vast enough to hold many flocks of sheep?

After a while we can only conclude that there are only so many impossible things we can take before recognizing that it is not necessary to take this story literally; we have to spew it up before breakfast to function rationally. While we can accept that Homer has inherited this story of the Cyclopes, it becomes clear that some aspects of his tale could lead us attentive readers to entertain the possibility that Odysseus may not always be literally truthful; although certain of his famed traits are on display, these very qualities only lead us to distrust the veracity of the songs he sings of his wanderings. Though we cannot dismiss the possibility that Homer's listeners, who by and large believed in the gods, would have been loath to admit some of the other monsters and metamorphoses of the *Odyssey*, we may definitely discern a trend towards offering us a parallel human account of the amazing things that our bard is duty-bound to sing about. In short, the boulder marks a boundary between ordinary and mythic reality, poetic truths and massive, boulder-sized lies impossible for a normal man to swallow. We must abandon all hope of literal truth here. It is not for nothing that the most hapless Ithacan is called Elpenor or hope.

We can only escape the cave of the Cyclopes when we can separate the sheep from the goats, in the sense of distinguishing the elements of divine truth hidden inside this mighty yarn. Even as Odysseus is telling the Phaiakians who he is, he is also offering them both entertainment and truth; it is up to the discerning to elude the deadly grip of wordy Polyphemus and leave the cave with a better grip on elusive Odysseus. Our hero is truly *outis* or "nobody" to the extent that he does not offer us a tangible look at himself; instead we must see that we can only view him indirectly, by paying close attention to his lies and seeing that he wishes to be known by men able to decipher the meaning behind his artful ways of revealing and concealing. In this tale, Odysseus presents himself at a most vulnerable point in his life; no more than his blinded victim who strove vainly to grasp his tormentor, Odysseus himself was quite lacking in the self-knowledge that could only be gained by consciously and deliberately repudiating the very behavior and reputation he treasured greatly. To this extent our storyteller is glory-drunk and oblivious to the deepest significance of his tale; this may be what Socrates meant when he said that the poets, though quite often divinely inspired, turned out to be the least capable exegetes of their own art.

But before moving on to interpret the allegorical significance of Odysseus' meeting with the Cyclopes, as the dialectical character of what we have discovered demands, let us first attempt to summarize the lessons imparted by the first exoteric level of our text. There is clearly a division between Odysseus and his crew. This was first shown to his advantage in the reports given of their conduct towards to Kikones and Lotus-eaters. In both cases Odysseus' rule was frustrated by the several passions that possessed his men; they first succumbed to drink and then to lassitude. In the Cyclopes' cave however it is Odysseus who comes out looking bad. His reckless and feigned concern with finding out whether the Cyclopes respected the laws of Zeus and hospitality, led to the loss of half the men he took into the cave. Even worse, his angry impulse to taunt Polyphemus, despite the anxious pleadings of his shipmates, incurred the hatred of Poseidon and eventually led to the loss of all his men and the delay of his return by ten long bitter years. While Odysseus seems to suggest that he had a run of bad luck, even a literal reading of his tale leads us to conclude that he failed his men as a leader; his powers of mind do not compensate for his inability to either anticipate or command their passions, and Odysseus' own passions of pride and curiosity turn out to breed results that are at least as dangerous to his men as the needs brought on by their natural desires. We must not let him escape judgment.

As we now go beyond the purely literal level of meaning, in striving to grasp the fullest significance of this celebrated and unforgettable story, it is important to bear in mind that Odysseus has yet to fully overcome the vices that brought about his downfall. In other words, this recounting of his adventures is a true apology in both senses: it is a confession that still contains elements of a defense speech. Odysseus is most interesting to us because he is far from perfect; he is a work in progress always on the way to grapple with new challenges that could possibly yield further insights into his soul and ours. While we have already seen grounds to infer that his songs are revelatory, and as such do not give him the same insights that the hermeneutic community built around him will subsequently enjoy, it should also be noted that the soul of Odysseus is not the kind of substance that can easily be disclosed to other men, even when its bearer claims that he is doing his very best to do so! There is something essentially Protean about Odysseus' soul. This means that he can never be seen as being completely on the side of order and truth; his nature is best viewed as a way of being, as a disposition that never allows the human spirit to subside into its tribal, animal, or material nature. He is trouble, more Heraclitus than Parmenides.

If we assume that the blatant physical impossibilities in the Cyclopes episode proves that Odysseus and/or Homer is also operating allegorically, this means that his other impossible adventures, most notably Circe's turning his men into swine and the trip to Hades, must also be interpreted in this same subtle vein. In other words, we are here offered a series of myths, albeit myths that conceal, contain, and offer the attentive reader a truer account of the heroic aspects of reality. This approach is also more than consistent with the twin themes of deflation and inspiration that were seen to be the essence of Telemachus' education about the Trojan War. By so artfully bridging the impossible gap between divine heroes and their epigones, such a logos preserves and fosters the conditions necessary for the return of genuine heroism to a disenchanted world. This is what is most divine about Homer's *Odyssey*.

One of the most pointed suggestions given by the Homeric text itself as to how it should be read comes in Book 8 when disguised Athena praised an unrecognized but angry Odysseus for his skill in throwing the discus. Noting that even a blind man could tell the difference between his mark and those set by the others, she draws our attention to the second rock thrown by the blind Cyclopes. This second near miss came from "a stone far greater" than "the peak of a mountain" which he hurled when Odysseus' ship was just half the distance away. The Phaiakians are likened to sailors ducking before this mighty cast that just misses them. Quite apart from anticipating the fate that Zeus and Poseidon contemplate visiting on the Phaiakians for aiding in Odysseus' return, this image both compares

Odysseus to his erstwhile enemy and draws our attention to the extent by which he stands head and shoulders above other ordinary men. In other words, Odysseus is very much like the Cyclopes said to have terrorized the Phaiakians in their native land. While these words, in their own context, describe the great problem posed by the vastly superior man to a political community, which is obliged to either ostracize him or become enslaved, they also unexpectedly point out the ways in which Odysseus resembles his most monstrous adversary, Polyphemus. Indeed the Cyclopes' very name, which means something like "abounding in songs or legends," may be aptly applied to Odysseus. We see this in the 'many-wordiness' of the once modest guest who now boasts of his war exploits.

While this curious connection between Odysseus and his most notorious adversary could readily be viewed as representing his prodigal mind's alienation from the body of his parent's son, or showing the extent to which this craftiest of strategists had become estranged from his long suffering men, it could be the case that an even deeper and closer identity is being indicated here. What does it mean for Odysseus to be seen as, or become, the very thing he hated most? Does this not explain the blinded Cyclopes' cry that no one (or nobody) has done this to him? Can Polyphemus be compared to Oedipus, that great solver of riddles and conqueror of the Sphinx who blinded himself after receiving a most unwelcome piece of self-knowledge? There is something deeply primal about this vision of the Cyclopes; any attempt at decoding the *Odyssey* cannot avoid, delay, or deny confronting this sublime image.

To the extent that Odysseus has been blown back from his post-Trojan encounters with the Kikonians and the Lotus-eaters, we may see that the effects of these winds could be temporal and well as spatial; in other words he has been blown back to his own past. This accounts for the extent to which the raid on Ismaros summarizes and epitomizes the first nine years of the Trojan War. This connection is further pointed towards when we recall that each of Odysseus' fleet of twelve ships easily bagged nine goats apiece on the island across from the Cyclopes; here it is also worth noting that twelve times nine is one hundred and eight or the number of Penelope's suitors!

The next stop, at the land of the Lotus-eaters, suggests that while the brutal events that took place at the end of, or after, the campaign were especially worth forgetting, insatiable Odysseus refuses to allow his men this necessary indulgence. Thus, in the cave of Polyphemus, while the bulk of his men sleep off the effects of food and wine, Odysseus must come face to face with his greatest enemy: himself. If we assume that no creature as large as Polyphemus could have existed, let alone entered the cave, then it would follow that Odysseus merely sees himself, enlarged by the shadows cast by the fire in the cave and rendered uninhibited by the potent wine sack, which resembles both the bag of winds he acquires just after this event and the unleashed memories that will drive him to Hades itself. Now he is like mad Ajax slaying sheep.

While the figure of Polyphemus is literally polyvalent in its over-determinate power, so much so that one is irresistibly reminded of Oedipus' equally complex and deadly Sphinx, many of the shadows cast by it remind us of the horrible Trojan War. Just as the generation of Telemachus was haunted and held hostage by long windy tales of gruesome heroism, the actual participants—or the greatest generation—could not but have been scarred by the atrocious deeds they performed or witnessed. They would have seen Ares the war god, that hated two-faced money changer in lives, he who returned urns of ashes to those whose loved ones followed his paths of glory. Even-handedly killing off Greeks and Trojans, two at a time, this deadly and gigantic embodied power of rage bears a striking resemblance to the Cyclopes as he cold-bloodedly fulfills the plan of Zeus and rids the world of the tiresome race of heroes.

By the war's end they would surely also have seen revealed the true nature of that other ultimate wine-sack, great Agamemnon, the cowardly Achaean commander who used violated hospitality and his sluttish brother's wife as a pretext to wage war on the wealthy city of Troy. As angry Achilles finally saw, the ruler of Mycenae took the lion's share of the booty while leaving the actual fighting to his lieutenants. While we shall become reacquainted with Agamemnon upon turning to Book 11, we cannot forget Odysseus' repeated insistence that he shared out all booty acquired equally, even though his men usually added on an extra item. Does he protest too much? Is the suspicion of his men, voiced when they are within sight of Ithaca, that he saved the best things for himself without grounds? We know from the *Iliad* that Odysseus was probably Agamemnon's most trusted advisor; even the celebrated quarrel with Achilles was said to be over tactics, whether to rely on raids and a strategy of attrition or direct attack. This could lead to the suspicion that Odysseus was, like his superior, more raptor than warrior. Did Odysseus prefer endless raiding to coming home to boring Ithaca? This discovery would surely have disturbed his men.

If my reading of the three songs of Demodokus is correct, then Odysseus himself fell very much under the influence of Ares. His Athena-inspired qualities of mind were turned away from strategy and towards destructive rage. Such a man would take perverse delight in the pseudo-divine power of violence. As we surmised, this transformation of our hero's nature would most likely have occurred through his emulous rivalry with Achilles. Just as Achilles' accursed armor blinded him and all who wore it to everything but the short-lived rapture of nihilistic mayhem in the *Iliad*, so too does the winner of these arms become as blind as Polyphemus to the worth of home and hospitality; the one turns into a mere storehouse for booty and the other is but a plausible pretext for an endless career of raiding and ravishment. Just as Hector, whose wife's identity Odysseus momentarily assumed as Demodokus sang of his greatest deed, foolishly refused to return to Troy for fear of being chided for recklessness even though this involved abandoning his wife and infant son, this Odysseus-turned-Cyclopes will renounce his famed temperance to pursue fortune. He will become the infamous Ulysses figure of legend, an uncanny outlaw scorned by Sophocles, cursed by Euripides, hated by Virgil and feared by exiled Dante. Alcinous asked his guest if there was someone dear to him who had died at Troy; the answer of course is that it was Odysseus' own "Ulysses" aspect that he mourned so piteously.

Odysseus, at this point in his life, its moral nadir, is as lost and lawless as his *bête noire*, Polyphemus. Even as the latter tends his flocks and keeps as neat a cave as Eumaeus, these several assets are as distinct from him in kind as King Odysseus is separated from his human body and crewmen. It also follows that by blinding the Cyclopes with a mast-sized stake of wood, perhaps the very winnowing fan Tiresias spoke of, Odysseus has also effectively turned the Cyclopes—or his own bodily aspect—and crew into a port-less ship. He steers by sheer force of mind despite having blinded himself/lost self-knowledge by the same deed. It can be seen that in this symbolic account, contrary to his narrative, Odysseus did not blind the Cyclopes; instead, by blinding himself through his violent hubris, he has become Polyphemus, a monstrously uncanny source of trouble and terror to comrade and enemy alike. In other words, his once temperate soul has become a monstrously intemperate will.

Although Odysseus prided himself for tricking the literal-minded Cyclopes by calling himself no-one or nobody, there is another quite literal sense in which he is truthful, albeit unwittingly so. Although Descartes famously proclaimed that he existed insofar as he thought, thus separating his intellectual substance from his extended body, this effectively means that his mind is somehow separate from the categories and conditions of time and space. By thinking he thus becomes nobody and is truly situated nowhere; what better explanation could be given of Odysseus' mysterious sojourn in Calypso? While Achilles is divine rage trapped in a mortal body, Odysseus *qua* angry mind is pure potential in the sense that he cannot truly appear as himself.

Alternatively, in Sartrean categories, his existence is pure being-for-itself; absolutely self-created and free, especially to the extent of destroying and/or objectifying the freedom or integrity of everything or being-in-itself that he comes into contact with. This account of his "essence" also accounts for Odysseus' odd desire to test others by asking them what kind of man he was. It is not sufficient to focus on his lying stories about himself without realizing that there is a real sense in which he does not know who he is. This wordy and famed Polyphemus lacks self-knowledge; only when he is truly aware of this deficiency is Odysseus ready to set out on his long journey home. And even then, like Achilles pursuing his own armor while Hector wore it, Odysseus will continually be menaced and pursued by this "poly-phemic" *alter ego*, the aspect of his soul that still rages in a way befitting the grandson of Autolycus, the wolf itself.

In Simone Weil's essay, *The Iliad, the Poem of Force,* she speaks of "the armor of the lie," saying that those who does not wear this protection "to conceal the harshness of destiny from their own eyes . . . cannot experience force without being touched by it to the very soul." Laboring in the forge of necessity Odysseus has become a Cyclopes; like Hephaestus, he makes his own armor that protects his body and blinds his soul. We must see through this bright shining lie and drag Odysseus away from his rage.

After his encounter with Polyphemus, his other self, Odysseus is figuratively split in two. His stake in the Cyclopes' eye becomes a mast and the

Cyclopes' body the ship that conveys him on his subsequent psychic voyages. It is this foul body that he must give up to come home to himself. He is now one-eyed himself. This monocular vision is what gives the shadows on the cave wall reality.

This transformation of Odysseus seems to occur through a combination of the ugly exigencies of war and his burning envy of Achilles. When Troy still stands, even after his glorious rival's death, it is Odysseus who by some combination of trickery and stark force earns his reputation as the sacker of cities. Although Odysseus could very plausibly argue that his only wish was to end the interminable war, the means that he used, coupled with his insatiate desire for recognition, necessarily involved the slayer of the Cyclopes becoming one such himself. As a result, he cannot leave Troy; it becomes his Cyclopes' cave, a carapace that protects, conceals, and corrodes the soul of its sacker wherever he goes. If we take towering Troy to be the Cyclopes, the enemy attacked by Agamemnon and his men under the pretext of avenging violated hospitality, we can then see how Homer's myth tells us how unimpressive-looking Odysseus punished this great city and tore down walls built by Poseidon himself. Also, just as Odysseus imprudently shouted his name out to the Cyclopes, thus giving himself credit for an act performed by no-body, so too did Odysseus emerge from disguised obscurity previously earned on his spying missions inside Troy and call himself the sacker of cities. We know from Euripides how much fear, hatred, and infamy he gained as a not fully unwelcome result. Now we see how his Cyclopean mind has made him an immoral giant, ostracized by men and even feared by himself.

The word Cyclopes literally means "circle-eyed"; if Odysseus is the Cyclopes, this image suggests that he is trapped within a circle or vicious cycle that literally exists within his own wounded head. While, as we argued earlier, his blind condition has to do with his loss or lack of self-knowledge, Odysseus is also aware of his accursed state and prefers not to advertise his identity, least of all before his hour of triumph. This character trait, which is consistent with his earlier Athena-pleasing nocturnal owl-like hunting ways, also complements his reputation for smooth and duplicitous speech. It was not coincidental that Odysseus was the addressee of Achilles' famous diatribe against "the man, whom he hated more than the gates of Hades, who hid one thing in his heart and said another." It would seem then that

Odysseus' naturally suspicious way of doing things is its own punishment. Like many of the accursed in Tartarus, he is condemned to continually outsmart himself; even as his thirst for victory and lust for adventure drive him to seek increasingly audacious goals, his human bodily aspect is tortured by his very invulnerability in the heel. To the extent that his thirst for victory enables him to absorb seemingly unlimited amounts of punishment, Odysseus' prodigious powers of endurance thus turn out to be his greatest weakness. Dante saw this predicament best when he placed the damned in Hell within circles they ceaselessly traversed. Odysseus has put out his own inner eye and fallen into the deepest parts of his psyche; he has bought his bottomless subjectivity at the cost of self-knowledge. The moral experience of conscience—literally meaning "knowing with"—thus cannot be experienced by his soul when it is in this psychopathic condition. This is why at this stage in his narrative, just like Polyphemus, he can only vomit up mangled fragments of the truth; until the Cyclopes' cave inhabited by his soul is found by him to be Hades, his restless quest will go on.

Book 10

While Book 9 of the *Odyssey* represents its subject as a raging Cyclopes, ensnared by his willful rationality within the cave-like confines of his inverted ego, Book 10 then reveals something of the ceaseless futile motion he undertakes within this encircled domain. This while Book 9 shows Odysseus' psychic state at the Trojan War's end, Book 10 sets his soul in endless activity and begins to depict its descent into Hades.

Like Glaucon, Odysseus was led by his concupiscence into a cave where he could see his nature writ large; he naturally recoiled from this ugly sight, this denial in effect blinding him. Yet wanton deeds inevitably circle back to visit terrible scars on the soul doing them; this *ananke* cannot be averted, least of all by those who refuse self-knowledge. By falsely invoking necessity to serve and justify their own selfish purposes, they merely lock themselves deeper into a vicious spiral or moral tailspin that eventually makes it impossible for the sinner to deny the truth. Otherwise put, even if Odysseus betrays everyone else to Scylla, Charybdis eventually gets her man.

Some explanation is needed for several otherwise extraordinary events in the first half of Book 10 that must be explained if they are not to compromise the integrity, not merely in a literary sense, of the whole *Odyssey*; we must prove beyond doubt that the meaning of this part of our text is not to be read as an accurate geographic account of the journeys undertaken by our hero. This is also why the credibility of our narrator is called into question by even his long-suffering crew; Book 10 shows that Odysseus has lost the confidence of his men; even if they approve of the brash conduct that caused the loss of six men on the island of the Cyclopes, they are still led to believe that their king, who takes great pains to tell his listeners how he divided up their spoils equally, has been selfish enough to keep some especially valuable prize for himself. Perhaps their discovery of the truth about Maron's wine led them to conclude that Odysseus did not share everything with them; indeed we ourselves are tempted to derive similar conclusions from the threadbare quality of some of his yarns. In other words, we too have ample cause to believe that Odysseus has not provided a true tale of how he lost six of his best to the Cyclopes; this leads us to feel that excessive audacity is not the least of his crimes; it becomes clear that Odysseus, just like Achilles, has gotten us drunk on glory and hidden his truly egotistic agenda.

This dishonesty is further underscored by Odysseus' next tale; he tells a story of two distinct encounters with King Aeolus, the keeper of the winds. By this account our hero visits a remarkable floating island ruled by the aforementioned Aeolus. After being questioned closely about his adventures Odysseus is given a bag containing winds that will, if properly used, give him safe passage home. Even though Aeolus somewhat resembles Zeus, he is willing to trust the veracity of his guest's account until he finds ex post facto that Odysseus neither trusts nor is trusted by his crew. As a result, they open the bag when he is sleeping, exhausted by the effort of staying awake and navigating for ten straight days. When the winds escape and Odysseus' fleet is blown back to Aeolus, the king drives them off, telling Odysseus that his return shows him to be "the least of all living creatures and hated by the gods." We see also that even if the gods can give him a fair wind, they cannot bring him ashore. This applies to his crew and ultimately also to the situation in Odysseus' home and soul. The only function King Aeolus serves is that of separating Odysseus' successful escape from the Cyclopes, albeit at the cost of six men, from the loss of the rest of his fleet to the equally gigantic Laestrygonians. The Cyclopes thus serves to provide our hero with an alibi for an event that supposedly took place when he was back with his fleet after being expelled by Aeolus. Because he chose to take on Scylla, Odysseus contends that he is not to blame for Charybdis. But the tale's logic suggests that the very way he took on Polyphemus and Scylla made the other two disasters inevitable.

Just as Zeus himself remarked at the start of the *Odyssey* that mortals falsely blame the gods for their misfortune, so too does it seem that the gods punish evil instead of causing it. Odysseus is to blame for not being able to either rule or trust his men. As he does not describe things clearly, he is either a liar or being punished for sin. In other words, Zeus and/or Aeolus punish us when our own actions show signs of vice. Aeolus has seen *prima facie* evidence that his guest's tales consisted of boastful lies. Further, since the court of Alcinous very much resembles the island of Aeolus, it may also be inferred that Odysseus is being offered another chance to make amends for his boastful account of his deeds; this also suggests that all that occurs after this tale is entirely in the psychic realm. Odysseus was first blown back from Ithaca after the sack of Ismaros. He then understands himself as the victor over the proud Cyclopes. But since this is also too hubristic, he must now deal with Circe and enter Hades. In other words, the truth of the war is not raging Ares (the Cyclopes in Book 9), or even wanton Aphrodite (Circe in Book 10); this tale of sound and fury finally must be seen to only signify Hades or death; this is why he must enter the underworld in Book 11.

We could also interpret this story as an alternative version of the quarrel between Nestor and Odysseus that led to the former returning safely while the latter went back towards Troy. Coming on the heels of the debacle with the Cyclopes, this would better explain resilient Odysseus' desire to commit suicide upon being turned back within sight of his native land. From Odysseus' perspective it would appear that his army had become one gigantic Leviathan like beast, a savage Cyclopes who revolted against his tyranny, killed the men loyal to him and forced him to resume his travels with only a single ship. His men however would see their king as a savage Cyclopes, one who held them hostage to his will and refused to lead them back home. While between them hero and men would add up to a powerful two-eyed body, their being at cross-purposes would have disastrous consequences for all of Ithaca. While we will duly consider other possible explanations of what happened to Odysseus after Troy, it is also quite likely that the Ithacans rebelled against his insatiable appetite for knowledge and plunder. They might have finally called him a bloated windbag; this would surely account for the sack of winds that Odysseus gained from Aeolus being made of skin taken from a nine-year old ox. The bag of winds would thus be full of Odysseus' windy words about exploits made possible by the sacrificial deaths and mute suffering endured by his ox-like men over the nine previous years of the war. The real bag of winds could also be a wine-sack; this is quite consistent with Odysseus' contempt for the drunken behavior of both his men and the Cyclopes and his use of wine to manipulate the much stronger Polyphemus. The human mind and body seldom have much sympathy for each other's ruling passions or addictions. We see how Odysseus could very well have come under the spell of (and even begun to believe) his own windy lies, the more his mind came to be ruled by his gigantic ego. Odysseus' already-noted tendency to behave as if he were nobody or divine mind only makes things worse; we saw how this attitude reduces his men to the status of lowly animal bodies. But the underlying truth of the matter is that as he moves from Athena and towards Ares, Odysseus' mind only became enslaved to his intemperate will. This is true whether or not the unlikely events he recounts actually occurred.

What we have seen so far suggests that Odysseus is, at this point in his long journey, whether epic or merely psychic, is on the brink of losing control over both his mind and men. Perhaps the best sign that the Odyssey is really about the voyage of a soul is the laconic manner in which the biggest disaster of all, the loss of all but one of his ships to rock-hurling giants, is described. This is aptly complemented by the cavalier way in which critics and readers of the *Odyssey* ignore or minimize this event; it would seem as if the real circumstances of this loss are both too embarrassing to be recounted as well as being inconsequential to his own tale. His real tale is of himself; the skeleton crew of the ship that accompanied him on his visit to Polyphemus is only required to account for his being able to visit so many strange places. As early as the incident with Aeolus' windbag, he speaks as if the eleven other ships were lost already; even though he blames all his men for this act of envious folly, the crews of these other ships could not have been blamed for opening the bag on his vessel.

The Laestrygonian disaster sees Odysseus play an uncharacteristically passive role. Though he dispatches scouts to check out the land, our hero moors his own ship far behind the others; this mirrors the disaster on the island of the sun where the cattle are killed as Odysseus prays. The curious incident of the normal-looking girl at the well who takes them to her monstrous parents recalls Odysseus' meeting with Athena a day earlier; Odysseus could be suggesting that it was Athena who led the men into this very dangerous place. Could he be hinting that it was the gods who stoned the other ships as savagely as Zeus wrecked Odysseus' last vessel at Thrinacia? Is this a working out of the curse of Polyphemus or can it be that the gods had it in for him for some earlier offence, the very reason for which Agamemnon delayed offering a sacrifice before leaving the devastated ruins of Troy? Or does this also suggest to readers that the tale of this ill-starred prior meeting was based entirely on what had recently happened to him in Scheria? In other words, is the comic encounter with Nausikaa the sole factual basis for this tragic tale? A third possibility, that the vast majority of his men were massacred before or after a gigantic defeat, albeit in a context different from that described in the *Odyssey*, will be taken up later in this book. We must not blame gods or giants for the results of our actions. Odysseus' brief discussion of this disaster lends further support to the suspicion that this whole episode has to do with psychic rather than actual events.

It is easy to see how the loss of all but one of his ships would have made Odysseus very reluctant to return home; so disastrous an event would be far more likely to cause even one possessed of his iron heart to seriously contemplate suicide. It is not just a matter of shame; the relatives of these six hundred men would clearly blame Odysseus for their going off on another expedition instead of returning from Troy. This would lead us to suppose that his men did not challenge Odysseus' leadership; it could very well be that he is trying to deny blame for the loss of these eleven ships, but it is also self-evident that he alone survives to tell the tale, just as he will claim to have emerged from Hades or to have slayed the suitors in a fair fight; his victims, or collateral casualties, cannot tell their side of this sad and sorry story. Odysseus may have tricked them by false promises into following his plans. Dead men tell no tales and Odysseus has claimed to have travelled and returned from the land of the dead.

In any event by the time they are guided by some god to land safely on Circe's island, known by the mournful name of Aiaia, Odysseus and his men have little heart or appetite to do anything more than tearfully lament their terrible ill-fortune for two whole days. Finally, on the third day, Odysseus summons up the spirit to scout the terrain and finds smoke, a good indication of human habitation on this desolate isle. He divides up his men—now only forty-six of the original seven hundred and twenty remain—into two groups and places one under the command of Eurylochus who, we later hear, is related to him by marriage. When lots are drawn it is this group that ends up having to go deeper into the woods and investigate the source of the fire.

Odysseus' story shows him to be far less reckless with his life and with the rump of his crew than before. He also shows active concern for their welfare, first killing a mighty stag to feed his men before returning from his first exploration, and even has recourse to drawing lots rather than impetuously choosing the best men of his crew to accompany him on his latest perilous adventure. Even if these events never truly happened, they still reveal that our hero's character has become more considerate and temperate as a result of all that he has been through over time, if not in space. Blown back to reflect on his egoism towards the Cyclopes on Circe's island, and the consequent devastation of all but one of his ships by the Laestrygonians, led him to see that his own interests were not distinct from those of his men. This is why their bodies, of Odysseus and his crew, all seek rest and resuscitation. Ares is drawn to Aphrodite just as cowardice needs sex, flattery, and forgetfulness. But Odysseus' mind must go deeper; he must enter Hades, the very collective unconscious of Hellas. This is because the therapy and punishment meted out by the cycles of Circe or fortune measure up to bodily necessity, collective guilt, and acceptance of chance and randomness; they are insufficient to purge his psyche of its deliberate sins.

Just as the confrontation with the Cyclopes slyly revealed the deep truth of the first song of Demodokus, Odysseus' tale of his dalliance with Circe will expose the real meaning of this second song. Although there was a seemingly great divide between Achilles and Odysseus, there is here an insurmountable gap between men and gods that is flouted when our hero plays the role of Ares dallying with Aphrodite. Even if Poseidon or nature looked indulgently upon Ares' actions, he surely does not extend this toleration to a mortal, especially towards a lover who is more like Hephaestus to the extent that he uses artifice to outwit nature. In other words, Poseidon and the god of fire exchange places in this recasting of the original comic story; furthermore Odysseus has violated something far more fundamental than a contract of marriage. He plays the role of a disguised god, seemingly testing men to see if they conform to divine laws of hospitality but actually exploiting them to serve his own wicked ends.

But if our hero is worthy of punishment, why then does Hermes enable Odysseus to defeat the wiles of Circe? The answer seems to reside in this god's role as mediator between the earth and Hades. Just as it was Hermes who brought about the release of Odysseus from oblivion or Calypso's clutches, here we see him originally deliver him to the captivating arms of Circe; it is also noteworthy *en passant* that the two dangerous goddesses are aunt and niece. Here Hermes is delivering Odysseus to the goddess. It is not that he will not be punished; his penalties will be customized for his unique soul. As we have seen, he invariably lets his guard down after his moment of triumph. The pattern persists with Circe; he is only ensnared after she declares him the victor; we have likewise seen Helen employ these cloying means to make Odysseus reveal the secret of the Trojan Horse. Then, serving the will of Aphrodite, Helen seduced Odysseus and turned Athena's favorite away from her. Now, in order for Odysseus to regain the favor of Athena, he must understand his errors, own up to his misdeeds, and prove his ability to withstand the charms of Aphrodite. Only thus can he gain his passage home and bring about the final triumph of Athena. The proof of this claim will be seen in the extent to which his deeds in Ithaca will be found to be in keeping with the real meaning of the true lies that get Odysseus home. The over-determined myths deployed here are necessarily circular; the Cyclopes' eye, encircling Circe, and the endless repetitions of Hades, all convey the tale's richness. Of course, Helen's dalliance with Odysseus, told in Book 4, is the factual basis for this. At a wider level, the Circe stories are based and located around Jason's *Argonautica*.

Many of the strangest details and perplexities emerging out of Odysseus' encounter with Circe can be explained by the hypothesis that he has already entered the outer limits of Hades' realm; Aiaia, the very mournful name of her island, provides us with preliminary evidence in support of this claim, as does the "forgetfulness of their own land" which afflicts all who eat food in her house, even as "they retain their minds." We also find much suggestive symmetry between Odysseus' piercing the eye of the

Cyclopes, certainly a phallic act, and his aggressive overcoming of Circe with a drawn sword, a deed that ends in a far more conventional form of physical penetration. Yet, on final analysis, both of these celebrated adventures only serve to draw him deeper into dire solipsistic straits from which he cannot free himself without Athena's help; as Circe's name suggests, he is caught in circular cycles of compulsive consumption.

While the gods have not forgotten Odysseus, his mortal part cannot elude penalty; he is like Heracles in Hades to the extent that while his divine aspect is fed ambrosia, as Odysseus himself was spoilt by Circe/Calypso, the human offender must suffer in Hades. It is by Circe that Odysseus is re-embodied; now his body must be punished.

It cannot be gainsaid that Circe is as much an echo of Helen as the Spartan queen was a physical proxy for another child of Zeus and her half-sister, Aphrodite. Neither can we ignore the way in which Helen stands opposed to her cousin Penelope; even though Odysseus' wife bears a certain resemblance to Circe to the extent that she too will weave and effectively turn her suitors into drunken swine by her strategy of divide and conquer, the ends to which she employs these devices are diametrically different. It is also striking that Athena seems to be counseling Penelope as she tries to hold her besieged household together; she is far more teachable than her son. We must infer then that to the extent to which deluded Odysseus is following the lures of Aphrodite and Helen, as he continues to wear the cursed arms of Achilles and feel the power of Ares, he is also placing himself in a zone of illusion and non-being that somehow lies outside Athena's ability to connect with him or offer aid. To the extent that Circe seems to satisfy Odysseus in ways that Athena cannot, at least when he is under the perverse influence of Ares and Aphrodite, she has literally encircled him. Simply put, Athena cannot infuse him with her power when he is under the aegis of another god. We could even say that Athena is also weakened by this defection; the gods seem to know themselves or become fully actualized by acts of human virtue. Odysseus looked like Ares at the sack of Troy but it was only with Athena's help.

To discern the true deep meaning of our text we have to see the hidden resemblance and connection between these two famous encounters with Polyphemus and Circe. In each case, Odysseus' very greatest triumphs, which curiously imitate Diomedes' victories over Ares and Aphrodite, have now turned out to be devastating defeats; he has been sucked or suckered into these pyrrhic predicaments by a wide variety of temptations that are unified by the common quality of being non-physical; he is constantly enticed by a desire to be pure non-being, destructive disembodied prime potentiality that only seeks to reveal itself in a moment of vaunting delight. Perhaps we could best express this dark force as the most primitive expression of Athena embodied as an owl; while the concealed nocturnal power that delights in ambushes and betrayal seemingly has very little in common with the brutally overt thuggish ways of Ares, there seems to be a desire to exult in victory that makes one who is intellectually superior somehow envy the master morality of the bad blond beast. Likewise, the un-sublimated energy of a soul that never quite succeeds in turning its continence, however prodigious, into true temperance is easy prey for a Helen or Circe. Just as Helen could mimic the voice of any man's wife and lead him astray, Circe excels in enticing what was banal and bestial from the depths of a human soul; she could then spell it backwards by commanding a man in the name of his most animal and chthonic desire. This evil child of the sun uses this dark light to enslave and dehumanize all who came her way. Though she seems to meet her match in Odysseus, their complementarity in cunning completed this couple in the worst way. United in smug self-knowledge, the two become Aristophanes' "circle-man."

Hermes has given Odysseus immunity from the power of Circe by uprooting his very soul from the earth and giving it to him in the form of Moly, but this exposes him to greater dangers. Perhaps this is what makes him attractive to her and vice versa; they are truly likeminded now that the Moly makes him fully disembodied. This is why he must be reborn of his mother in Hades. This reading is consistent with our hypothesis that this most famous part of the *Odyssey* is really a *mythos* of a soul.

What does Circe offer Odysseus that keeps him from wanting to rejoin Penelope? In the symbolic economy of this story she seems to represent the earliest figure of fortune, down to her wheel and name. When Machiavelli valorized the pursuit of the fickle pagan force that Boethius made infamous, he famously pointed out that this goddess was drawn to virile young men. Hermes' advice that Odysseus advance upon Circe with a drawn sword and not refuse her offer to make love makes her Aphrodite to his Ares. We recall Hermes, according to Demodokus' second song, mockingly telling Apollo that he would gladly risk public exposure and even wear thrice the shackles placed by Hephaestus if he could sleep with golden Aphrodite. This quality of shamelessness, even lamented however disingenuously by Helen, seems to be completely lacking in Circe. We also note that like Machiavelli's goddess, she is never jealous and quite willing to separate from those no longer able to desire her; simply put, Circe is as incapable of love as she is irresistibly drawn to violent sexual energy. In this respect she is very much like Odysseus in his insatiable and impersonal curiosity. They both use men as means in the service of their appetites, plying their victims with wine or drugged food while professing to value hospitality; the difference is that while Circe only dehumanizes her guests, Odysseus' own men are brutalized by their inability to keep up with one who is invulnerable in the heel.

Now that Odysseus is finally trapped in the outer limits of the Underworld, Circe informs him that he may only leave by journeying through Hades itself. He must meet the blind prophet Tiresias and recover the self-knowledge symbolically lost by his snakelike entwining with his *alter ego*: Circe. Or less poetically we could say that Odysseus must atone for his sins, and sing his way out of hell, by bringing mankind a new account of the price of glory. But first, in order to return to life, Odysseus must acknowledge where he is and admit to what he has become. This stage of recovery corresponds to his weeping moment of self-recognition at the third and last myth of Demodokus, the song that the prophetic bard sang at his request. This final journey through the Underworld and beyond will strip our boastful hero of all and any vain delusions of power and virtuosity he had held about himself. This Ulysses must die *qua* virile hero and be reborn in a feminine form, all the better to serve Athena!

Book 11

While the first two songs of Demodokus were spontaneously rendered, the third was sung at Odysseus' request, yet even here the Bard says enough to remind our hero of what truly happened. The joyous climax of his efforts at Troy has a tragic essence that cannot be denied, even by one being feted as a god. Tragedy and comedy cannot be split any more than Ares and Aphrodite or male from female. His seeming apotheosis as the sacker of Hades, when recollected by Demodokus is also his moment of greatest shame, sorrow, and self-knowledge. Now he must pay tribute to the name-less women he resembled when he wept over his glorious reputation. This is the side of his soul that forbids glory, literally Anti-klea. In Hades Charybdis' whirlpool spins backwards and it exposes the blend of trauma and untruth that imprison a soul in Hades. Our hero only escapes when he is willing to jeopardize his legend, intact as long as he's *hors de combat*, and reenter history as a desperate reprobate. Only now can Athena assist him. Once he implicitly accepts the truth about himself, and explicitly sub-jects himself to humiliation, he can finally reenter reality as an antihero. First he's the equal of Achilles or an avatar of Ares; next, he is lover of Helen or Aphrodite; lastly, the sacker of Troy must admit that he is (in) Hades. Until he admits to this dark truth the winds will blow him back from home.

The first time he is prevented from returning with a cargo of lies occurs after the Cicones; this was repeated after the Cyclopes and it is then that he is sent to Circe and/or Hades. This is why the transition from his ship-wreck in Book 12 to Scheria skips over the time with Calypso. Odysseus also has monocular vision; this explains the doubling or splitting of the vis-its to Aeolus, Cyclopes, and Laestrygonians as well as the link between Circe & Calypso. It is only in Scheria that his mind and body are reunited, as he formally renounces the Ulysses in him. Hades is where he meets Antikleia, the mother's voice he strangled like Antiklus in the horse; simply put, Pene-lope's voice, mimicked by Helen, had no allure for him since he was already intent on glory; this is why it was easy for him to show temporary restraint.

Hermes guided the furious motion of Odysseus out of a Dante-like dark wood to Circe, a Homeric precursor of Fortuna. While Odysseus sur-vived these exploits, we have seen him lose control over his body and almost all his men. When he is ready to end his fling with fortune and head home, our hero finds that he is already in Hades and playing with the house's bad money. As in Vegas, what happens in Hades stays in Hades because you can beat the house but you can never beat the system. Just as with Troy, Odysseus must storm Hades and extract its murderous essence if he is ever to escape its dire power. He must destroy the *Iliad* itself; the siren song of Ares, the tale of death and glory, must be overcome by a new song, albeit one that has nothing to do with what really happened over the ten years between Troy and Ithaca. Just as the ten years raiding around the Dard-anelles were not described in the *Iliad*, so too does the *Odyssey* convey psycho-mythic meaning rather than giving history. By this new myth of Hades, Odysseus admits that his own obsession with rage and glory had made him oblivious to the toxic psychic forces that brought him there; only now can he begin to rebuild his psyche and prepare for the voyage home.

Hades is the collective unconsciousness, the cultural treasury of Hellas. This is also where we must consider the identity of Odysseus' audience. The court of Alcinous may be viewed as being representative of the floating isle of Aeolus and the court of Zeus. But there is also Penelope, to whom Odysseus recounts this very tale at the poem's end. We must also bear in mind the Thresotians, of whom more will be said later, and Homer's own audience—both then and now. These are confessions just as much as they are boastful tales of exploits and explorations. Just like Augustine, his most celebrated descendant, for they are connected by Virgil's epic, Odysseus' task also has to do with his renunciation of glory. To this extent, his voyage to Hades has to combine aspects from both the *Confessions* and *City of God*; the sack of Rome was really executed by a man who was as familiar with its values and poetry as our hero was with the *Iliad*. They came to bury Achilles and/or Caesar, not to praise him.

Homer as Demodokus cannot change the official story. But he subtly undermines it by means of the bard's three songs, songs he uses as the basis for his accounts of the wanderings of Odysseus. One year in Circe's world corresponds to the year in Egypt after Troy. Hades stands for the much longer time spent in concealment with Calypso. The song's conquest of Hades or Troy thus means nothing more than his resurrection or victory over death. We also see how terrible Hades and heroism was. This is why Achilles now prefers abject slavery to ruling over the dead, in the sense of choosing victimhood to active envied vice. Socrates echoes this choice at his trial; even the fear of death will not deter him. In less glorious terms, albeit Platonic terms, Odysseus must save his soul rather than pose as the sacker of Troy. Before this, however, he must save his body. For this reason he must give a long account of his trip to Hell and back to win favor with King Alcinous and gain his passage home.

As Aristotle reminded us, the mind is in a sense all things. In the present context this means that Odysseus' matchless mind discloses its power to represent all that has happened within him as an extended journey to Hades and back. This deep psychic voyage is no less real for its being represented physically. We cannot forget that those in Odysseus' audience at Scheria are more like Olympians than mortals, to the extent that they have never truly experienced pain or privation. If his tales are full of exaggerations, this is because human events would appear in this way to those who, like the gods, had never known what it was like to be mortal. He must teach through poetry since their souls are too shallow to empathize with what he truly underwent.

In books 9-12 Odysseus ensnares us, as both Circe and Penelope did, in a web of words that has nothing in common with the realities under its surface; these words or myths are only connected to other words—earlier myths—and not to real events. We must distinguish between the Ares/Aphrodite horizontal axis and the Master/Slave vertical axis, both formed by Odysseus' desire to emulate Achilles. He not only misses his Ulysses aspect, he also weeps over himself *qua* once and future slave. Wanting to recall past glory, he is driven back to the past. It was the mast or oar in Polyphemus' eye that became the basis for his fabulous trips. His mythic path leads from (9) Achilles/Cyclopes, to (10) Aphrodite/Circe, to (11) a literal experience of Hades, and then back to (12) Calypso/Circe (this time he *experiences* Hades with Calypso and leaves her), and then to Scheria where he repudiates Achilles' way.

Odysseus' meeting in Hades with his mother, Anticleia, is far more important than the briefing from Tiresias Circe required of Odysseus. The goddess provides all the information that our hero needs to get home; she knows more than Tiresias. Instead it seems necessary that Odysseus must be reborn of his mother, thus negating his polluting penetration by the spirit of Ares, before he returns home to Ithaca; it is in this respect that he must be seen to resemble Tiresias, who was also reborn as a woman. This reversal also explains Circe's telling Odysseus that he, having returned from Hades, has died twice. Like Tiresias, he has regained his old identity while retaining his mind. After this meeting with his mother, he is sought out by women who were raped by gods and disbelieved by men. Of all living men, only Odysseus has the ability to know what they underwent; this mingling of human and divine seems unknown or impossible after Troy. His need for Antikleia confirms my interpretation of his being likened by Homer to a woman weeping over her dead spouse's body. But though he has given birth to his new self, Antikleia's son finds it hard to lose his Ares identity. This process requires courage and a male midwife.

Blind Demodokus, upon first meeting disguised Odysseus, was moved to sing of an *agon* between Odysseus and Achilles, thus suggesting that he could not tell who was standing before him; this leads our hero, who continues to mythologize his recent experiences, to tell Alcinous' court of his encounter with blind Tiresias. But in the symbolic economy of his tale, it is crucial that Odysseus return his wayward soul, which thieving Hermes (Autolycus' father) just gave him, to his mother, Autolycus' child, so he could be restored to his original humanity. Also, the rites before Hades must be seen as being as much for Antikleia and her son as they are for Tiresias. Odysseus may only leave after denouncing wanton glory in its very treasury. As the *telos* of this process, his heroic image must suffer failure and ignominy in Book 12. Yet, at least by the time this story is told, Odysseus recognizes that he must become feminine and productive/creative rather than masculine and destructive of life. This is further reason for him to sing the tales of the "mothers"; now just as androgynous as Tiresias, he must prepare his soul to join with the virgin goddess Pallas Athena.

While Homer is truthful, Odysseus tells lies from beginning to end. Demodokus is the transition between the two. In response to his revelation of the Achilles and Helen/ Ares and Aphrodite themes, Odysseus wants the story of his famously heroic deed recounted. Yet this too pales in comparison to his involuntary recognition of the suffering undergone by his victims, those in Hades who are either slandered or forgotten entirely. This is why after the essential truth of his Ares/Aphrodite phase and his addiction to Circe is revealed, he must do the impossible deed of descending to Hades and dragging out, as he once dragged Helen from Troy, the true nature of echoing glory itself. Even the greatest hero, monster-slaying Heracles, testifies to the ugly reality of his labors. His prudently esoteric reference to the second Heracles, Theseus, also implies that this hero was no better than the original violator of Helen.

This harrowing of Hell, revealing the nihilistic nature of the vertical dimension, is a necessary precondition for the establishment of what we would view as democracy, the horizontal extension of the friendship between Theseus and the demos that overcame the destabilizing effects of the destructive glory-seeking ethic and brought out the true goodness and capacity for virtue in the obscure many. By flipping glory into the underworld, and bringing out true virtue into the light of day, especially by exposing the horrific torments sustained by the greatest heroes/sinners in Tartarus, Odysseus turns the tragic cosmos upside down, a feat more dramatic than that of the Eleatic Stranger, and makes possible a far better understanding of Athena and Zeus. Whether or not he's a liar, as Alcinous suspected, his tale of Hades effectively sacks Troy and the warrior ethic based on Achilles' deeds and Glaucus' words in the *Iliad*.

Seeing that violence and lust are for cowards, the means through which they try to recover qualities of Ares, somewhat resembling the way he successfully gained the arms of Achilles, Odysseus no longer boasts of his own famed exploits; instead he mourns the sad fates of his comrades, while not openly confessing his own sins, and gives prophecies about his future. Just as only Tiresias could compare male and female sexual pleasure, only Odysseus can tell the truth about the Trojan War and compare his career to Achilles'. But if Odysseus is to regain his kingly identity, he must fully confess all he underwent: the good, the bad, and the shameful. Between this reunion with his feminine side and his final confession, he must be punished fully for his misdeeds; this occurs in the events described symbolically in Book 12.

Odysseus brilliantly tells tales that match up to the three divinely inspired songs of Demodokus. It is for this as much as anything else that his hosts reward him. The essential elements of the myth are "true" but Homer improvises with the details of his story, just as his character Odysseus would have done. We recall also that since Homer inherited many elements of the story of Odysseus, the matter of the tales is not necessarily as pregnant in meaning as the suggestive form in which they are set. Beneath the true meaning of his lies about his adventures we find the transformed account of the human condition he claims to bring out of Hades itself, an exploit worthy of Heracles. Though this change cannot occur in our hero's own time, or even Homer's, it is here that the truest and deepest treasures of the *Odyssey* reside. Even the popular albeit mournful tales of Achilles and Agamemnon that the more "truthful" Homer tells are meant to protect and preserve the deeper truth of the lies of Odysseus; they must mature like fine and unmixed wine in the dark cellar of Hades.

At this point Homer in our narrative seems to reveal the poet's power over the hero, when we see Odysseus draw his story out for more profit and pander to his wealthy audience's needs. A good poetic tale of divine ancestry can give luster and legitimacy to even the most tawdry of tyrannies. This power also hovers over the *Iliad*. Once seen, it undermines its fine tales of gods and heroes; instead we are left with poetry and the poet's shrewd insights into the human soul. Everything else is abandoned to birds and dogs. Simply put, Odysseus' tale emulates and surpasses the bard's tale of his conquest of Troy. Here he not only exposes the ugly truth about those sackers of Ilium; he also sacks the very cultural underworld based on tales of heroic feats of undying fame. In revealing the sad condition of the Trojan heroes' souls, he exposes the ugly horror of it all, Odysseus takes on the name, sex, and sad wisdom of his own mother; now he will be a womb, teeming with stories and identities that enable him to indirectly convey his own story and experiences during and after the Trojan War.

Tiresias can only come after Elpenor is lost. As we recall, Hermes gave Odysseus his soul along with hope on mournful Aiaia when all seemed lost. Now our hero must move past false hope and interrogate his own inner feminine soul. We recall that Elpenor, the unknown soldier of the Trojan War, asked Odysseus to bury him in the name of his wife, father, and son. The very striking omission of Antikleia suggests that the loss of hope accompanies news of her death. Elpenor, whose name means hope, replaces the mighty stag that gave hope to the Ithacans when they landed at Aiaia. Circe takes a soul for the one taken from her. Just like Orpheus' wife, all who eat at Circe's table are doomed. Hermes' gift of Moly may be equated to the self-knowledge that saved Odysseus from this ugly fate. Dante saw this; his claim that we must abandon hope before entering Hell is from the *Odyssey*. This means that our hero must become as vulnerable as Andromache. Only then can Athena help him again, as she now assists his wife, who labors like Hector to defend son and city. While the *Iliad's* Priam and Hecuba are replaced by Laertes and Antikleia in the *Odyssey*, it is striking that Laertes assumes a feminized slavish form. He is like the dog Argos. Legend has it that Hecuba who was to have been Odysseus' booty from Troy is turned into a dog. Her soul could not endure any more.

A prophet sees the present clearly. Tiresias will speak to him from within only after he abandons the blinding hope of glory. This is equivalent to mourning his betrayal of his mother. Helen first weakened him, as she made him feel Aphrodite's power, and this led him to turn his intellect toward intemperate ends. Now, later, finding out about Antikleia and

Agamemnon plunges him into a downward spiral/Charybdis. We must also see his Antikleia tale as a virtuoso performance that quite surpasses the bard's song about the triumph of Odysseus. It also both erases and exceeds the sorrow of an unknown soldier's wife that he had emulated earlier. In one sense the old Odysseus is dead, as dead as the hopeless Elpenor; but he is also responsible for many of the dead, including one whose daimon-like name warned against false glory, his mother, and the living, by this implied account of the meaning of life.

His emulation of Achilles was the cause of Odysseus' mad infatuation with Circe or Helen and the eventual loss of his men, manliness, and freedom. This was seen in Book 10. As he travels to Hades, before leaving on his final doomed voyage, the tale gets increasingly surreal; fabulous feats are replaced by fateful apparitions. Book 11 is the most didactic part of our epic; even Book 12 takes us back to the allegorical. We soon find out that while Agamemnon was self-centered to the end, Achilles comes to regret the lust for violent glory that led him to abandon his father and son. There are no second chances for the dead to change how they have made themselves.

If Aiaia stands for Aias, the mournful name of the hero who defended his comrades, just as Odysseus did on Circe's isle, then Agamemnon represents for the Cyclopes (and Aeolus' deflation of this windbag) and the earlier Laestrygonian episode sums up what was most despicable about Achilles, his betrayal of the other Greeks. This seems to point towards the separate deal Odysseus makes with the king (of Egypt?). Perhaps Hades also signifies his own experience of self-forgetfulness, derived from a condition, perhaps of enslavement or captivity, that reduced him to little better than a beast. Scornful Ajax is as silent as the eleven ships lost in the Laestrygonian episode.

We see Odysseus first testify before the very gates of Hades itself to the hollowness of glory in Book 11. Then in Book 12 he will endure great temptations, and finally suffer more than any of his victims on account of his greater consciousness. He will thus mourn his former vainglorious self, *qua* crafty Ulysses, as bitterly as Achilles did when he stalked himself thinly disguised as noble Hector. The *Iliad*, the epic tale of the madness of Achilles, is about the end of a brutal age and not a fallen flag to be picked up and unfurled by eager epigones. It is not about the many unspeakable atrocities performed at the sack of Ilium; neither does it tally all the terrible long-term results of the Trojan War. Yet, sadly, this eager misreading is one of the most frequent and lasting deleterious effects of the moral breakdown that occurs in the wake of a disaster. We learn from wrestling with great works of literature; we are not supposed to imitate images, or even meant to illustrate these works at all. Only literature can charm the poisonous roots of fury out of the mimetic human soul.

Odysseus cannot admit to his crimes though he does eventually experience their material results. This is Hades; it is an autonomous state of self-pity; the dead soul cannot see itself or take responsibility. Instead Ares persists in visiting Aphrodite; this cycle is embodied by our hero in Circe. Odysseus must discover that he is in a Hades of his own making. But only he has a chance to relive his own errors and take blame for errors that are not his but caused by his own neglect/selfishness. At the end, his material desires are purged; the only residue is his indomitable will. By contrast, while all that remains of Agamemnon is self-pity, Achilles, stripped of his armor, is belatedly concerned about his father and son; an Ajax is simply titanic pride. There is no sorrow for the victims of the War; indeed there are no Trojans in Hades. However, this is Odysseus' take on them. Homer's account follows much later.

Odysseus' meeting with manipulative Agamemnon explains how he became this way; it describes his inner rift between mind and body, reflected in an increased alienation from his crew. His meeting with Achilles shows what he became when he lost himself. Lastly, the scene with Ajax hints at the deep internal shame he carries; he is bound to his false identity and also disgusted by it. Invincible Ajax's contempt undermines any glory accruing to Odysseus from outlasting the other two or sacking Troy. It is a body blow, delivered by the bravest Greek, that reminds him of his sins.

Like Heracles, one part of Odysseus suffers in Hades while he claims to be with Calypso. Even if he is a liar, nothing really happened as he described, he is divinely gifted and must be rewarded accordingly; he is a poet who literally makes reality by his power to fashion the categories by which lesser mortals regard it. This is what makes Hades rich; it is a storehouse of meaning. We see Odysseus' poetic power in his reducing Agamemnon and Achilles to the banal noumenal residue of the evil they unleashed for power, pleasure, and profit. Hades thus reveals a soul to itself as much as it hides its fate from others. Achilles, as Odysseus sees him, despite the company of his beloved Patroclus, is now belatedly concerned with his father and son. Only by returning home, Odysseus will best him; likewise revealing Penelope's fidelity will mark his superiority to Agamemnon. But even as Socrates' life and death do not refute the values of the Peloponnesian War, which seems to be driven by the desire to emulate Agamemnon and Achilles, Odysseus' confessions cannot preempt the eternal return of strife to the human soul. In Hades, however, reflection does not occur nor is there repentance; the shades are basted eternally in tears of self-pity.

Agamemnon, who as Demodokus saw, ruled by a strategy of divide and conquer, had claimed to be ruled by sad necessities only he could understand. It is easily inferred that this approach divided him from his wife and eventually incurred her utter fury. Odysseus comments on the irony of Agamemnon losing his wife while fighting for Helen but, as they both know, and the *Odyssey* well reveals, this was but a pretext. While the self-pitying king is stunned by his wife's cruelty in butchering his mistress before his eyes, a scene exquisitely rendered by Aeschylus, we must see how our own hero's own egocentric behavior, based on his mental superiority, has alienated him from ordinary morality and left him in a place of great vulnerability vis-à-vis somebody like Penelope who, like Aeschylus' Clytemnestra, is very much his equal.

Achilles' tragic choice must now be exposed and rejected. As Nietzsche may have put it, that Myrmidon died too soon. He does not see that the soul is feminine; it follows that he has yet to grasp the fullest meaning of what his pregnant soul learned. His earlier meetings with women testify to Odysseus' newly feminized soul; they are drawn to this quality that he once possessed to a superlative degree. He can once again feel for others and regain the self-knowledge that his mad quest for glory, in Achilles' unfeeling arms, had lost. Achilles' armor was mentioned when Odysseus met Ajax and regrets their contest. Figuratively or literally, Odysseus must have worn this armor in the horse. This is why he does not weaken before Helen's song. Odysseus also had this armor on when he sacked Troy, looking like Ares or Achilles, and also when he blinded the Cyclopes. It is only when Antikleia disarms him that he's symbolically able to feel again. Thus Circe both did and did not keep her promise not to un-man him; it was this very clinging to his Ares-derived false masculinity that kept him in her domain. Odysseus will symbolically don this armor again when he encounters Scylla. He does not wear it when the Sirens sing to him.

Ajax stands for more than the contempt a good soldier feels for Odysseus' betraying his comrades for personal honor or safety; He also represents the unvoiced hatred of the eleven missing ship-crews as well as the anger towards their absent king that has overrun and given power to the suitors. Yet Odysseus must also be reminded, through Agamemnon and Achilles, of the wife and son who still await his return. While Agamemnon and Ajax are fully enclosed in their own armor of perfect self-pity and rage, Thetis' unarmed son belatedly sees that he has neglected old Peleus and his son. Sadly, Neoptolemus turns out to be just as bloody-minded as his sire; he is like Orestes to the extent that they are both haunted by the ghosts of their wicked sires, demanding that their error-filled lives should be vindicated. Odysseus must ensure that Telemachus will learn from his father's sins and become a better man. Although his visit to Hades symbolizes a triumph over Achilles, thus gaining greater glory than the sack of Troy, since . Agamemnon also pays homage, the humiliations and losses he undergoes on Book 12 are preceded by the deep glimpse Odysseus gets into his own soul in Hades. Seeing he is yet a monster, our hero fears exposure to the Gorgon; his fate as statue or influence as icon would be no better than that of his old comrades. He cannot risk looking back, teary eyed, into the gaping womb of Hades. The victorious Greek camp turns out to as desolate as the raped city of Troy. While the surface of Book 11 is of family, father and sons, Hades itself is a political unconsciousness or cultural substrate. The Trojan city has been destroyed along with the cultures of honor and glory that Trojans and Greeks stood for. A true Greek city must be built along lines different from those of either Priam or Agamemnon.

After meeting his three comrades from Troy, Odysseus then sees some of his own predecessors, men enduring endless self-torture for crossing the limits separating gods from mortals. Sisyphus, Tantalus and Tityos were all punished in ways that involved eternally recurring ordeals they could never escape from; their plights can only remind us of the centripetal nature of Odysseus' own psychic trials. It is as if their evils have been writ large as represented in the physical realm as trials for both body and soul; they have already been judged by Minos. It seems to be implied that the three dead heroes of the Trojan War may well have to undergo the same scrutiny; surely instigating the war and all related raids and atrocities deserves at least as much punishment as offenses against the gods committed in the past.

Lastly Odysseus meets the only other man who entered Hades and escaped to tell the tale. It is we who must take note when this hero is struck by his resemblance to Odysseus; it is Heracles who reminds us again that all we have seen is image and not real. When Odysseus says that he only met Heracles' wraith, claiming that the real hero was eating Ambrosia with the gods, the truth may that Odysseus was in Hades all the time he supposedly spent treated as a god by Calypso or Alcinous. There is also a profound insight into the nature of trauma; even if Heracles is actually being feted the Olympus, part of him will always remain in the darkest recesses of Hades. This forces us out of Hades along with our anti-hero's deepest insights into the toxic effects of glory on the soul. Our hero now goes on his last fantastic voyage while we must read between his lies; we are still in Scheria or Olympus, being entertained or deceived by a trickster whose inner nature and true motives still remain concealed. This newly feminized figure clinging to his old self will be duly chastised in Book 12.

After this ugly self-knowledge Odysseus is reborn if not redeemed, chastened if not continent; he will face punishment in full awareness of his crimes. It is different for his men. Elpenor's cremation also signifies their end. Just as the elaborate obsequies for Patroclus, though directed by Achilles truly marked his own death as a man, the soon to be drowned shipmates of Odysseus are given the consolation of being present at their own funerals. No other shipwrecked sailors would be as fortunate. Odysseus however has to look beyond the past and family; he must come up with a solution to the problems facing the post-war world we have seen in Books 1-4.

Book 12

The final episodes of the great wanderings of Odysseus, as told to the rapt court of Alcinous, tell of his ship's last disastrous voyage. After returning from Hades, a feat Circe regards as a second death, this unhappy body is now ready to journey home. As noted before, there was no need for Odysseus to gain Tiresias' advice here; Circe knows all the details of their itinerary, and advises Odysseus about the difficult choices he will face. The trip from Hades to Circe's palace of sorrow is easy, thus confirming the suspicion that they entered the gate of Hades at *Aiaia* and are still within the realm of non-being. It could be that all Odysseus' adventures in this book will only expose him to aspects of his unredeemed past rather than with spatial locations to be escaped; this unsentimental journey must even include the ultimate un-digestible event, the sack of Troy. This means that Calypso's isle could be as much a part of Hades and his psychic inferno as Circe's. The torturously circular dialectical paths of punishment literally conceal what they hold captive in their orbit, whether as speechless beast or lifeless shade. It follows that numberless dead are too undifferentiated to have a distinct existence, even as lies or myths in Hades; they represent those whom Odysseus has tried to suppress memory of: his eleven abandoned crews and the even larger number of souls killed or enslaved during the years spent 'fighting for Helen'. Even entering Hades proper, and becoming part of the Greek collective unconsciousness, could be seen as a great deed. This was the hope of Elpenor, the 'Unknown Soldier' who fought for ravished Helen. But to save soul, family and people, Odysseus must escape Hades by confessing his sins and renouncing his false heroic identity, even as he uses it as a raft to survive physically.

Now that the adventures corresponding to the three songs of Demodokus have been produced, all that remains to be told is the inside tale of how Odysseus dealt with the other famous adventures he was known to have had on his voyage home. This means that while *what* happened is well known, the *how* and *why* of these strange events must be accounted for. Homer's version of the ending to this part of the story suggests that these many un-heroic trials are part of the process by which Odysseus himself finally escapes the infernal circle of Circe he was trapped in. In other words, our hero must divest himself of all the heroic lies that dragged him down to Hades; he must deconstruct his own immortal legend to become a mortal and return home. This process is prefigured in the scene where Odysseus wept like a widow over the corpse of her husband. He must remove the blinding armor of Achilles; he has to separate from his Ulysses identity and resume his ugly all too human form. This deconstructive aspect makes Book 12 something of a satyr play with regard to the tragic trilogy set forth in Books 9-11. The effectual truth of this story, as well as the essence of the great wanderings, is epitomized in the image of our weeping hero. It is also possible to see him as clinging desperately to his former identity as a heroic warlord, even as his vain pretensions to glory and virtue as stripped away from him.

The Sirens correspond to the Lotus-eaters. Their songs offer soul-cloying pleasures that may compliment the, equally dangerous, physical comforts offered by Circe. It is striking that they do not consume the flesh of those who entranced by their song. In a sense, they represent the outer limits of Hades; a 'first circle' where death comes in the gentlest form of self-forgetting, after sympathetic recognition of all that was endured. They are not unlike muses; remembering so that we may forget, they take over the burden of bad memories and offer men absolution at history's end. Even if their tales may be false and euphemistic, the relief they give gives us closure. Just as his men were willing to languish to death, eating the cloyingly sweet lotus, so too is Odysseus now tempted to waste away while listening to the Sirens' sweet flatteries.

Here once more, Odysseus is separated from his men. Circe realized this when she gave him the opportunity of listening to what his crew could not be allowed to hear; indeed this distinction is presupposed in the very fact of her briefing him privately. It may be that only Odysseus is capable of regaining continence after having time to reflect on what the Sirens had to say; his crew could not be trusted to reject the wish to return to this place after they had experienced its temptations. We also note that unlike the case of the Lotus-eaters, it is Odysseus who is to be tied up by his crew. By this point of his story all of these enchanting exploits must be spelled backwards.

The burial of Elpenor, which took place even before Odysseus and his crew rejoin Circe, represent this abandonment of hope that mires them in Hades even after it has seemingly been left behind. This fatalistic mindset is appropriate because the events that will take place *have already happened*. Only this explanation can account for their nightmarish quality and the need for Odysseus to endure them one more, this time from the perspective of the helpless victim. Even though what will happen to them is thus predetermined, how Odysseus will respond to them is not. The way he reacts will condition whether or not he will escape the circles of Hades; this also means *a fortiori* that how he tells the story determines whether or not he gets home. Circe informs Odysseus that while she will tell him all he needs to know about his voyage, "the very god will make him remember."

Otherwise put, his recollection will have a deeper basis than her words; something already in him will recognize them.

While the encounter with the Sirens is unavoidable, Circe seems to suggest that Odysseus will then face something resembling a choice. One course leads his ship towards the rovers, clashing rocks that no living thing, with the sole exception of the *Argo*, has gotten past; Circe says that this miracle occurred through Hera's great love for Jason; we infer that Odysseus' strong connection with Athena no longer holds. It seems to follow that our hero must accept his disgraced mortality and choose the other path. Circe does not tell what would happen were he to escape these rocks. Yet as noted, a god, Hermes, did rescue Odysseus from something equivalent to these very rocks, the continual dialectic between Ares and Aphrodite that saw Circe stand for the erotic feminine that Odysseus, *qua* Achilles, is drawn towards. But since this gift of the gods only led deeper into Hades and did not save him from the vicious circles he was trapped in, it follows that Odysseus must now choose the other path. Here he faces another choice, one that will further separate him from his shipmates.

The celebrated disjunction between Scylla and Charybdis amounts to the ugly choice between a certain minor loss and the prospect of losing everything. By electing to avoid the clashing rocks, Odysseus has already lashed himself with the scourge of cowardice; he then exposed his own incontinence to his men by his conduct before the Sirens; our hero must now act in a way that draws attention to his selfishness. Due to the recollected nature of these events, and the intelligence he has received from both Tiresias and Circe, Odysseus knows his own life will not be in danger. His fate is to incur the odium of cowardice/selfishness and lose the trust of his men. As Circe sees it, it is reckless and stupid for him to try to take on immortal Scylla; this will only lead to the loss of six more men. Instead he is urged to call on her mother.

The final ordeal Circe describes has to do with the cattle of the Sun. She repeats the warning of Tiresias against slaying them and mentions that these cows and sheep, three hundred and fifty of each kind, are immortal and do not reproduce. Although these actions incur the vengeful wrath of the gods, it now seems that mortals have power to perform actions greater than the blinding of Polyphemus; they can even kill some immortal beings. Further, as Odysseus told the blinded Cyclopes, even the gods cannot reverse the effects of certain human actions. This is why men outside the law are a threat to gods, nature, and each other. We now see why it is incumbent that Odysseus rejoins the order of things; part of his atonement must include an account of the bad influence he had on other men. Tales of the rage of Achilles and the confessions of Odysseus teach others of the unprofitability of rage and piracy.

The meeting with the Sirens goes just as Circe has predicted, though he tells them that Circe ordered him to listen to the Sirens, instead of giving him the option of doing so. Odysseus has his men tie him to the mast so he can hear their songs. This action, though permitted by Circe, shows that Odysseus' curiosity is still not under his control; further, his men see evidence of their king's incontinence when he pleads to be freed from his bonds. Though they only followed his earlier instructions when they tightened his knots, the men acquit themselves better than their master.

Odysseus' relationship with his crew deteriorates after their terrifying encounter with Scylla. This time he does not tell his crew what Circe had told him. Neither does he follow her advice that he should not fight the monster. Thus, by his being armed when Scylla attacked, the men realized that Odysseus was not being honest with them. Though Odysseus says that Scylla's victims crying out to him was the most piteous sight he had seen on his travels, meaning that Achilles' armor no longer shielded his iron heart from pity, his men must have been horrified by this sign of his perfidy. It is also worth wondering if Circe had been completely honest with him. While Tiresias too had warned him of the Cattle of the Sun, her directions left them undermanned and hardly capable of rowing past Thrinacia; after having lost six more men, he now has fewer than forty of the sixty who should have manned his ship.

There are several indications here that their encounter with the Cyclopes is still being reprised. It is not just that six men were lost here too; they were lost as part of a calculated "executive" decision by Odysseus, albeit one forced on him. Moreover, Odysseus himself alludes to this adventure when he seeks to hearten his men, just before they approach Scylla. We also recall the wanton curiosity that led him into the cave of Polyphemus; is this also paralleled by his desire to listen to the Sirens? It is also the case that Scylla's residence is also a cave. There is also the odd symmetry in the choice of Scylla over Charybdis here, and the parallel disjunction between losing six men to the Cyclopes as opposed to the loss of all the other ships, a disaster that much resembles the total destruction Charybdis represents. This also confirms our suspicion that the Laestrygonian episode does not occur after the defeat of the Cyclopes but is synchronous with it. The assailants in both cases were giants; the evil Laestrygonians just do what the Cyclopes would have done, had Polyphemus not been outwitted by Odysseus. In other words, it seems as if the other eleven ships were stoned and destroyed when Odysseus left them to visit Polyphemus' cave. Even if these events never really took place, the logic of the story shows a parallel between the forms of these different lies. This also explains the minimal attention that Odysseus gives to the biggest disaster of his voyage. His neglect *qua* storyteller thus parallels the way he actually neglected the other eleven ships under him. Again, even if these events never occurred, they still show that Odysseus was not aware that he should have explained the loss of 90% of his fleet, even in his lies. Otherwise put, the lies he does *not* tell point us towards moral failings he is quite oblivious to.

While Odysseus has shown restraint in not provoking Scylla to further depredation, this conduct does not appear in the best light to his long-suffering comrades. Even as he comes to feel more empathy towards them, his men become less prone to trust him; while his conduct towards Polyphemus was reckless folly, it seemed brave to his men. Now, conversely, his moderation appears as selfish cowardice. This theme is resumed later on Ithaca, when he can only speak the truth while seeming to lie. By these two antiheroic actions he has finally escaped the realm of the Cyclopes that stands between the island of Circe and the reality he is seeking to reenter. This suggests that his final ordeal somehow involves where he was before embarking on these mythic voyages, the Trojan War itself. We must see that the songs sung before Alcinous both tell the story of how Odysseus lost his way after Troy and also become the way by which he somehow overcomes his past by recounting his errors. This too suggests that the end of his sorrows, which deliver him to the arms of Calypso, may also provide some account of their origin—the tale of how he lost Athena's favor.

The final tale of his nostos, one that ends with our hero clinging for his life to a piece of wood like that used to blind the Cyclopes, in a way reminiscent of how he then resembled a war widow clasping the corpse of her slain husband (or the Trojan Horse) is the incident of the Sun's cattle. Here the separation of Odysseus from his crew is completed; his piety is contrasted to their desperate greed. While the whole debacle seems set up and unavoidable, closer examination of the tale reveals several points at which the crew's fate could have been averted. In the first instance, they could have rowed past the island, even thought their just depleted numbers would have made this harder; secondly, they could have resumed their voyage right after eating instead of stopping overnight to wallow in their sorrow; and lastly, they could have survived on fish. Thrinakia means "trident." While this reminds us of the triadic structure of this part of the book, complete with three warnings and three ordeals, we cannot forget that the Cyclopes and Charybdis are not primarily flesh eaters; while Polyphemus seems to live off milk and cheese, Charybdis also consumes sea creatures, i.e. fish. Wayward sailors are but substitutes.

This suggests to us that it would have been possible for the crew to have survived a bit longer by living off fish, a lifestyle Homer's own audience would have practiced; in other words, the rebellion against Odysseus led by Eurylochus was animated by motives other than absolute hunger. We must also note that the crew continued to feast on the cattle for seven more days; there is no sign that they only ate what was absolutely necessary. It was once suggested, by an authority no less renowned than Xenophon's Socrates, that the famed gift of the gods that Hermes gave Odysseus was moderation; he did not become a pig because he did not eat any more than what was truly needed. While this Talmudic gloss is not essential to my argument, it provides collateral support to the view that the hunger felt by the crew was more thumotic than physical; the bestiality Circe spawned seems to have corrupted their appetites. Alternately, his men seem to be taking on the qualities Odysseus is being purified of; it is as if they are back on Circe's island and his men are now reduced to consuming cattle they well know to be transmogrified men. As we recall, Circe merely allowed the crew to indulge their basest appetites when they first visited her island. On this instance, in her absence, their bestial natures reassert themselves once more. While the ultimate responsibility for these misdeeds is Odysseus', since he spawned these appetites, like Frankenstein he can no longer assert his authority over his monsters. As Aristotle saw, we are as responsible for our habits as we are for our children; bad traits once easily governed by us grow independent and unruly when left unpruned. Now Circe, who is a daughter of Helios, the owner of the cattle, has Odysseus at her mercy. Neither can we forget that Calypso, to whose hands our hero passes, is the niece of Circe. We are reminded of Jason and his relationship with Medea, another one of Circe's nieces. Medea is to Jason what Circe is to Odysseus. As her own name indicates, she encircles him so he keeps returning to her as Ares did to Aphrodite. In other words, her sailing instructions brought him back to her as Calypso. While it is literally hidden, this is as bad as the vicious cycles Tantalus and Sisyphus were in.

Tiresias told Odysseus that they could only escape Thrinakia if they controlled their spiritedness. Even Odysseus' prayers could not save his crew; the gods just put him to sleep. The sleep of reason breeds monsters whose base deeds offend the gods. In other words, instead of saying that the gods lead us to act wickedly, it seems as if the true guilt resides in our unruly desires; the fault is not our gods but in ourselves. To the extent that the adventures recounted in books 9-12 truly describe a psychic journey, what we have before us is a process by which the mind of Odysseus, that tireless engine which escaped the rule of Athena, has been chastised. Yet, just as the hero is detached from his crew and leaves them to pay the full penalty for their sins, the physical part of Odysseus must also atone for crimes that his mind now laments. While this part of his confessions, their factual or material basis, will only be made later, it must also be noted that unlike all his other stories, which have their basis in some recent event, the unprecedented origin of the tale of the Sun's cattle must have been those unspeakable actions following the sack of Troy that evoked the rage of Athena. In this case also, great atrocities were performed that would both have gone against the strict warnings of the gods and also exceeded any measure of justice. It is Ares rather than Athena who is associated with the mad hubris of revenge; if those acts of mindless violence and impiety described by Euripides happened, they must have alienated the goddess from Odysseus in particular and the Hellenes in general. We recall again that the parallel from Scheria was the sad image of the soon to be enslaved war widow; she represents the events following the sack of Troy. There has to be a link between the apex and apogee of Odysseus' life. He is somehow both the conqueror of Ilium and the war's most abject victim; like Achilles in Hades, he chooses being a landless outlaw to lording it over the dead. He is left holding the mast/spear used to blind Polyphemus that will later be his beggar's walking stick.

Perhaps, ultimately, the three famous adventures/humiliations of Book 12 both correspond to and deconstruct the Cyclopes episode, which in turn epitomizes the entire career of Odysseus during and after the war. Thus the Cyclopes episode that begins with his wanton desire for glory, marked by the wholly unnecessary raid on Scheria, leads then to the sacrifice of six, just as in the case of Scylla; it culminates in the loss of control over his last crew on Thrinacia. Left unspoken is the unwritten Charybdis episode, the loss of other men to the Laestrygonians, which seems also to reflect the choice of Scylla over Charybdis. It is also possible to match the Cyclopes, Circe, and Hades to the three songs of Demodokus; the bard's accounts of Achilles, Ares, and Aphrodite and the sack of Troy serve as counterparts to the songs rendered by Odysseus revealing the deeper psychic significance of these myths. The factual truth is only told much later. If I am right, it appears that the maker of the *Odyssey* contributes these three songs of the bard, described but never sung, to explain the three songs of Odysseus, inherited by him and duly sung, though not decoded. We can't forget that Books 9-12 are almost certainly the oldest parts of our story. Odyssey wept in part before Alcinous' court because they could (and should) not ever understand him or what really happened at Troy; not for the first time, the truth is told as a temporally inconsumable and thus eternal fiction.

Although the events in Books 9-12 never took place, and are literally impossible, it is still possible to draw legitimate inferences about what our poet may not speak about before his impossible audience, if he is ever to get home. Bluntly put, both the economy of the *Odyssey* and the heroic code require that some deeds stay unspoken of. They may be reconstructed by looking ahead and seeing what he tells Eumaeus and the suitors about what befell him *qua* beggar. Here he does not talk about gods, magic or monsters but explicitly confesses to human crimes such as treachery, incontinence, and selfishness. While these qualities seem to undergird the character of the narrator of Books 9-11, and are allegorically exposed in Book 12, they can only be confessed to by one of the lowest social standing. With one or two notable exceptions, the men to whom these disclosures are made will soon be dead and disgraced. Only Eumaeus has heard the most damning of these accounts; he was not privy to the fabulous tales Alcinous heard; even the doomed suitors hear nothing about his treacherous surrender in Egypt. It is only when all three incompatible tales are juxtaposed that we can reconstruct what happened when Odysseus faced the Laestrygonians and shamefully lost almost all of his little force from Ithaca. If the truth were publicly known, Odysseus could never resume his position as king; we may add that even his wife and son would find it hard to accept so polluted a sinner.

While the story told by Odysseus about Thrinacia is that he was engaged in some act of piety while the blasphemous slaughter of the cattle took place, a story that so weirdly resembles the tale of Moses and the Golden Calf that some plagiarism on the part of the writer of *Exodus* can be suspected, it also parallels the separation from the other eleven ships when he visits the Cyclopes cave and, even more strikingly, prefigures his hanging on the fig tree, like Jesus on the cross while his last comrades die. While the egotistic distinction between Odysseus and his divine mind from his body of men is bad enough, his use of this disjunction to escape their fate and even become complicit in it is surely the ultimate violation of the *Iliad*'s heroic code. If we follow this logic, it could be the case that Odysseus fled Hades before the five to six hundred of his men lost to the Laestrygonians came to accuse him. At the least, the disobedience of the men led by Eurylochus shows his loss of control over them.

Book 12 strips Odysseus of the false virtues he laid claim to, especially if his tales are taken literally by hearers of Books 9-11. Our hero is no longer a Polyphemus figure, an eloquent giant among men, when we see how his own stories expose his soul. We realize that he is as incontinent as the Cyclopes, as manipulative as Circe, and just as selfish as Agamemnon and Achilles. Later, when we study his revised account of his travels to Eumaeus, we shall see good grounds for suspecting that Odysseus may have betrayed his men by surrendering in the face of overwhelming odds; he did not merely blame his men or lose control of them as he lost mastery over his passions. It is easy to see why he wept as a woman over his old self while being led into slavery. He was as incontinent as the Cyclopes, cruel as the Laestrygonians, dehumanizing as Circe, deceptive as the Sirens, murderous as Scylla, and dangerous as Charybdis. All those who sailed with him died. He is his own dark Hades. Now he must save Ithaca.

Odysseus is Scylla—an Octopus six-armed consuming six men apiece. He must arm to confront himself . . . cry out to her mother, ie Antikleia! Like the octopus, Cyclopes, he too had/has only one eye, two arms as Antinous and Eurylochus.

Chapter 4
Gods, Slaves, Outlaws, and Fugitives: Books 13–16

Book 13

Odysseus' physical return to Ithaca is actually quite anticlimactic. As the poet completes his marathon session of storytelling and receives twelve cauldrons to reward his twelve antiheroic labors, he is likened to a ploughman who has worked the field, up and down, all day. We are now reminded of the themes or motifs that our poet has skillfully repeated to give symmetry to his work of art. The details of his voyage home to ordinary reality out of the enchanted element of Scheria are as much a mystery to inspired Odysseus as the process by which a blind man is transported from place to place is to Homer; yet upon arrival even though the bard's location is invisible to him, he still possesses the precious stock in trade that is his story. Otherwise put, we are as blind to the poet's mythic reality, the master narrative of meaning that he steers us through, as he is to the physical space surrounding him. Only his muse can dispel the mist; this Athena will begin to do, more surely than Poseidon could cure his blinded son.

Such a reading also explains how Odysseus, our bard, sleeps so mightily once he performs his shaman-like feats; we also "see" how his crew could be perplexed by the fact that he only possesses a bag of wind, an insatiable belly that yet takes him everywhere. We also better comprehend the transformations from ugly old beggar to divine hero and singer that Odysseus regularly enacts with the aid of his muse. Just as the Trojan Antenor marveled at the Ithacan's transformation from a short, sullen, and even stupid-looking man into one who became the master of the field as soon as he spoke, Homer's readers and auditors must appreciate our polymorphous hero's ability to change from nobody into Athena's dearest friend and change agent. Without Athena, he is nobody; through her and with her he is transfigured in beauty.

119

Concomitantly, even as Odysseus is "translated" from wandering vagrant to hidden king, an equally dramatic metamorphosis occurs in the land of his sometime hosts. Enraged by their treatment of his enemy, Poseidon demands that Zeus punish the Phaiakians for this implied disrespect towards him. How could Alcinous and his people have shown so much hospitality towards the self-confessed enemy of their patron? Although this seeming impiety seems inexplicable, unless we conclude that the obligations of hospitality trump those of piety—a claim that places the universal values of Zeus above the local hegemony of Poseidon and thus subtly shows why the king of the gods freely consents to the "punishment" of the Phaiakians—it leads to the sealing off of Alcinous and Nausikaa from the rest of the story. As with Calypso, what happens in Scheria stays in Scheria and our hero is safely deposited on his island. In his dearly regained reality there will be no more fantasy. Then, his lying words were accepted literally by all; now whatever he says will be automatically discredited as coming from the lips of a self-confessed Cretan liar. There they gloried in tales of the Trojan War, here he has to deal with the bitter aftermath of those ten years of war and the decade of neglect that followed. The heroic age is over in war-depleted Ithaca; brave new modes and orders of rule are needed to restore the land. Just having a "mighty mind" won't do it. But there is another good reason behind this sealing off of Scheria. It could be that Odysseus does not want the real story of his return to Ithaca to be known any more than he wishes the truth of his time after Troy to be told. He's happier to conceal this tale in fantastic myths that are as pleasing as they are false. It is only with Eumaeus that the Prodigal Prince shares the truth about his passage from pigsty to palace.

Just as he seemed to cause the Phaiakians' fall from an effortless golden age into a Hesiodic time of work and pain for the many, one that would engender reverence towards gods previously regarded as their equals, Odysseus is also destined to lead his own people out of this age of aristocratic oppression and towards a new proto-democratic dispensation. We saw that he ruled Ithaca in the past as a benign despot, albeit with some popular consent, as shown by the institution of the assembly; now he will be seen to take steps that overcome the division between the few and many. This basic distinction between warriors and farmers, raiders and nomads, could very well have been the truest cause of the terrible Trojan War.

Otherwise put, the acquisitive temptation, one never totally alien to him even in his antebellum days, duly separated Odysseus from his own people and even caused him to be alienated from Pallas Athena, his divine patroness. The son of Laertes must now truly earn the reputation, which he formerly possessed undeservedly, for being a just man and kind ruler. This again can be seen to parallel the challenge facing the Phaiakians as they enter the age of Zeus; they too must come to see that only those who share in the human condition of incompleteness can display the virtues of hospitality and piety. Their previous state of Disney-like complacency made it impossible for them to perform deeds that would be truly pleasing to the reformed gods of the *Odyssey*. It is also possible for us to infer that these terrors of the open sea served to make men more piously attached to their birthplace. Poseidon is the god of both earth and sea.

When Odysseus awakes to find himself left ashore on *terra incognita*, his very first impulse is characteristically suspicious. He wonders where he is and laments having left Phaiakia before having made the acquaintance of a powerful king who would have escorted him home. Indeed, Odysseus even curses his blameless hosts for having abandoned him in a strange land where his very possessions make him all the more liable to be killed whilst defending them. He cannot as easily become no-body. We may infer from this that Odysseus himself has not fully internalized the lessons that he so brilliantly imparted to his audience a day ago. His words do not quite measure up to the desires and disposition of his restless and troublesome soul. This predicament may be interestingly contrasted to his plight upon landing on the shore of Scheria; there he chose deliberately to be awoken by his fighting spirit, instead of allowing his body's desperate desire for sleep and death overcome him.

But even as Odysseus, prematurely as it turns out, bemoans his lot while counting his spoils, he is met by Athena disguised as a delicate and beautiful shepherd boy. Yet, though our hero is elated to hear that he is indeed home, he promptly responds to this news with an elaborate lie. Odysseus claims to be an exile from Crete; there he ambushed and killed a man, the Cretan equivalent of Achilles in being the fleetest of foot, for trying to deprive him of his fairly won share of the spoils of Troy. Here we must note that Odysseus is warning the lad that he is (a) a liar, (b) a murderer, and (c) desperate enough to kill again. While the famous paradox that all Cretans are liars, known even at the time of Homer, calls the last two claims into question, we can surely see that (d) all liars are not Cretans and even infer that a true Cretan liar would not and could not make such a claim about himself. It follows then that wily Odysseus is testing his interlocutor's mettle and seeing whether he can be trusted. If the young man thinks that the stranger is speaking the truth, he will not emulate the Cretan's last victim by running away from so dangerous a man. If on the other hand he realizes that the stranger is posing a riddle, he is intelligent enough for Odysseus to do business with. Agamemnon's warning still rings in Odysseus' head. He needs assistance before going about the difficult task of reclaiming wife, home, and crown.

There is a further reason for Odysseus' choosing to depict himself as a Cretan. This was prefigured in his meeting with Polyphemus and implied all along in the account he gave of his adventures to the Phaiakians. In the court of Alcinous Odysseus the sacker of Troy was hard pressed to describe what really happened to an audience grown well used to cartoonish accounts of what the Achaeans endured for ten long years. This was also why he chose to depict his post-Trojan travails to the eager Phaiakians in terms that were more mythic than literal. Supporting my claim is the strong attraction he felt towards the Sirens and Circe; they either claimed to know or possessed the capacity to absorb the unspeakable things that he had learned and experienced. To all other mortals, and even to himself to a significant extent, he is truly no-body; his is a furiously active fevered mind, possessing knowledge of many souls and cities and yet paradoxically unable to share this logos with a single other human. In other words, he is a Cretan to the extent that he can only convey the truth about himself by artful myths and seemingly tall tales. We recall Homer's poignant image of the man hiding a precious burning log amidst a deep pile of ashes on the off chance that it will survive the winter. It is up to us to decode these true lies. Our goal is not to burn Troy a second time; we merely wish to see Ilium through his eyes.

Just as readers have long read the *Iliad* through the lens of a prior conviction that the Trojan War was a noble struggle for family values, and that Achilles was a noble hero standing beyond good and evil, the *Odyssey* in turn suffers from a too-willing suspension of disbelief. We don't want to take Odysseus at his word when he calls himself a liar. This leads us to focus our attention towards either the vertiginous center of this story or its bloody conclusion; we want either a magical Disney story or a gory Western shootout where evildoers are exterminated. Given all this, it is small wonder that Odysseus the antihero is almost impossible to detect; we too take his mythic lies for literal facts and concomitantly discount some tantalizing clues about what really happened over those missing years. If my reading is correct, and the truth about Achilles and the awful Trojan War is best gained from close reading of the *Iliad* itself, then the *Odyssey* is a continuation of a "great motion" that began in the first work. As its result we see a profound change of the way in which the gods and the very meaning of human life itself are viewed. This revaluation is our topic.

While we shall go on to examine good reasons for believing that Odysseus' Cretan lies are not quite as false as they are meant to seem, our immediate task at this point pertains to Athena and her self-proclaimed deep connection with the son of Laertes. Her words, as we shall see, are amazing. Their import would be quite blasphemous; Odysseus would immediately qualify for special tortures in Hades, alongside such worthies as Sisyphus and Tantalus, were he to make such a claim in his own voice. This is why it is fitting to begin with Athena's revelations before turning to look at how Odysseus is transfigured by them. His self-knowledge only comes through her. In the first half of the *Odyssey* we have seen our hero confess the meaning of all the many misdeeds he performed, for "Confessions" including those of Augustine almost always pertain to meanings rather than facts, when he was alienated from her grace.

Just as Odysseus, the first true man, is radically incomplete without Athena (though Penelope his long-suffering spouse is the best human embodiment of virtues that the goddess represents minus the not unattractive attributes possessed by Circe) we must understand how it is that Athena herself cannot fully exist without Odysseus; herself born from Zeus's head, she only becomes truly activated through our hero. The words she addresses to him, when speaking and appearing as herself, deserve very careful attention; this epiphany reveals the deepest meaning of the *Odyssey*. By the actions of men like Achilles and Odysseus, the Olympian gods undergo change.

What does it mean for Athena to discard her previous disguise as a noble shepherd boy, the "look" of Hermes when he appeared to Odysseus on Circe's isle, and now be present to him as "a tall beautiful woman skilled in fine handiworks"? We could now even rudely ask the blind bard how on earth, short of wearing a Girl Scout badge, one could appear to have a mental skill? Still, regardless of how this was done, we are struck by the fact that it is even more difficult for Athena to appear as herself than it is for Odysseus. We can only wonder if she seemed less sexually alluring than Helen or Circe, both of whom were skilled weavers, while yet conveying something of the wickedly intuitive intelligence that so delighted Odysseus. Would it take an equal or complementary mind to penetrate her ultimately inadequate guise and see what the great virgin goddess could or would not show to any other human being? Is it possible that Athena was angered by Odysseus' attraction to these false images of herself? Would she prefer to be represented by chaste Penelope? We recall that wise Athena competed with Hera and Aphrodite for the title of the most beautiful.

The question could be posed in another way: are Athena's divine powers somehow limited by differences in psychic potential of the humans she works with? While this would clearly not be a problem for such primal divine powers as those represented by Hades or Poseidon, or even the more social passions such as jealousy and sexual allure that Hera and Aphrodite stand for, we could easily see how the powers of Apollo, Hermes, and Hephaestus are unequally distributed among men. Indeed, we could even say that they exert their influence by exploiting our human differences.

One important aspect of this question is raised in Plato's *Euthyphro*: do the Homeric gods create virtue *ex nihilo* or do they recognize, foster, and reward human erotic striving? As far as the *Odyssey* is concerned it seems that Homer's answer is clear; it is also very consistent with Zeus' complaint that mortals should not blame the gods when they are penalized for acts of hubris and excess. Zeus' rueful words suggest that while the gods both warn and punish us, they do not control human freedom. However, this does not mean that mortals are free to be or do anything they want. There is ample evidence to argue that human differences are inherited through their parentage, whether human or divine. As a result, different mortals are best suited to embody and reflect the virtues or powers that the gods possess to a superabundant degree. But since the Olympian condition is one of effortless ease and immortality, the gods' signature qualities have no real meaning as far as their own lives are concerned; this means that thumotic or self-asserting satisfaction can only be had indirectly. The gods only know themselves in relation to the tragic realm where mortal men act out and fully experience the truest meaning of the divine attributes. Only this can explain the passionate interest the gods take in the affairs of humanity.

Yet Odysseus is quite exceptional; it is a terrible thing for a human body to contain the spirit of a living god. As we saw in the case of Achilles, a powerful precedent that will be illustrated subsequently by Attic tragedy, such a person's life is almost necessarily as short as it is glorious. Those who are the means by which the gods know themselves inevitably come to think themselves divine. The resultant hubris along with the sheer physical burden that comes with expressing divine power by means of mortal flesh leads to envy, overreach, and madness. While it is quite hard enough for a hero to reach the level where he can interact meaningfully with the gods, the return to the human realm, and the awareness that one is but human at the end of the day, is an impossible task that no mortal can perform. This is why Athena's intercourse with Odysseus makes even the case of Achilles lose its luster.

Although not of divine descent, Odysseus somehow manifests qualities of wit and guile that are of the utmost consequence to Athena's own development or growth in power. To this extent, just as Achilles' career and explosive self-understanding was to bring about a diminution in the hegemony of the tyrannical Zeus of the *Iliad*, it is Athena rather than Apollo, that jealous guardian of the limits separating the human from the divine represented in the *Odyssey* by Helios the sun, who redefines the new meaning of human life. This was to become the basis for the Classical Age of Greece. Apollo's role in tragedy is to warn the eponymous Athenians against the excesses of their own free and creative nature. While his qualities of prophecy and harmony represent the fated or determined aspects in life, Athena comes into her own in the democratic age. She overcomes limits and advances progress. Enlightenment that comes through her is not the blinding insight given by Apollo; it occurs more in the nocturnal way of the owl. By careful planning at night she weaves meaning into life.

Athena works best with rational mortals; she is not able to animate those who act impulsively or intemperately. This is why she lost contact with Odysseus in the years after the war; at this time he was enthralled by Aphrodite and Ares. Thus her words after he reproaches her for having left him for so long when his "heart was torn to pieces" in his breast are deeply significant: "I never did have any doubt, but *in my heart* always knew you would come home, after losing your companions." Perhaps the companions in this case, those who tore apart the integrity of his heart and soul, were Aphrodite and Ares? In other words, Athena is stating that Odysseus' return, *especially as himself,* was not predestined. This is also why she rejoices to see that he does not succumb to anger or sorrow on his return, but resumes conducting himself as the crafty rational planner she loved. It is through, with, and in him that Athena can complete her metamorphosis from the vengeful vulture, seated beside a similarly disguised Apollo as Ajax and Hector dueled, into the Goddess of Reason. While she can guide and test others, like Telemachus who is being prepared by her to understand the ways of his father through his sojourn abroad, it is only Odysseus who can actually see Athena herself through her iconic disguises and artful designs. This is the same capacity by which Odysseus is able to express deep ineffable truths by the indirect means of myths that are in a strictly literal sense lies. We shall soon see Odysseus pay tribute to Apollo, the muse of the oracular art, order, and the bow as he plies "archery by the dark of the moon" to restore harmony and peace in Ithaca.

Book 14

Although Athena has promised Odysseus that she would throw her invincible power behind him, and made it very clear that she expects the suitors to pay the ultimate penalty for their hubris, we have already seen that the goddess acts through human agency rather than *force majeure.* Just as Athena could only hope that Odysseus would return to her range of influence, and Odysseus' failure in turn stemmed from his mind's inability to rule over his body and crew, their joint alliance ultimately depends on "boots on the ground." It is only fitting then that Eumaeus, the person to whom she sends the now disguised hero, sets eyes on his master while he is in the act of fashioning a new pair of sandals; the best parallel with the *Iliad* is Thetis' visiting Hephaestus in search for new armor for her son. This playful parallel persists when we note that Eumaeus is about to make himself relatively invulnerable in the heel! Yet just as Athena sends Telemachus on a wild goose chase with a definite intent in mind for the inexperienced youth, Odysseus too will find that he must depend a great deal on his swineherd, even to the humbling extent of having to recite one of his famous true lies for the mere sake of a robe to keep warm overnight!

Although I have called Odysseus "the first man" this in no way discounts Homer's description of "the city of swine" that Eumaeus rules over. The swineherd seems to have built himself a homestead and way of life that is almost enviable; when his master, attempting to promise the skeptical Eumaeus of Odysseus' return, claims to "hate more than the gates of Hades" a man who utters lies under the constraint of poverty, we hear a powerful echo of Achilles' famous condemnation of Odysseus' "hiding one thing in his heart while saying another." Yet we are just as irresistibly reminded of Odysseus' own report, from the very same Hades, of Achilles' belated preference for the life of a day laborer in the service of a landless slave over his own useless glory in the Underworld. Here we see described the hospitality enjoyed by Odysseus in just such a humble relationship; indeed, it could even be the case that here alone is he able to speak, relatively truthfully, of the wanderings after Troy.

Our first indication that Eumaeus is no ordinary man, and certainly no gratuitously humiliating Eurystheus to Odysseus' Heracles, is provided when we find that he has built twelve pens within his compound, each housing fifty breeding sows. These numbers strongly remind us of the roughly equal number of men (several of whom were turned into swine) and ships that Odysseus lost. Further, the stock of three hundred and sixty males being consumed by the lawless suitors match up to the Sun's seven herds of fifty oxen that were depleted by Odysseus' last impious crew. We are invited by these numbers to infer that Eumaeus, being a better ruler of his irrational beasts than Odysseus, could teach him a few things about kingship. It is also necessary that we recall Proteus' revelation that Odysseus' own basic nature is swinish. This matches up with the beggar's laments about being ruled by his belly.

At the very outset Athena ensures that Odysseus *qua* beggar should owe his life to the swineherd. When the dogs guarding the swine attack Odysseus, he displays the kind of prudence one learns from resisting the violence of Scylla or the seductions of the Sirens and plays dead. After the dogs' master finally comes to his aid Eumaeus' first words are of his absent King whom he supposes is either dead or wandering about in just such a condition as his visitor. These sentiments are amplified further when the swineherd brushes aside his guest's blessings and renders a definition of the laws of hospitality commanded by Zeus that is both simpler and far deeper than either Agamemnon's justification for invading Troy or the pretext used by Odysseus when he raided the cave of the Cyclopes. While what he offers isn't much, Eumaeus is well aware that, with Ithaca in its present state, sacred hospitality is as necessary as it is dangerous. He has no doubt that the gods reserve the harshest condemnation for the suitors. While even those desperate nighttime raiders who pillage farmers have the decency to feel shame and fly the scene of their crimes, Penelope's wooers shamelessly remain, feasting and reveling as they defy the gods in the light of day. The implication is that while property rights are not sacred, the household itself must be held inviolate; it is the basis on which the laws of hospitality are founded. This could very well be the basis for the gods' unanimous condemnation of the Achaeans' disgraceful behavior after Troy's fall. Wanton rape and destruction are never justified.

Yet Eumaeus' next words must cause even more shame in his guest; as the retainer proudly lists the riches of his beloved master, it is very clear that Odysseus had no cause to go raiding abroad, having more wealth than the next twenty richest men in Ithaca put together. His love and loyalty for his absent master prevents, even deters this slave from returning home to the parents and land he was taken from as a child. Eumaeus is even reluctant to pronounce his master's name; his greatest longing is to see his absent master return. Saying "he loved me greatly in his heart" of his absent lord, one notorious for not acting in accordance with what was in his heart, the loyal slave trusts Odysseus implicitly. He is thus very unlike those on our hero's last crew. Only in such a context can his suspicious, disguised master feel confident to promise Eumaeus, even swearing by the gods, that Odysseus himself will soon come home.

Now following the customary formula of hospitality, the swineherd goes on to ask his guest who he is and how he came to Ithaca; he asks that the stranger tell him the tale of his sorrows. Even though the host has gently rejected the nameless beggar's sworn word that Odysseus would return in the space in one revolving moon, he is still curious to know something about the man he is hosting. Since Athena has sworn him to secrecy, Odysseus clearly cannot disclose his identity to his slave at this time; yet his very anonymity, coupled with his humble surroundings, gives the

128

disguised hero a certain freedom to reveal far more literal truth than he could share with the childlike Phaiakians. They desired entertainment and totally lacked the capacity to appreciate anything of the suffering that he had undergone; Eumaeus however fully deserves to be told the truth, even if it cannot be connected to the name of Odysseus. While the court of Alcinous will only know Odysseus by name and reputation, the true facts of his odyssey can only be disclosed to one believing him to be no-body. He is freer to tell the literal truth when it is not connected to his name and legendary reputation; by talking to Eumaeus, who is already disposed to regard him as just another vagabond with a hard luck story, Odysseus can finally unburden himself of the most shameful details of his story. We could even argue that he only becomes truly free to take possession of his kingdom after he has confessed his sins to one of his subjects. Until then, he is doomed to continually test others, asking them what they thought about Odysseus, as if he himself were a stranger to who he really is; as we noted earlier, his desire to be being-for-itself or pure mighty mind, only ends up turning him into a bad imitation of Ares: angry, insatiate, and duplicitous. Eumaeus thus seems to play an underappreciated but critical part in the restoration of his master. His name, which could mean either "nobly born" or "good midwife," suggests that its bearer creates a hospitable ethos, one where Odysseus can finally overcome the ugly estrangement from his body and obligations that has all but wrecked Ithaca. Otherwise put, just as Demodokus's songs made it appropriate that Odysseus tell the story of his life in a manner that is not literally but poetically true to people who know him only by name but could never understand the sufferings that his very name itself suggested, so too does his disguise make it possible for his long-suffering host, a man who knew and loved Odysseus but could not penetrate his disguise, to hear and understand an account of a troubled soul and its travails. Though the lost king of Ithaca could not recount this tale to his slave, it could still be shared and understood by men of noble birth, men who had known similar sad experiences of betrayal, kidnapping, enslavement, and life in exile far from home and loved ones. It is also noteworthy that neither party tells the other his name; the story is sufficient. Eumaeus merely asks his guest what man he is, who his parents were, and how he got to the swineherd's home. Indeed, Eumaeus' own name is more a description or claim to be of noble origin told by a confused child not familiar with his real name; the slave who was once probably called young master, is also a nameless stranger.

While the story Odysseus tells in response is much shorter than that he has just told at Scheria, it yet contains almost all the same elements, thus giving fascinating insight into how a bard tailored his performances for different audiences. Odysseus begins his tale of sorrows by repeating what he told Alcinous: his is a tale that would need more than a year to tell fully. Nevertheless, even as he proclaims himself to be a lying bastard from Crete, he promises Eumaeus an accurate account of his origin, life, and journey to Ithaca. Despite being an illegitimate son, the stranger tells how he gained a rich wife through his courage in battle, a gift from Ares and Athena. Yet this very prowess in combat and strategy only meant that hard work and household tasks never appealed to him; he was different, always drawn to long ships and a life of piracy on the seas. We could add that this quality is consistent with the pleasure in lies that Eumaeus has already seen in the Cretan. Yet, after nine successful raids and much plunder, he was coerced by popular pressure into joining the Trojan War. Here too he was successful but then, after only a month at home, a "spirit within" led him to take nine ships for an expedition to Egypt. The motive was clearly mercenary; no feigned outrage at Helen's abduction here, but the results are just as disastrous.

The Cretan's description of this post-Trojan raid matches well with what Odysseus told the court of Alcinous about his foray against the Cicones. Here too, after early success, his men succumbed to indiscipline and began to plunder and pillage. This brought on massive retaliation on the next morning from the allies of the coastal people they had wronged. As piracy rather than trade was the whole point of the expedition, it was clear that just like the Ithacans' ill-fated raid on Ismarus the error lay in remaining on the scene of the crime instead of swiftly departing with their ill-gotten gains; this we recall was just what the swineherd found to be most evil about the suitors—they were as brazen as those who claimed to defend poor Helen's honor.

While poetic Odysseus told Alcinous that his twelve crews raised three cheers for the three men per ship who were lost at Ismarus, the Cretan beggar's claim that he raised nine ships to leave for Egypt suggests that Odysseus lost three ships, a full quarter of his men, before leaving Troy. Things got far worse once their effortless cruise down the Nile ended;

instead of simply sustaining the heavy losses reported by Odysseus, the beggar claims that the entire force was routed and defeated once their over-extended incursion was reported in town and the main body of either the Ciconians or Egyptians, equipped with chariots and fully armed infantry, came down to punish the lightly armed pirates. This disaster, the equiva-lent of the Laestrygonian episode (one where Odysseus played a curiously passive role, perhaps because it occurred while he was occupied with the Cyclopes), also ends in total defeat. His men all either massacred or en-slaved, the narrator throws his arms down and falls weeping in a posture of abject submission before the king. Although many of the Egyptians, as naturally angered by the raid as they are disgusted by this pusillanimity, strain to kill him, the king shows mercy and, honoring Zeus the protector of strangers, takes him into his own home. Here he remains for seven years, growing rich in servitude.

This remarkable tale, besides having a ring of truth to it, also resonates with many other parts of the *Odyssey*. We are first reminded of Homer's de-scription of the weeping Odysseus in the court of Alcinous; there our hero was suggestively albeit incongruously compared to a woman who, having seen her spouse fall in battle, is just about to be led off into slavery. Then and there we were reminded of how very difficult proud Odysseus found it to achieve separation from his former heroic self; here and now we see this image become a literal fact. Once we place it before rather than after his encounter with the evil Phoenician, his story also seems to offer us an explanation of what really happened over those seven or eight years he sup-posedly spent with Calypso. Finally, the essential elements of this story also remain in the final version of his wanderings, told by Odysseus to Antinous and the other suitors, in his own home. Here too, although he is enslaved and taken to Cyprus in its wake, the essential elements of the story of his post-Trojan Egyptian raid remain. These three different accounts he pro-vides of (a) the drunken conduct and imprudent delay of his men, (b) the arrival on the next day of massive reinforcements, and (c) his later total de-feat, all suggest that Odysseus is here disguising truth as falsehood.

Though it is only in the third version, that told to the suitors, that he actually admits to being enslaved, we see how its likelihood is supported both by Homer's image of the weeping widow and the simple fact that being under the protection and in the household of another, when others have both the right and desire to take it, both mark the beneficiary as someone who is not an outlaw; this is the one thing worse than being a slave since an outlaw both deserves to and can be killed with impunity. There is something incorrigible about the outlaw that makes him incapable of either ruling himself or obeying another; while it is good for a natural slave to be ruled by another, an outlaw's matter is too unruly to accept order. Since this has to do with the very trait that the nameless Cretan confessed to the swineherd—a dangerous disinclination towards manual labor or household values—Eumaeus could only infer that his guest served as a skilled mercenary soldier under the king's protection. He may even have been in command of the last remaining survivors from his original force, a number that would approximate the last crew that Odysseus had with him. Such a life would also clearly measure up to the Ares and Aphrodite theme that we observed earlier, while it also could in theory be a way of accumulating wealth, just as he *qua* Cretan claimed earlier to have been generous in distributing booty with his fellow fighters, the accompanying destruction and dissipation can only have made the once and future Odysseus yearn all the more for his family and kingdom.

This is why the Cretan's account of his year-long association with the cunning man from Phoenicia matches up with its mythic equivalent, covering the same time that Odysseus spent on Aiaia. Just like Circe, whose clever wickedness clearly captivated Odysseus, this new companion's excellence in craft and deception would surely have offered him the sort of fellowship enjoyed by those who help friends and harm foes. Yet, as the *Republic* well depicts, associations of this kind are as short-lived as they are dangerous. The Phoenician inevitably set out to betray Odysseus and probably turned his own men against him; when we are told that he meant to sell the Cretan as a slave, it is hard to avoid the inference that the captive's dramatic escape from his bonds brings him to the shores of Scheria. The story of the storm and shipwreck, a disaster that Odysseus alone escapes by holding to the mast, could well be another way of depicting the way he escapes the clutches of Poseidon, who as god of the sea would not have approved of the profane use made of his element, and symbolically blinds and/or escapes the Earth-shaker's justice. We also recall that the Phaiakian ship bringing Odysseus home thrust itself halfway into the ground at the very sacred place where Poseidon made love and fathered Polyphemus. This could represent the original act of hubris, which later turned into the blinding of the Cyclopes by nobody.

The likely reality is that Odysseus, fleeing his captors, was washed up on the coast of Thesprotia or Scheria. Here he was found and succored by its king's son or daughter. It is from Thesprotia/Phaiakia that he finally gets to Ithaca. We cannot but take note of the Tiresias-like way the sexy women in his tall tale told at Scheria are replaced by bad men once the story is re-told at home. The type of his audience and his own needs ultimately determine what kind of story emerges from our bard's cauldrons.

What really happened? We can never forget that nobody can answer this question, not even Homer, whoever he was. Among other things, my purpose here is to show how many different ways of singing this story, with as many turns as its hero, exist. We are dealing with the saga of a self-pronounced liar, a body of stories that Homer himself inherited, enhanced, and passed to us. We have to avoid both Lotus-eating gullibility and the Cyclopes of reductive skepticism while following yet another path through the multiple layers of lies that somehow, when put together, add up to or point towards something that far exceeds the sum of its parts. We must delight in our hero's glib storytelling while never losing sight of either the sublime universal insights that he conveys or the tragic substrate of suffering endurance underlying it. In other words, the basic difference between Odysseus and Ulysses is never fully overcome; this is why the lying Cretan arrives in Ithaca just ahead of good King Odysseus. The untamed core of our hero remains a mystery, even to Athena, Homer, or himself; his is not a pre-spun essence, but a way of being, suffering, and enduring.

The swineherd's response to his visitor's remarkable story is a mixture of sympathy and skepticism. Even as his spirit is troubled by all of the sufferings described by the Cretan, he is yet unwilling to believe his words about Odysseus. Far too many prior visitors have raised false hope in Ithaca by telling tall tales of their king's imminent return. Eumaeus expects to be neither encouraged nor entertained by his guest. The simple hospitality he provides comes both from pity and a sacred duty enjoined by Zeus, the protector of strangers. He refuses to forsake this simple code of virtue.

As much as he yearns for Odysseus' return, Eumaeus believes that the gods hated his master. This is why they condemned him to an obscure and inglorious death at sea. Perhaps this has to do with a peasant's deep dislike for the ways of warfare and piracy that produced equally injurious effects in both Troy and Ithaca. Odysseus is made to experience a way of life completely unlike everything he had experienced since his departure for Troy. The swineherd's simple goodness has already made it possible for him to divulge far more about what really happened to him after Troy. Now the combination of a hot meal, wine and good companionship lead him to let his guard down and address Eumaeus by his given name. While it is quite possible that he could have heard one of the swineherd's hands use their master's name, this curious slip, on the part of both Homer and Odysseus, reveals how much affection they both have for this thoroughly decent individual. It is not for nothing that, of all the characters in his *Odyssey*, Homer only addresses Eumaeus in the second person.

Still, the warmth of Eumaeus' welcome cannot keep the chill of the cold night from entering his master's bones through the rags Athena dressed him in. Accordingly, the Cretan tests his swineherd by relating a story about Odysseus that shows a far closer familiarity with the latter than he had previously admitted to. The stranger tells how Odysseus secured him a cloak for the night by sending a younger man on a fool's errand that required the discarding of his outer garment. The ostensible goal of this story is to make Eumaeus find a cloak that the stranger could sleep in. But while the swineherd sees this and promptly provides the requisite item of clothing, he does not notice that only Odysseus, or someone uncannily like him, would deploy a story from the past to make things happen in the present. Odysseus has already tested his swineherd's moral virtue and seen evidence of his temperate nature; he is now trying to find out if he has an ally cunning enough to cooperate with his plans. He will soon discover the perfect comrade, one quite his equal in wit and deception. In the meantime, Eumaeus, perhaps slightly suspicious of his daimonic new friend's identity, has hastened to keep watch over his pigs. Perhaps the Cretan's tale disposes him to take precautions against those Thesprotian pirates; there is also the chance that his guest could be one of them. The Cretan is every bit as wily as his master. We must never forget that Odysseus built up his own flocks by acts of piracy. As we shall see, the difference between piracy and natural justice is very subtle indeed. As the pirate reminded Alexander, only the scale of their deeds separated the two men. In other words, the difference between them is purely quantitative and not qualitative.

Book 15

Many instances of Athena's subtle weaving together of the various elements in her grand strategy now begin to emerge. Matching Odysseus in testing and deception, she enters his son's mind as he tosses sleeplessly, urging him to return home and protect his property. She instills in him the belief that Eurymachus has gained the affections of his mother and adds the misogynistic suggestion that it is natural for a woman to augment the household of her new husband and forget her old family. Telemachus also sees that if the suitors were to try to ambush him, and they would be fools not to, the natural place for such an attempt would be between Ithaca and Samos. He should instead try another, more indirect route home; this line of thought would also lead Telemachus to leave the ship as soon as possible, a route that would take him to the swineherd's compound. Whether or not these ideas were Athena's or his internalized prudence, the end result is fully consistent with her grand design.

Once Menelaus, who many years ago famously made a similar catastrophic mistake of leaving his wife and household at the mercy of his enemies, understands these fears, he immediately concurs with his young guest's desire. The king presents his young guest with the gift he was earlier promised, a beautiful mixing bowl made by Hephaestus himself, remarking that it is as bad to delay the departure of a guest as it is to hasten that of one not ready to leave. These words of moderation are thus well consistent with his gift. All that remains is for the son of Odysseus to bid farewell to Helen. His aunt sends him off in her typically unmeasured fashion, presenting him with a dazzling robe woven with her own hands. She asks him to have his bride wear this at her wedding, thus ensuring that he would not forget Helen on the occasion. This implied contrast with the selfless purposes behind Penelope's weaving is striking. Helen also volunteers an interpretation of a striking sign from the gods that occurs just as Telemachus' chariot is leaving. When an eagle steals a great white goose from the yard and passes to the auspicious right of the chariot, the Queen promptly tells Peisistratus that Odysseus, like the eagle, will come down from the mountains and kill the homebred suitors. While Telemachus promises to worship her as a goddess if these words come true, thus unconsciously echoing a similar promise made by Odysseus to Nausikaa, we might observe that the sign could very well indicate that Odysseus did come home by way of Zeus' shrine at Dodona, just as the Cretan said.

Telemachus now persuades Peisistratus that he must leave as soon as he reaches his ship, thus denying the latter's garrulous father, Nestor, another opportunity to spout forth his limitless advice. Even though his friend complies with this prudent request, the young prince must deal with one last unexpected request before he leaves Pylos. He meets Theoclymenos, a prophet who had killed a man and grants him sanctuary. While it could well be that he needs a prophet's aid to evade the suitor's ambush, we also see Telemachus behaving more as a king and less like a frightened mama's boy. Though Menelaus and Nestor have failed to offer him any military help, he has come to understand the Trojan War and see what it is for a kingdom to lose a generation of fighters. This is the best reason for their otherwise inexplicable failure to aid him.

Meanwhile, back in Ithaca, Odysseus asks after his parents and also hears a sad tale of his host's life; while Eumaeus' story sheds light on both the subtle workings of Athena, and the ethos of piracy that continually menaces the Mediterranean world of their day, we also come to appreciate his role in the *oikos* of Odysseus. It seems that the swineherd is the closest thing to the brother Odysseus never had. He will be to Odysseus what Patroclus was to Achilles. Both the *Iliad*'s tragic outcome and the "happy ending" of the *Odyssey* are related to the fortunes of Patroclus and Eumaeus.

Odysseus is first told what he has already learned from Tiresias in Hades or Zeus at Dodona. Both his mother's death and his father's miserable retirement are the result of his failure to come home. The swineherd would not wish these sad fates to befall anyone he cares for. We also discover that Eumaeus was in the habit of visiting Antikleia and engaging her in inquiry and banter. The daughter of the great trickster Autolycus does not seem to have gained the same kind of intellectual stimulation from either her gentle husband or taciturn daughter-in-law. Her son, from all we can learn about him, seems to take after his mother rather than his father; as Odysseus told Eumaeus earlier, domestic and bucolic pursuits held very little interest to him.

We also discover that the swineherd was brought up alongside Odysseus' younger daughter Ktimene of whom nothing else is ever mentioned beyond the fact that she married and left for Samos. Although

Eumaeus is treated as almost the equal of his playmate, once she was married off he was given a new set of clothing and sent off to tend the swine. Though Eumaeus has raised his pigs with great success, he greatly misses the intelligent conversation and community that went with life at the palace. Apart from the education this intelligent slave-boy received from Odysseus' mother, there seems also to have been a sense of community that formed around Antikleia. This pre-political order, which must have outlasted the Ithacan public assemblies that ended with Odysseus' departure for Troy, ceased to exist once Antikleia died; things only became worse once Penelope was forced to use dissimulation to keep the suitors at bay. Even Eumaeus could not have been told that she was infantilizing her son and toying with the affections of the suitors; they would have killed her son and overthrown the kingdom of Ithaca had she not followed this very risky strategy.

While the suitors' "home invasion" was shameless and disgusting, we cannot forget that Homer is depicting a culture built and shaped by the constant threat of piracy. The "un-harvestable sea" rules all things around Ithaca and the Mediterranean setting of the *Odyssey* in general; even Athena must respect Poseidon's prerogatives. This is why Eumaeus' sad tale of his abduction is also relevant; we wonder at his strange reluctance to make his way home almost as much as we were amazed at the unwillingness of Nestor and Menelaus to offer Telemachus any military help at all.

The swineherd's reluctance to leave Ithaca can be attributed to a mixture of loyalty to his new home and genuine fear of both the sea and the anarchic savagery that existed outside Ithaca, especially after the overthrowing of the last person with the power to unify the piratic Hellenes: Agamemnon. It would seem as if a king ruled by virtue of his ability to offer protection from pirates and/or booty from his own raids. In the aftermath of the massive loss of manpower brought about by the glorious but pyrrhic Trojan War, there could not have been much appetite for excursions abroad. In such a disenchanted postwar context, even a relief expedition to Ithaca could only have been raised by dangling the prospect of booty before the few men available to risk life and limb. Rhetoric about the honor of hated Helen's cousin would not have been very persuasive. Of course, this would only have meant that the remedy would have been just as bad as, or perhaps even worse than, the problem of the suitors.

The distinction between piracy and permanent occupation that Eumaeus himself made is undergirded by a more fluid view of material property that necessarily exists in times of scarcity and deprivation. The laws of hospitality are based on the sober recognition that since those refused temporary shelter and basic sustenance can potentially drag us all back to a war of all against all, our rights of ownership over property cannot be considered absolute or sacred. However, as sacred laws promulgated by Zeus they go further, creating a network of relationships based on generosity and gratitude that fosters cooperation and eventually overcomes much of the suspicion and scarcity that marked the original condition. Otherwise put, the conditions of scarcity and violence after the Trojan War had everything to do with the way Agamemnon, far more than Paris or Priam, abused the laws of hospitality, and the permanent relationships between patron and clients stemming from them, in order to increase his own prestige and property. While Book 1 of the *Iliad* makes this case in a nutshell, its ultimate dire consequences are indicated in the *Odyssey*.

Very simply, a culture without hospitality consists of static households and roving pirate bands. While households now include the remains of kingdoms, this is one reason why Menelaus could not mount an expedition to relieve Telemachus even if he had the stomach for it, they are still hierarchized formations of non-equals; by contrast, pirate bands are essentially egalitarian and as anarchic as the sea itself. Menelaus would thus cease to be king the moment he left his household. We could then say that the best regime unites the stability and hospitality of a household with the egalitarian inclusiveness of a pirate ship; it would synthetize qualities of trader and raider, merging the decency of Main Street with the efficiency of Wall Street.

In such a reality, most people would be either slaves or outlaws. While the slave gives up his liberty for the stability of an object with a name, a pirate or outlaw is a no-body like Odysseus who gives up his pre-established meaning for pure freedom. Furthermore, since pirates also deal in slaves as well as property, and in this sense serve both as traders and slavers, they could even be said to optimize the situation of any given slave by finding him or her a household that can give them security. In other words, slavery and piracy become the purest instruments of the free market; they place one who chooses to become a slave, by refusing to fight for his freedom, in the best place to sustain his choice of work and security over liberty and equality.

Returning to the text after this extended time at sea, we observe that Eumaeus was originally abducted by a slave as part of her own unsuccessful attempt at returning home. He does not wish to emulate his nurse's conduct in any way, certainly not at the expense of Telemachus. The swineherd's loyalty to the *oikos* that educated him may yet seem to be slavish, were it not for the fact that he has actually achieved a fair deal of success and self-realization, even to the extent of buying a slave of his own; slave ownership in this sense clearly carries with it a strong sense of reciprocal obligation and protection. By contrast, taking to the sea in hope of returning to Scheria would be physically dangerous, for he would run the risks of being shipwrecked or sold to another, and could also end in disappointment. He could very easily find that his family has no place for him or has even ceased to exist. It is only in Ithaca that he has a given name and identity. Scheria is but a mythic origin. This is why Odysseus *qua* Cretan beggar claims to envy Eumaeus. Even as he told Alcinous that Achilles would have preferred being a landless man's hired hand to his present state of gloomy pre-eminence, this hero disguised as an outlaw now extols the lot of the just slave. We shall soon see Odysseus prove these words to be more than idle flattery; the noble swineherd has taught his lord much about virtue. These lessons will be incorporated in the new political order the *Odyssey* leads us towards. This was why Athena told Odysseus that the path to his palace led through Eumaeus' hut. Perhaps it is also why the nursemaid who abducted Eumaeus from Scheria, the tall beautiful women skilled in handcraft, turns out to be identical with the way Athena chooses to appear to Odysseus. Perhaps this is how she provides Odysseus and Telemachus with the kinsmen that the brother-less line of Laertes could never provide. As Odysseus said of Circe, "whose eyes can follow the movements of a god, unless the gods so wish it?"

There is a good reason why Eumaeus is the only party Homer's *Odyssey* addresses in the second person; just as the *Iliad's* primary addressee in the vocative, Patroclus, is the only man whose love could keep the divine fury of his adopted brother Achilles in his human body, and prevent him from self-destructive apotheosis, so too does the aptly named good midwife, Eumaeus, help raging Ulysses to be safely reborn as spouse of Penelope, father of Telemachus, King of Ithaca and human form of Athena. As a result of the education he received at the feet of the daughter of Autolycus, the wolf itself, the swineherd is well prepared to understand the means by which the seemingly lying tales of beggars, outlaws, and tricksters may yet be seen to reveal much truth about the chaotic realms of reality inhabited by them. As such, he will revel in the tales told by the nameless stranger from Crete, the haven of pirates and land of liars, for they remind him of his happiest days spent chatting with Antikleia.

Book 15 ends with the swift return of Telemachus to Ithaca. We are not told how he eluded Antinous' ambush. Perhaps this happened with the help of Theoclymenus, the prophet who is now part of his ship's party; perhaps it also had something to do with Athena's warning, however imparted or internalized, that the enemy ship would be in waiting between Ithaca and Samos. But regardless of how it occurred, the feat reflects well on the young prince and adds to the suitors' fear of him. On the conclusion of the voyage we see Telemachus faced with the problem of what to do with his new comrade. He fears to bring him to his home and risk having to fight the suitors in defense of him. While this course of action is not imprudent, it also shows that he does not yet quite trust the gods, even though they have seen him through a very risky journey and made him aware of another uncanny dimension in human life. But this could also mean that he is still learning how to strike a proper balance between piety and prudence. At this most critical point in his young life it seems that Eumaeus is the one person he can fully trust; Penelope could very well be under the power of Eurymachus, and none of the other adults in his life have any real power to help him. The time is right for our young Ur-Hamlet to meet his father's ghost.

Book 16

Odysseus receives two powerful reminders of just how estranged he is from both his land and family when his son Telemachus finally arrives at the swineherd's house. Eumaeus' watchdogs, ready to behave like wolves towards the beggar, now conduct themselves like good guardians when they recognize their young master. As long as he continues to wear his Ring of Gyges and remains removed from his family and kingdom, he cannot expect to be treated in a way commensurate with his rank. In other words, natural right does not entitle him in any way; all that he can hope for is sanctuary and hospitality according to the very law of Zeus he previously abused.

Secondly, and even more poignantly, Eumaeus and Telemachus tearfully embrace with the swineherd being addressed in words that could be taken to mean "father" by the son of Odysseus. As it is safe to assume that Odysseus left for Troy before he ever heard his son speak, it is surely painful that the first words he hears uttered by his son are spoken to another, when they should properly be addressed only to him. Once again, Odysseus is literally no body. Like Antikleia in Hades, he cannot hope to be embraced, even by his only son. All the credit he had gained with Eumaeus the previous night somehow fades to nothing; Odysseus is also acutely aware that a good part of the affection the swineherd expresses towards Telemachus is also sympathy for a child effectively abandoned by his father. Here again, we see a clash between what he is entitled to as father or king, and what he deserves on account of his dereliction of these fundamental and natural duties towards those he should love most. His mind's cupidity is coupled with his ego's power lust to cause this quite unenviable state of affairs. Nothing he could ever do would truly make up for this. All the cauldrons and other treasures he brought back from Scheria mean nothing.

Homer underscores this point by what he likens the reunion of Telemachus and Eumaeus to how "a loving father welcomes his grown son for whom he has spent ten hard years in a distant land." The simile is doubtless Odysseus' own, the bitter thought that crossed his own mind when he saw his son embrace another man with a love he had forfeited any right to. The image suggests strongly that Odysseus did make a choice not to come immediately after the fall of Troy, this regardless of how much freedom he possessed *after* making that fateful decision. This inference is also supported by the story he told Eumaeus about being the kind of person who chose ships and piracy over a life of hard work spent plowing a field and raising a family.

This curious distance from Telemachus is maintained even after he enters the house and graciously refuses to occupy the beggar's seat but instead chooses to sit on the brushwood and fleeces that the swineherd laid out for him. After they have eaten the leftovers from the previous day's meal,

Telemachus questions Eumaeus about the beggar in his very presence. Yet again Odysseus is treated as if he is nobody. This curious slight must surely add to his already complex feelings of guilt and alienation. Perhaps this reminds him of how he, *qua* pure intellect, ignored his men's feelings?

Eumaeus and Telemachus argue over whether it would be possible for the young prince to take the beggar into his house under his protection, and Telemachus makes it clear that he fears to do so, for the reason that he could then be forced to protect the nameless Cretan from insults and injuries that could not be directly leveled against the prince himself. Although Telemachus is prudent in recognizing that such a strategy could very well be employed to bring about his assassination, Odysseus yet reacts passionately. His purpose is to test his son's fighting spirit; the qualities of a Nestor are of very little value and could indeed be positively dangerous in the ugly bloodbath that is almost certain to follow. Even if it is the case that Telemachus absolutely loves him and is protective of his sire to the highest degree, these very qualities could become their greatest vulnerability. While we will soon see that Telemachus is well aware of the danger posed by Penelope's protective instincts, the quality of the utmost importance here, given the unsurpassed strategic powers of Athena and Odysseus, is simple cold-blooded but bloody-minded courage. The dogs fawning at Telemachus' feet must now be roused to fight for his rights.

Earlier Telemachus had referred to Odysseus' great bed lying empty and covered all over with cobwebs; while this state of affairs suited Odysseus perfectly well from a purely egotistic standpoint, it also surely suggested that his son was not up to the task of doing what he seems to have done at a similar age: casting kind but impotent Laertes aside and taking over direct rule of the kingdom himself. In other words, he should have occupied the bed of Odysseus himself! While his failure to do so could reflect poorly on Penelope, the blame could be traced more directly to Telemachus and/or Odysseus himself. Although Athena has tried to overcome some of the gap between the shadow of the father and the situation of the son, a proper resolution of this daunting disparity can only come about through their direct interaction.

The Cretan beggar's impassioned words defending the rights of his imperiled host are designed to make Telemachus reveal his own assessment of the plight he faces at home. Odysseus asks if his oppression is involuntary, popularly supported, or divinely ordained? Does Telemachus not have brothers on whom he may call for support? Perhaps the disguised father is still wondering whether his beleaguered son will blame him for abandoning his little family? Perhaps Telemachus would have responded differently before his trip to Pylos and Sparta? On the other hand he could very well reply that the honor of the household does not exist anymore. All he feels and knows is his lack of honor. Is it better to have lost what one never knew in one's own life or to never have had it, either in known memory or perceived right?

By speaking passionately while slyly pretending to be ignorant of what he very well knew, Odysseus has forced Telemachus to reveal the deeper passions underlying his prudent speech. Telemachus denies being hated by the people but admits that, by being the only son in a long line of only sons, he lacks blood kin to defend his rights; Eumaeus seems to be the only real "uncle" the young man has. As Telemachus sees things, he's left all alone; we find that miserable Laertes has totally abdicated all responsibility for the family, a truly pathetic response to his departure for Pylos, while Penelope seems to be unable to decide which of her suitors she will choose. Even though Telemachus is willing to have the swineherd let his mother know he's arrived safely, for reasons not completely unconnected to the desire to let her know that she should not marry thinking he's abandoned Ithaca and/or is lost to her for good, he does not think it worthwhile for Laertes to be informed directly.

There seem to be two important Homeric hints worth exploring here. The first is that Telemachus may not be really the grandson of Laertes; just as Achilles was not truly Peleus' son and depended on Patroclus to maintain the eponymous "glory of the father," Eumaeus (the only person in the *Odyssey* addressed by Homer in the second person singular like Patroclus) performs a similar function in the household of Odysseus. He too will be the literal "good midwife" who will serve as the brother Odysseus never had and help secure his kingdom. The second point follows from the first; Ithaca, by virtue of the royal line's very minimal production of sons, is well suited to be governed in a far more egalitarian manner. Once Odysseus, following Athena's plans, wipes out the decadent suitors and their claims to oligarchic power, the way is cleared for democratic reform. The casualties sustained in the war also support this; Ithaca not only lacks a warrior class, there is also an unwillingness to be drawn into any further wars having to do with the rights of the nobility or their lust for riches. Merit should replace blood as the criterion for civic power; evidence supporting this lies in the fact that the suitors themselves were far more interested in liquidating the household wealth of Odysseus than ruling over his kingdom.

All of this lies very much in the future though, for the present our concern is with the long-awaited reunion of Odysseus with his only son. While the swineherd's departure for the palace prepares the way for this event, it is Athena who appears to Odysseus and tells him that the moment is right for him to reveal himself. It is quite noteworthy that she once again chooses to appear as a "tall beautiful woman skilled in weaving." Here again, Homer seems to be suggesting that it was Athena who took on the disguise of Eumaeus' nurse and brought him to Ithaca. We see now how vital it was for Odysseus to have an adult brother in arms to stand by him in strife. Still, here again, the focus is not on family but community; this is the unit of consequence.

Although Athena is invisible to Telemachus, the dogs see her along with Odysseus. The goddess chooses to appear only after Eumaeus has departed; is Homer subtly indicating that he would have *recognized* her as his nursemaid had she chosen to be visible in this guise, just as Odysseus recognized this look from their more recent meeting? Although Athena only wants Odysseus to identify himself to his son after Eumaeus has left for obvious reasons, we see why this choice of disguise is either superfluous data or far more likely a way of disclosing things inconsistent with the reverence that is due a virgin goddess. She is not identical with Eumaeus' nurse.

When the glorified Odysseus appears to Telemachus he is mortified that his son prefers to worship him as a god instead of accepting the embrace of his lost father. It seems to Telemachus that the transformed beggar cannot be Odysseus since only a god can undergo so magical a transformation, this despite his having heard Helen tell of Odysseus having performed a similar trick at Troy. Even if we allow for the possibility that Athena made Odysseus look more impressive than a hand-washed beggar could ever be, Telemachus is still implicitly denying that even a god could effect such a change in a mortal. Even granting that the gods could make a man old or young, he cannot accept their power to bring about such an apparent apotheosis. His prior experience has not prepared him for the experience of a genuine hero; all three famous figures he had met earlier—Nestor, Menelaus, and even Helen—turned out to be all too human. Although they spoke repeatedly of his father's close ties to Athena, Telemachus could not imagine such things occurring before him, in Ithaca.

Odysseus bluntly tells his son that it did not become him to doubt his own father. "No other Odysseus than I myself will ever come before you." He gives all the credit for this to Athena, explaining that she can turn him into whatever thing she pleases. According to him, it is easy for the gods to glorify or degrade a human. He does not add that it is far harder for a mortal to remain at the levels of glory he is elevated to. This shift away from claiming to appear as himself to giving all credit to Athena also tacitly avoids any reference to how difficult it is for *Odysseus* to appear as himself; in other words, every appearance of Odysseus will be deceptive if the viewer believes that what he sees is the literal truth or the man in full. The appearances only point a mind towards the unyielding substance underlying its many turns and contortions. Even though Odysseus "up to now unyielding" had wept when he embraced his son, Telemachus had been too impressed by his divine appearance to appreciate the far more genuine passion of the great liar. Gods do not weep. It is of course highly ironic than Odysseus is only disbelieved when, for once, he tells the truth about himself.

Only after Odysseus resumes his unyielding posture and sits down does his only son finally embrace him. Father and son are compared to birds of prey in their weeping, terrible raptors robbed by men of their young before they were strong enough to fly. While the Homeric texts are filled with bird omens, mostly involving predators, only here are men likened to birds. Now, instead of raiding farms, these two regal birds mourn their own pillaged nest. They have lost no fewer than twenty of their young, precious irreplaceable years that cannot be compensated for by cauldrons of gold. Yet, even among the tears there still are doubts; Telemachus cuts short his weeping to ask his father how he got home. The mistrust cannot be drowned in a sea of tears. But we ourselves, unsure of how exactly Telemachus eluded the suitors' ambush, must also wonder how the ship bearing Odysseus from Scheria got to Ithaca. Could the fast Phaiakian vessel have served as a decoy pulling Antinous out of position? There is only more cause to wonder at how well Athena synchronized everything.

Telemachus' practical doubts persist even when Odysseus begins to plan the death of the suitors. He tells his father that there are a hundred and eight suitors and then, rather absurdly, asks a man absent for twenty years where they could look for allies. Although reassured by the promise that Zeus and Athena would be on their side, the young prince yet dissuades his father's plan to question the serving men to see if any of them could be trusted. Telemachus is too angered at the thought of the suitors squandering more of the household wealth to wait any longer; he promises his sire that his fighting spirits are aroused and will not bear slackening. This combination of impatient anger and skepticism does not bode too well for Odysseus and his son; even though the master strategist tells his son to clear the great hall of all weapons on the plausible pretext that they were being fouled by the smoke, the odds are still too long for two men, one barely an adult, to take on over a hundred drunken thugs. Meanwhile father and son continue to deliberate. The key element of the winning strategy has yet to be found; it will be furnished from a most unexpected source.

Another element of Odysseus' still to be completed plan has to do with using his disguise as a beggar to test and incriminate the suitors. After being the butt of their hubris and wanton violence he will then be justified, if not expected, to retrieve his honor by taking bloody vengeance on his wife's wooers. But crucial to all this is the element of surprise; as with the Trojan Horse, the enemy must be caught off-guard. It is also vital that Telemachus' location be known only to Penelope. As we shall see, the suitors desire nothing more than to have the prince end up trapped at Eumaeus' place or ambushed as he made his way back to the palace. When, however, the herald from his ship brings word of Telemachus' successful return this is sufficient to make humiliated Antinous even more resolute and intemperate in his desire to kill him.

Now grudgingly admitting that the young prince is smarter than he had been given credit for, thanks to Penelope, Antinous is quite frightened. This very fear only adds urgency to his violent intent. Addressing an urgently called meeting of the suitors outside the palace, Antinous now proposes a *coup de main*, the very course of action Penelope most feared all along and strove to frustrate by her flirtatious "divide and conquer" strategy. By making each individual suitor hopeful that he could win all of Odysseus' kingdom and household, Penelope managed to prevent them from uniting to divide up the assets among them. But at this point Antinous realizes that by their earlier unsuccessful ambush they lost the tacit support of the towns-people; further, there is always the risk that Telemachus has found allies abroad. The suitors are all too well aware that twenty men at arms would be more than sufficient to rout them.

This is why Antinous now proposes that the suitors collectively kill Telemachus and divide up Odysseus' estate and property; Penelope and the royal palace could be left intact and given to the suitor who marries her. The status quo cannot continue. The only other alternative is that Telemachus be left in possession of his property and his mother immedi-ately forced to decide among the suitors. Antinous is now making explicit the fact that their palace invasion was really not about Penelope at all, any more than the Trojan War had to do with Helen's threadbare honor; the truest prize was the fabulous wealth of Odysseus. He is forcing the other suitors to admit that they were not really suitors at all. They are but a gang of pirates, plain and simple.

Several of the suitors are "stricken to silence," aghast at these blunt shameless words; many of them are not willing to admit that they have be-come what Antinous says they are. Their spokesman is Amphinomus, an otherwise sensible and decent man who was Penelope's favorite among the suitors. Arguing that it is a terrible thing to kill a man of royal blood, he proposes that they first ascertain the will of the gods. Amphinomus claims that he would be willing to kill Telemachus, but only if the gods allowed it; if however the gods forbade it they should desist. Here we must recall that Amphinomus was the first to laugh upon hearing that Antinous' mur-derous errand had been unsuccessful. Further, Antinous himself had earlier acknowledged that Telemachus had come home under divine protection. This being the case, it clearly made little sense for them to anger the gods, who like the townspeople had probably only been incensed by this intem-perate plan to murder Telemachus. The suitors are swayed by his words, even if this only means that the present *impasse*, which evil Antinous had correctly denounced as untenable, must continue. Just as irresolute as the townspeople, they troop back to the house to resume their feasting. It seems that the gods are not disposed to let them disperse without punishment.

The suitors' collective discomfiture and confusion is only increased when Penelope, having received word of their plotting against Telemachus, comes down to denounce them. She tells Antinous that, although reputed the very best among his generation in speech and leadership, he was simply foremost in violence and evil. Reminding Antinous of how Odysseus granted his father sanctuary when he was wanted by their allies for piracy, she accuses the son of now practicing the very evils he was justly accused of on the household of the man who rescued his life and property. She demands that he cease these evil ways and asks further that he stop the others too. At this Eurymachus takes up leadership and smoothly assures Penelope that no man alive will threaten Telemachus as long as he lived. Fondly remembering the old days when Odysseus gave him food and drink from his own hands, Eurymachus insists that Telemachus is dearest of all men to him and need fear nothing from the suitors. Yet, he sagely concludes, doubtless mocking the earlier more sincere words of Amphinomus, none can avert the plans of the gods. These oily ugly words seal the suitors' fate; not one among them speaks up to denounce the hypocrisy and evil of their two leaders. Not merely guilty of breaking the sacred laws of hospitality, they are now collectively bound together as a gang of liars, predators, and murderers.

Meanwhile, as the doomed suitors enjoy one of their last gaudy nights in the palace of Odysseus, the true master of the house along with his son are preparing a far simpler meal over a fire in a humble hut. They will share this dinner, made by their own hands, with Eumaeus their faithful slave. These three men will form the nucleus of a new kind of community, one based on virtue not blood. Eumaeus mentions seeing a fast vessel, filled with armed men, just arrived from a voyage. At this, both father and son smile grimly. Now all the suitors are back and ready for their deserts.

Neither man is part of his non-family without the friendship of a loving brother figure to keep him in the *oikos*. Eumaeus speaks of this closeness to Antikleia, one based on riddling speech rather than unspoken unity. This is closer to the polis than the *oikos*. Did Laertes abdicate upon finding that Odysseus was never really his son? After Odysseus returns from Sisyphus' home Odysseus restores him by remembering the deeds, the gifts Laertes gave him. A good midwife must be the domestic equivalent of a Protagoras, the first to speak (thus creating an agora or political space) before what has previously not existed has the power to speak back. The speech of a midwife is performative in this sense. Eumaeus later puts together the beggar's story about Odysseus with his way of telling the story and the very way the story serves as a request, turning a speech into a deed from his hearer. This performance he will repeat with Penelope. Vagabonds/outlaws cannot be expected to speak the truth. They could only testify under torture; perhaps because this was the element they were most accustomed to functioning in?

Chapter 5
The Prodigal Predator: Books 17–20

Book 17

We are now at the absolute nadir of Odysseus' fortunes. Even though the portents are all favorable, and Athena has promised him victory, he must still undergo a humiliating series of ordeals as he slowly moves from the swineherd's hospitable sanctuary to his own desecrated palace. Further, Odysseus must see that he, or even Athena herself, cannot turn back the hands of time. Even if he succeeds in defeating the suitors and regaining his wife, home, and kingdom, the very real material and psychic damage that occurred in his absence, most of which is surely due to his own delays and dalliances, cannot be undone or denied. Part of his just deserts must surely consist in this knowledge; Odysseus must feel—as indeed he should—very guilty indeed. There is something ritualistic about the long walk that Odysseus must take that reminds us of his tale about the voyage to the land of the dead. Now ill-shod and disgustingly clad, rather like the man Achilles hoped to be reborn as, the vagabond must accompany a household slave as his hanger-on and face ridicule in his own home from persons who would normally be set far beneath him on the social scale. This is why it is not un-fitting that it is Telemachus, one of the chief victims of his irresponsibility, who orders that the stranger be removed from the swineherd's hut and send on to town. This is surely the will and justice of the gods.

Telemachus' quite harsh words to Eumaeus concerning his "guest" in-dicate that the once impetuous youth is finally trying to dissemble; he is deploying the distinctive qualities of Odysseus that he first heard of in Sparta and has more recently seen in the man himself. Although this pro-nouncement about a man who has indirectly placed himself under his pro-tection seems to fly in the face of Telemachus' generous initial plans for him, Eumaeus, who knows his young master as well as anybody, seemingly suspects nothing. Yet Homer's listeners would surely be alerted to this change in Telemachus by his own claim to be a plain-speaking honest man; he is complementing the strategy of his father who spoke the truth while claiming to be both a Cretan and a beggar, thus proving his identity by being doubly a liar.

Odysseus, who is likely sensitive to this overly abrupt change in his son's attitude towards the stranger, now chimes in and tells Eumaeus that he'd prefer not to remain with the swineherd. Keeping with his self-description of a roving wanton man who preferred piracy over farming, he claims to be too old and too set in his ways to be of much use to Eumaeus; begging for his meals in town is far better than idling in the country as a burden on the land. Whether or not Eumaeus believes him, it is not worth his while to persuade him to stay. We also note that Telemachus has not asked the beggar to darken his doorstep; even the words Odysseus speaks agreeing with the prince do not suggest that he intends to establish himself as a beggar in the palace itself. If anything, his last words to the departing Telemachus seem to be desperate attempt to receive the change of clothing he had been previously promised. Both father and son are trying very hard to discount even the remotest appearance of collusion. This joint deception practiced against Eumaeus serves also to bring long-estranged father and son closer together; before departing for the palace, Telemachus has shown Odysseus that the trust he owes his gentle adopted father has been overridden by his genetic bent towards trickery.

While Telemachus' conduct, once back in the palace, must show the suitors that he has grown up, thus raising the stakes and making it impossible for them to not feel some hostility towards him, it is equally important that he serve as a decoy and turn their attention away from Odysseus. This, we shall see, is a role he plays quite well; in other words, the suitors must not know that their Trojan Horse is already well within the city walls. Telemachus must tempt them into wickedness and lead them away from immediate suspicion; any belated remorse or renewed vigilance on their part would only serve to frustrate the plans of Athena. They are dead men drinking. Even if they could be rehabilitated, such an unlikely development would not further the greater purposes that the daughter of Zeus has in mind for Odysseus and Ithaca.

On the other hand, Telemachus' behavior towards his mother, a quite deliberately measured mixture of coolness and cruelty, shows how far he is from full maturity. It is as if he both knows why his mother could not take him fully into her confidence and yet cannot forgive her for being prudent for his own sake. Telemachus will force Penelope to evince, endure, and express some of the pain she had previously refused to share with him; until she does so, he will quite deliberately attend to more manly and practical things pertaining to his newly asserted status as man of the household. It is significant that he pretty much ignores the feigned greetings of the suitors and takes his seat among the old men, the adults of his father's generation; here again he is signaling that his short stay abroad has brought about his elevation into manhood. From what has been seen of him earlier, we can hardly doubt that the former youth called Telemachus would not have held his tongue for an instant; instead he would have swiftly denounced the suitors for their treachery and precipitated a crisis. Now he merely tells the eager elders, a group of Nestor-like men, what he has learned of the Trojan War. He thus makes it clear that he has no secret intelligence that would necessitate immediate action by his enemies. Telemachus merely makes himself the focus of attention and makes it easier for his disguised sire to steal home. All he has brought back from his mini-wandering is his maturity. A necessary condition is met.

When Telemachus finally deigns to talk to his mother of his journey, after she sadly threatens to go back to her rooms and weep her eyes out, we notice that he leaves out some of the most interesting details. While he does mention seeing Helen, Penelope's cousin, he does not recount her story about Odysseus or her long-suffering spouse's rejoinder, even though these tales provided him with the best insights into his father's character. Telemachus only repeats Proteus' story that his father was held captive on an island by a goddess, without means of getting home.

While Telemachus does not mention Helen's interpretation of the augury at his departure, this omission is more than compensated for by the mysterious prophet, Theoclymenos, who has accompanied him home. Penelope is assured that Odysseus is already on Ithaca and is either already in the palace or on his way there. While this very strong assertion is welcomed by Penelope, we see why Telemachus would have preferred to take a more cautious approach. Still, there is also evidence that the good will of the gods cannot be contained by his not un-egotistic prudence; we must not ignore the hidden truth that valiant Penelope is the co-heroine of the *Odyssey*.

Meanwhile Odysseus himself is led by the swineherd to town. As they reach the water fountain, a site reminiscent of prior meetings with the Laestrygonian princess and Athena, they meet Melanthius the foul-mouthed goatherd. This man subjects Odysseus to a torrent of verbal abuse that is as nasty as it is unwarranted. It is as though he is the other extreme to the unconditional hospitality offered by the noble swineherd; this polluting language is quite consistent with his king's ugly exterior. While we recall ugly Thersites and his equally foul abuse of Agamemnon in the *Iliad* it cannot be denied that Thersites was correct when non-aesthetic moral criteria are applied. Odysseus then punished *him* on account of order rather than justice. In the case of Melanthius we see the first of several persons who do not wish Odysseus to return. Men like him thrive in the absence of law and order; they prosper in chaos. This is why the goatherd prays that Telemachus will have the same fate as Odysseus.

Regardless of what actually happened to Odysseus during the hidden years between Troy and Ithaca, it is through Melanthius that Homer depicts the full horror of what it was like to be an anonymous vagabond. It is not merely that one's character was deduced from one's appearance, as Telemachus' was in Sparta; we also see that those without the protection of a master or patron were but outlaws, literally in the sense of being outside the domain in which freedom was gratefully given up for a basic sense of security. To be an outlaw meant that one could be killed or kidnapped for the kind of destructive work that was done at a stalag or gulag in our day. This smug superiority that a house slave felt over one not thought to be worth enslaving, or punishing for running away, meant that only fear of Zeus—the god of hospitality—stood between anonymity and non-existence; yet, in the absence of effectual rule, these tales about the gods had little practical value. Odysseus' three meetings—with his goatherd, the dog Argos, and Antinous—reveal the effects of his long absence; in each case we see how poorly interior quality corresponds to external appearance. It is perhaps a king's role to rectify this disparity and midwife his subjects' potentials.

The beggar now convinces Eumaeus to take him inside the palace. He pretends to identify his own house by admiring the unity of its construction and also by sensing by the smell and sound that a feast was going on. After the swineherd has proposed that they enter separately, and urged the beggar not to linger outside very long for fear of being humiliated again, Odysseus promises him that his insatiable belly has made his spirit enduring enough to suffer all manner of blows and insults. If he is to be believed, even war and piracy have their origin in man's stomach. But this crass reduction of all strife and energy to bodily need is refuted by an unlikely authority, a moribund dog. Argus, once Odysseus' prized and magnificent hunting hound, has been lying badly neglected and flea-infested on a garbage heap by the palace. Yet, somehow seeing his master, this miserable beast makes a final effort to wag his tail and raise his ears before dying. While all his disguised master can do is to secretly wipe away a tear before entering the house, the dying dog's action somehow proves that love can be just as strong as bodily necessity. Still, the question that we are left with just as Odysseus enters his house concerns the nature of love. Is it exclusively a jealous devotion for one's own kin and property or can it also be a more generous kindness towards the needy other, best exemplified by the hospitable swineherd?

This matter is further complicated when Eumaeus, denouncing the palace servitors' neglect of the dog, opines that Zeus takes away half of a man's excellence the day he first becomes a slave. Yet *Aristeia*, the word he uses, only problematizes the matter here. Much as the distinction between Socratic and Aristotelian ethics is based on Aristotle's privileging of intellectual excellence above mundane moral habit, the code of aristocratic warrior virtue is based on each man trying to exceed all others. By contrast, moral virtue has to do with a cooperative morality that is often instilled by habit rather than being based on one's unique nature. But this can also lead to common norms that seek the good of the whole; these virtues are literally catholic in their concern for the good of all. By this ideal, Odysseus can be seen to become an enlightened despot who seeks to advance the general good of his people; otherwise put, he realizes the potential of simple hospitality and turns it into a political virtue. A good ruler must thus seek to foster and feed the potential for good in all his people.

As the disguised beggar-king crosses the threshold of his home he continues to find gross disparities between external appearance and moral virtue. While Melanthius sits beside Eurymachus, Telemachus is forced by necessity to demand that his father beg for food from all of those who sit around consuming his property; we note that this same logic forces the young prince to feast the very men who tried to kill him.

While Odysseus is happy to comply with his son's request, since it gives him a fine chance to study the character of those who are occupying his house, Melanthius somehow sees the need to continue his gratuitous malice against the old beggar. He tells the suitors that it was Eumaeus who brought the vagrant into their midst and this excites the rage of Antinous, the self-appointed master of their revels. While all the others feel pity towards Odysseus and give him crumbs of their food, Antinous is quick to denounce the swineherd for ruining their feasting. There is something truly strange about his Anti-nous, mind set against itself, that leads him to find fault with others who engage in the very actions he is performing, albeit with far better cause. Telemachus underscores this ironic situation when he accuses the suitor of acting towards him as a father treats his son, adding that one who takes should also give. When hubris-filled Antinous responds by brandishing a stool, and offering to make the beggar a gift he will not forget, wily Odysseus promptly seizes on the challenge.

Complimenting the young thug whom he once fed by hand, Odysseus asks him for the biggest handout of all on account of his being the best looking of the suitors. He then launches into an account of his travails that leaves out any reference to Crete and its flavor of untruth, and instead has him taken away in slavery to Cyprus. With these exceptions the basic outlines of the story he told Eumaeus are preserved. The raid on Egypt takes the place of Ismaros and no reference is made to Troy. In this iteration also, Odysseus depicts himself as a rich man led by the gods to travel with pirates. Once again, he faults his crews for acts of violence that let to their downfall. Left unstated is an implicit comparison and challenge: could Antinous learn from his example and henceforth conduct his own home invasion without hubris? Odysseus is giving him valuable advice before then asking for a crust of bread. When Antinous breaks in to denounce his "shameless" abuse of their "generosity," implicitly claiming to be lord of the house he had invaded, the beggar turns his back on him, mocking the parasite as one who thriftily denies a beggar crusts from another man's table.

These words have the desired result. Boiling with rage, Antinous hits the unflinching Odysseus in the back with his footstool. This gives the beggar ample reason to curse the son of Eupeithes; pointing out the difference between fighting for plunder and begging out of necessity, the curse of the belly, Odysseus calls upon the Furies, if there are gods looking over the beggars, to let his assailant die before his marriage. Antinous' behavior has even shocked the other suitors. As they angrily warn him about gods who disguise themselves to test mortals, Penelope finds out what took place from her women. But as they curse the suitors, bewailing their impotence, and wish none to survive the night, she herself singles out Antinous for her maledictions, telling them she hates him more than the others, indeed even more than the plague itself.

The beggar's exploit has also sparked Penelope's curiosity about him and Eumaeus does nothing to dispel this when he is asked to bring him to her. He compares the vagrant to a skilled bard, telling the queen that he held him entranced for the three days they spent together. Furthermore, the stranger claimed to be a family friend of Odysseus and familiar with his present whereabouts. While this news intrigues the queen, and makes her call him a bashful beggar when Eumaeus returns without him, Penelope is even more impressed when she hears that he has prudently proposed that they talk after her potentially violent suitors have left the palace for the night.

Book 18

So far, the behavior of the suitors has not been as objectionable as the conduct of their two leaders: Antinous and Eurymachus. With the exception of the former, they have treated the beggar with a modicum of respect and given him food. We could easily conclude that the majority of these young men were wealthy young drones; left without role models by the war, they naturally fell under the influence of the most persuasive and confident members of their own age group. This led them to wage their imitation of the Trojan War, the multi-year invasion of Odysseus' palace; they also came to believe themselves entitled to entertainment without exertion. In the last book we saw Odysseus experience some of the pain, sorrow, and disrespect that were the lot of an outlaw or beggar; here we see the truth about the way men of this kind were regarded by their so-called betters. Even though many of the suitors did not actively perform the outrageous acts of hubris they collectively shared in, and often remonstrated at the excesses of an Antinous or Eurymachus, we will see how they could be held culpable for refusing to peel off from this oligarchic mob.

Much of Antinous' hostility towards Odysseus was probably caused by the beggar's reference to his military experience; the suitor hates to be reminded that he is not battle-tested. The suitors are much like the young men Odysseus met in Scheria; while they look impressive they lack genuine heroic qualities. Like the Phaiakians, the suitors much prefer listening to songs about battle; it is this vicarious dimension to their spiritedness that will be exposed when their messenger, Iros, enters the hall. It is hinted that their moral corruption, though similarly expressed, is also gained by these very means; by mindlessly sharing in the fruit of Antinous' sin, they all fell.

By conferring the name Irus, the masculine form of Iris, a large lout renowned for his greed, on their messenger, the suitors implicitly elevate themselves above mere mortals; much like the bored gods of the *Iliad* who found their entertainment in pitting men against each other, these dissolute young men derived pleasure from manipulating the despair of men ruled by hunger; Odysseus has already called attention to the plight of a man ruled by his shameless belly, and the cruelty associated with grudging him his subsistence. Now he points out that this necessity compels him to fight a much younger man. That is why it is fitting that the reward offered to the winner of the bout between Iros and Odysseus is a stuffed goat's stomach. This prize, the bounty of Melanthius, also gives him the right to share in the goatherd's privilege to feast with the suitors. Yet while this motif is not accidental to Homer, the suitors are blind to their own hubris. Also, all the suitors are involuntarily ruled by their own greed or stomachs. Whether they like it or not, they will soon digest the effects of their own sloth. We may contrast Odysseus' appetite or stomach for trouble with their bloated acquisitive appetites. When they strip down, hulking Iros is seen to be bloated and flabby beside the short but muscular beggar. As we know, Odysseus has been underestimated all of his life. Once again, exteriors prove to be very unreliable indicators of human inner quality.

This is why the beggar's bout with Iros is actually a sign, sent from the gods though not through Iris. The promoter of the fight, Antinous himself, recognizes this clash as "the best entertainment that the gods have brought to the palace." But Iros is much more than a messenger. As Theoclymenus will explain, Iros is the sign itself—sent to warn the suitors of their imminent doom. The "bum fight" they have devised with so much hubris turns out to pit their greedy concupiscence against the rage aspect of Odysseus' psyche; it is not surprising that the scales tilt towards the Ares-like beggar. We shall also see that this contest is the earliest image of the Master-Slave dialectic. Eurymachus will learn this from the king who once fed him on his knee.

When the two fight, Iros struck Odysseus on his right shoulder. It was also where Antinous had hit him earlier; even Penelope saw fit to mention the location of this blow, the base of his right shoulder, to Eurynome. This is significant because it is the area of his body that Odysseus must rely on if he is to string and shoot his bow. In turn, when Odysseus strikes Iros, he does not deliver a killer punch that could very likely damage his own hand; by dealing relatively mildly with the braggart, bursting his eardrum and filling his mouth with blood, he also conserves his strength for the coming fray. His Athena-ruled strategic side rules his Ares-ridden appetite for strife.

When Odysseus drags Iros out of the hall and props him up against the courtyard wall, as a living scarecrow, the suitors fail to see that their deafened messenger is now an ugly sign of their inability to hear warnings from the gods. They congratulate Odysseus and wish that the gods give him what is dearest to his spirit, little knowing that they have requested their own doom. Odysseus is pleased by this good omen. He now receives his prize, the stuffed goat's stomach, from Amphinomus; speaking respectfully, the best of the suitors wish him prosperity and health for the future.

Odysseus responds to this courtesy by giving Amphinomus fair warning of what lies in store for them. After letting the well-spoken young man know that he is familiar with his ancestry, the beggar warns him not to trust in his present good fortune. Using winged words that will later be used by Sophocles in his *Antigone*, the pauper warns the prince that nothing is more uncanny, *deinos*, than a human being. Anyone who believes he will never suffer misfortune just because he presently has boldness and energy, does not know how contingent his happiness is. He himself, trusting too much in his noble blood and high-spirited companions, recklessly participated in excess and violence. He never suspected that a time for suffering and endurance was ahead of him. Amphinomus is thus warned not to forsake his sense of righteousness. Otherwise put, he must not let confidence or companions cover up his conscience.

The beggar predicts that Odysseus is close at hand to avenge the reckless outrages visited on his wife and property. He prays that destiny will take Amphinomus out of his path for there will surely be a bloody reckoning with the suitors. It is fitting that these words are said to one whose name suggests that he lives by two sets of norms. Yet, although the young man is deeply troubled by these words, for his spirit senses the evil, he still does not leave. We are told that Athena had already marked him out to fall to Telemachus. Perhaps this conflicted man had prudence without courage? It could be the case that one must build up sufficient internal fortitude to wrestle with his evil destiny and break with his bad comrades. Conformity is an insidious vice.

Meanwhile, as though to seal the fate of the suitors and ensure that none should leave the house of Odysseus until the hour of their doom, Penelope is impelled by Athena to appear, veiled, and remind the suitors what they were there for. It is possible that the queen was moved with curiosity about this stranger who has already done much to disrupt the regime that the home invaders had set up in the palace; all the recent omens, culminating in the avowal of Theoclymenus and the report given by the stranger to the swineherd of her dear husband's presence or imminent arrival, could well have added to her confidence at this time. Yet, she must also be concerned that the disorder introduced by the stranger should not turn into outright violence that would unite the suitors against the household they would share between themselves. This would undo all that she had done by dividing them up as her wooers, each set on having Odysseus' wife and estate all for himself.

When Penelope finally appears before the suitors at the top of the stairs, she first speaks to her son. But even though Penelope roundly admonishes Telemachus—for his neglectful hospitality towards the stranger—before addressing the suitors, she never once speaks to the stranger. It is left for us to wonder if either Odysseus or his wife actually saw each other. Was long-suffering Odysseus just content to hear her voice as he stood in a corner of the hall? Did Penelope let her veiled eyes wander towards the shadows? All we know of is Odysseus' pleasure as he hears his wife flirt with the suitors and trick them into bringing her valuable gifts. It appears that he marvels at her mind and enjoys her artfulness. He does not seem to be jealous.

However, Penelope's appearance has driven the drunken suitors mad with desire. Eurymachus speaks for them all when he tells the queen that if the princes of Argos were to see her—surpassing as she does, all other women in beauty and mind—they too would join and multiply the ranks of her wooers. Although Penelope smoothly rejects these compliments, claiming that the little beauty she had left when her lord left for Troy, leaving her to weep in her lonely bed ever since, she gives the suitors new hope. We recall that she has said nothing in denial of his praise of her steady mind when the queen claims to recall words Odysseus spoke to her many years ago.

According to Penelope, Odysseus left everything in Ithaca in her charge during his absence. Yet, knowing full well how dangerous the Trojan expedition would be, he also told her to marry the man of her choice once their own son Telemachus, then but a babe in arms, grew a beard. Though it seems highly improbable that Odysseus could have foreseen the length of the Trojan War and his long disappearance, all of this would be music in the ears of the suitors. It seems that Penelope is finally ready to choose a man. Even though she follows up on this acquiescence by demanding to be wooed properly, and makes the suitors send their henchmen scurrying off to find and bring appropriate gifts, it seems as if the siege of Odysseus' home is almost over.

It seems that Athena is resolved to maintain the state of tension that was dispelled by Iros' beating and Penelope's appearance. Even as she used the queen to prevent any of the suitors from leaving and escaping the just deserts, she now has several of the queen's maids—led by Eurymachus's bedfellow and Melanthius the goatherd's sister, Melantho—insult Odysseus as he prepares to meet with the queen. Although the maids are speedily driven away by the stranger's threat to report their insulting conduct to Telemachus, Eurymachus takes up where they left off and taunts him. It could be that he wishes to defend Melantho; he certainly abuses the stranger in language similar to that used by her brother, Melanthius, when he met Odysseus by the fountain, although it is more likely that the sycophant is imitating his patron.

The basic line his abuse follows is timeless. It is still used in our own day by the lazy privileged rich and their children against the poor and unemployed. Eurymachus, after first gratuitously mocking Odysseus' baldness, offers him hard work in fair exchange for food, shoes, and clothing. But he then goes on to claim that the stranger prefers begging from others to hard work that would feed his ravenous belly. In his response, Odysseus gets to the fallacy that lies at the heart of this hubristic vaunt. He knows all too well that the undeserving rich are at least as guilty of the crimes they are prone to accuse the poor of, regardless of whether they are deserving or not.

The stranger duly challenges Eurymachus to compete with him in working, instead of looking down on him from a position of privilege. He proposes three activities, each calling for skill and endurance: harvesting, plowing, and fighting; he suggests that he would surpass Eurymachus at all three of them. He ends by briskly advising Eurymachus that his height and powerful friends would be of little help to him were Odysseus to return home. He would then find that his eponymous broad shoulders would only be a hindrance in his hurry to get away from the home he had invaded. In effect, Eurymachus for all his glibness is little better than Iros. He is to his stooge what Odysseus is to the beggar. True worth has nothing to do with stature or birth. These words, whether spoken by king or beggar, call into question the aristocratic order that is being exploited by the suitors. The stranger is implying that the spoilt suitors are incapable of embodying the martial virtues that justify their privileges.

His words unerringly hit their target. Infuriated by his boldness, Eurymachus hurls another stool at Odysseus who ducks beside Amphinomus. When the stool hits a wine steward and drunken mayhem breaks out, the suitors angrily blame the beggar for bringing trouble into the house and ruining their pleasure. Of course, in doing so, they unwittingly name the one who successfully provoked Eurymachus: the master of the house. At this point Telemachus orders the drunken company out of the house and Amphinomus, intervening as peacemaker, scolds his fellow suitors for their bad behavior in response to words that were truly spoken. He persuades them to leave. The battle of words is over; the pauper has humiliated the princes and their pawns. The suitors will go to bed with the disconcerting awareness that their bluff has been called. This awareness will linger into the next day longer than a bad hangover ever could.

Book 19

As disguised Odysseus prepares to meet with his wife, two questions are uppermost in his mind. The first is tactical; how on earth is he to defeat this great throng of suitors? Even though he has very little respect for their military ability and despite the odds having been shortened somewhat by his removal of the weapons from his great hall, the fact remains that there are well over a hundred of them and only one of him. Telemachus his son is as much a liability as an asset since the suitors would surely see that the young man's survival matters very much to Odysseus. The other question concerns Penelope. Should he identify himself to her? Surrounded as she is by maids of doubtful loyalty, he would be running a huge risk by revealing his true identity to her. Just as one treacherous maid revealed the secret of the shroud to the suitors, it would be even more likely that either fidelity or falseness would give the game away. His secret being known, preferably without his knowledge, the stranger could be eliminated with ease, ideally in his sleep. Even the appearance of too close an attachment between Odysseus and son would attract much dangerous scrutiny.

The need for esoteric communication is underscored further when foul-mouthed Melantho subjects Odysseus to further abuse in her mistress's presence. She may well have been asked by her lover Eurymachus, already smarting from his tongue-lashing, to keep a close eye on the stranger. He, unaware of this connection, warns her not to place too much trust in her ephemeral beauty after asking what he had done to make her hate him so much. Odysseus warns her of what he would do to her upon his return. He even foresees Telemachus dealing harshly with the maids who disgraced his house when he comes into his manhood. Considering the eventual fate of the unfaithful maids, Odysseus could at least say that they had been fairly warned by him against fraternization with the suitors. Whether or not this reading of the riot act was merely formal, these maids were expected not to betray the household.

Penelope now sharply chastises Melantho. It transpires now that she knew very well that her mistress intended to question the stranger about Odysseus. Perhaps it was some primal instinct or fear that caused both of the disloyal children of Dolius to display so much unconditioned spite towards their master? Nevertheless, even after Melantho has been dispatched, Penelope still asks Eurynome the housekeeper to sit by her. While this would certainly be in keeping with propriety, it also makes it very clear that this is an intelligence test similar to that which Odysseus set the disguised Athena. If the stranger is the man he says he isn't, Eumaeus having already told her that he claims to be from Crete, or a trusted emissary from

Odysseus, the queen shows that she expects him to show discretion in communicating his news to her. We must also see that Penelope, right up to and beyond the denouement, reserves the option of deniability; despite her intelligence or perhaps due to it, she greatly fears being manipulated by gods and men. This caution has preserved her household.

We must also take note that this tattered vagrant is being treated very unusually by the queen. To begin with, they are seated on similar chairs and conversing as equals. Penelope begins their conversation by asking the stranger who he is, where he hails from and who his parents are. He responds by praising her to the heavens, likening her to a just and blameless king who brings great prosperity to his kingdom through his good governance, and courteously says that while he cannot fault her for asking, he cannot answer this question in her house. He is willing to answer any query but this; too full of sorrow to contain his tears and laments, he fears to disgrace himself. From this, Penelope can conclude that this man who freely shared his Cretan origins with Eumaeus, keeping him enthralled for three days and nights, is acting very oddly indeed. If on the other hand he is not a Cretan and is her husband, he has praised her running of his kingdom and voiced shame and grief for his long absence from her.

The queen's response first seems as if it were addressed to Eurymachus. She denies any claim to beauty, although the stranger has not complimented this quality, and says that her reputation would only be saved by Odysseus returning to Ithaca and taking care of her. Penelope then swiftly proceeds to describe her own beleaguered state in the palace and recounts the famous device of the shroud by which she was able to put her suitors off for over three years until some of her own maids betrayed her. Now, however, she is left without any way out. Her parents urge her to marry while her son, grown to manhood, grows impatient and angry as his inheritance is wasted by her suitors. Simply put, Penelope wants the stranger—whether or not he is Odysseus—to see that while she does not want to take the easy way out by leaving Ithaca and giving up on her beloved husband, she has run out of options. Her tale of desperation is equal to the burden of guilt and sorrow that rob her guest of speech; the queen is all but begging the stranger for news of Odysseus. He is her last hope. Yet Penelope is also warning him that any such news cannot be given in a exoteric manner; as noted earlier, she is asking that he both reveal and conceal his secrets.

Although Penelope knows full well that the stranger told her swineherd that he had recent news of Odysseus, her guest tells her now that he met her husband in Crete, twenty years ago, just after he left for Troy. By telling her now that he is a Cretan, he is warning her that she will hear lies; she must be ready to decode their meaning. If Penelope and Odysseus are still one mind and one heart this should yet be possible. It is vital that we recognize, and try to understand, why Penelope has a meltdown before Odysseus gives her clear signs that he is himself and not whom he claims to be. It could be that she recognizes his way of lying. Though Eumaeus was enchanted by his guest's storytelling, it seems that he did not know Odysseus personally; he is but reminded of Antikleia's riddling way of talking. But Penelope would notice these dark verbal pyrotechnics and pierce his disguise, just as Helen, her cousin, would.

Even though any speculation along these lines is necessarily conjectural, and could be part of Homer's artistry—thus letting his hearer experience the thrill of discovery that Penelope felt—we can support it by two other images the poet uses to describe Odysseus. The first is from the *Iliad* and describes what occurs when the seemingly foolish and sullen Odysseus speaks and "weaves the web of speech." The Trojan Antenor says, backing Helen's words about Odysseus, that "when he lets his voice speak and the words come down from his deep soul, as thick as winter snow, then no man could be compared to Odysseus and no one would mock his appearance." Here we note that Odysseus is compared to a speaker who weaves a web of words; the similarity to the woman with whom he is of one mind and heart is inescapable.

This is surely why when Penelope hears the stranger tell his Cretan tale of Odysseus held captive by the North Wind, "her tears ran over her cheeks as the South Wind melts the snow on mountain tops." She detects the long-hidden spark of genius that Odysseus and Athena hid in a beggar's rags "as a man buries a burning log in a heap of ashes, thus saving the flame in a remote place with no one around to rekindle it." Penelope had built her own frigid fortress of solitude, as secretive a state as Calypso was for Odysseus; where her husband employed windy lies and disguises along his journeys in *terra incognita*, she used evasion and silence to hold her fixed location.

Yet now, as her defenses seem to come down in a flood of tears, Penelope retains enough prudence to set this uncanny man a difficult, if not impossible, test. She asks him to describe Odysseus' dress, his character, and his companions. Expecting the Cretan to recall all these details from a meeting twenty years ago is quite absurd; it follows then that she does not expect the truth from a Cretan. To answer her fully he must lie; it is from the quality of this lie that she will find out the truth about him.

The response of the stranger shows quite clearly who he is. If he really was who he said he was or a lying vagrant, it would be easiest for him to speak of the well-renowned character of Odysseus and claim to remember very little of his dress or companions. Stunningly, he chooses the opposite approach; it is as if he were to ignore Hamlet and dwell lovingly on the attributes and apparel of Rosenkranz and Guildenstern.

The stranger claims to remember exactly what Odysseus wore when he met him. It is quite possible that had this meeting actually taken place, Odysseus would have been scantily clad after his long and terrible battle with the storm winds. But the stranger knows that this is not the answer that Penelope sought. Instead, he tells her exactly what Odysseus wore when they parted; these were the very clothes she gave him when he left for Troy. Only Odysseus could be expected to remember this; also, the fact that he recalls this moment also reveals how much it meant to him. In other words, Penelope is told that he loves her just as much as he did twenty years ago. In this way, the enigmatic stranger does reveal Odysseus' character. Like Turandot, his name is love! Or better, this is what brings him home to Ithaca after twenty years. As if to rub the point in, he apologetically tells her that these may have not been what she remembered him wearing when he left home, knowing well that they were. Only Odysseus could have spoken the right untruth about this imagined meeting in Crete.

When the stranger goes on to casually describe Eurybates, the herald who was well loved by his master, we must see that he is trying to divert the attention of anyone else in the hall from the hidden import of his reminiscence. Eurynome, Penelope's chaperone, may well have known this man although she probably would have been less familiar with her long-lost master. This detail merely serves to underscore the false fact that the stranger entertained Odysseus twenty years ago and deserves to enjoy the hospitality of his home. But Penelope cunningly signals her recognition of her husband when, after acknowledging him as an honored guest, she laments her inability to welcome her husband home from that other unspeakable place, Troy.

Meanwhile the beggar hides deeper in his own disguise by repeating a tale he had earlier told Eumaeus, of Odysseus' imminent sailing in from Thesprotia. In effect, as with the Trojan Horse, he seems—at this time—to be trying to turn the attention of the suitors outside so as to engineer some sort of coup d'état within the palace. By speaking of the great riches that Odysseus will bring home, it seems as if he is trying to make the suitors even more eager to fight him on the beaches or ambush him at sea; such a story would also serve to soften the hearts of those holding grudges for the lives lost at Troy. However, Odysseus still does not seem to have a plan of action; the stranger tells Penelope that he is asking the Oracle of Zeus whether to return openly or secretly. He makes his solemn oath—swearing by Zeus, friendship, and her hospitable hearth—that Odysseus will return soon, before the next moon has waned.

Penelope meanwhile pretends not to take these lies at all seriously; the queen gently reproves the stranger, telling him they both know that Odysseus will never come home. Neither, she says, will her guest ever board a ship that will take him away as his reward for bringing this news. While she attributes this inability to produce his conveyance to the absence of Odysseus, the truth of the matter is quite different. In effect, the queen's words mean that Odysseus can never come home because she knows him to be there already. Further, the stranger will never be given passage simply because she will not permit him, her husband to ever leave their home again!

Now, even though all seems to be well and the suspicious Penelope has secretly acknowledged that the stranger is indeed Odysseus, she may have yet another test in store for him. Claiming that she could hardly live up to his high praise of her rule over the household if she were not even to offer him a bath and a bed to sleep in, she summons her maids to extend these rituals of hospitality to her guest. Although he gently refuses most of these attentions, Odysseus does consent to have his dirty feet washed, opting however for an older woman of the house rather than a young maid. As his nurse point outs, this is a natural response to the rude way the maids acted.

While we do not quite know whether Odysseus wants this, or if Penelope planned to have her perform this service all along, the person chosen for the task is Eurykleia, his old nurse. The danger dawns on him too late; his nurse would certainly identify him by the scar he sustained as a youth, when boar-hunting with Autolycus. While he, not for the first time, has let his guard down after accomplishing his mission, it is possible that Penelope has been both too clever and suspicious. What if his nurse is unable to contain her feelings upon seeing him? As Odysseus knows, the body, like the heart, has its reasons. Penelope has set her trap but can she trust her agent and prey not to betray her? Odysseus is like the great wild boar that scarred him on his leg. If he poked too much, the primal beast within will emerge maddened from the hidden depths of his psyche. He is after all the grandson of Autolycus, the wolf itself.

Mercifully the test, if intended, concludes without the stranger's cover being blown. Odysseus, who just managed to avoid showing emotion when his beloved dog died before him, evinces only savage fury when his wet-nurse, who has already noted his strong likeness to her dear master, recognizes his scar and causes his foot to fall back into her basin with a loud clang. When she looks towards her mistress, whose eyes we are told, were averted by Athena, Odysseus threatens that he will kill her along with the other bad maids if she does not keep his secret. Eurykleia duly gives her word; her desire to rejoice gives way to Antikleia—caution and fear of hubris. We also note that just as Helen was the only one to outwit Odysseus when he snuck into Troy, only her cousin Penelope could figure out how to penetrate his disguise. In this case though, she will offer Odysseus invaluable help instead of betraying him.

This incident, along with the longer flashback to our hero's childhood that was given along with it, seems to sum up the two aspects of the man. Odysseus the good king and loving husband cannot be separated from the restless, nameless sacker of cities. This dichotomy was set up by Autolycus who, as the favorite of Hermes, "surpassed all men in thievery and the art of lying" when he named his grandson "odious" or "distasteful." This was the uncanny inheritance of our hero through his mother's line. We will hear later of what he received from his gentler and far less assertive father.

Meanwhile Penelope, whether or not she was truly "distracted by Athena," has not been woolgathering. The queen tells her guest she herself is deeply conflicted by the alternative courses of action she is faced with. Hinting that she fears endangering her son, the queen wonders if it would be better for her to quit Ithaca and leave him his inheritance; she doubts his ability to defend his estate without her protection. We come to see that she is pondering a course of action that would involve a great deal of violence and risk when she asks her guest to interpret a dream she just had. Penelope has digested what he has just said and realized that Odysseus has come back without allies or resources. Perhaps she also heard his threat to kill the maids. This is why she tells him of Odysseus taking the form of an eagle with a crooked beak to kill her flock of twenty geese, pets she has fed for many years. The eagle himself interprets her dream, claiming that he is Odysseus come to slay her suitors.

When Penelope asks the stranger how she should interpret this curious interpreted dream, she is told that its meaning is clear; the suitors will all be killed. The queen responds by telling the stranger that dreams come from two different places: the gate of ivory and the gate of horn. While the dreams that come from the first gate deceive, the second gate breeds dreams that accomplish the truth for those who see them. This means that true dreams coming from the ivory gate do not just predict the future; rather they cause or inspire the dreamer to act and fulfill their truth. We have already seen Odysseus traverse the no man's land between truth and falsity as he uses stories to express deeper realities. Differently put, mere words that cannot bridge the gap between speech and deed come from the gate of ivory. The ivory here turns out to be the material of the teeth from which these boasts emanate; this is why some of Homer's characters chide one another for letting certain base words escape their mouths and we still speak harshly of people who lie through their teeth.

Penelope expresses her fear that the eagle's words may emanate from the gate of ivory, as much as she and her son would like to see him make good on his boast. She then goes on to confide another important secret. The very next day she intends to set up a contest at emulating a feat of archery performed by Odysseus himself. The entrants would have to string the bow of Odysseus and then fire an arrow through twelve axes lined up on the floor. The winner would gain her hand in marriage.

The stranger is quick to approve of this plan. He assures her that Odysseus will be there before any of the suitors can perform this feat. The truth of the matter is that this inspiration has originated, literally, from the gate of horn. Bows of this time were made of two animal horns. Further, just as dreams from the gate of horn had the ability to make words become deeds, Penelope has handed Odysseus the ideal means by which to greatly shorten the odds against him. Given the right context, one man with a bow could ambush and kill dozens of enemies, especially if they were drunk. We can see why Penelope is the perfect match for Odysseus. Like Athena, she has come up with the idea; it is up to him to make it become flesh and draw blood. We may even say that this can only happen by Odysseus going deep within his soul. Yet such an internal journey will inevitably bring up what is most enigmatic about him; we cannot tell which aspect of him will appear from his cavernous psyche. Even the gods, let alone Penelope, cannot predict the twists and turns of his spirit.

Book 20

When Eurykleia finally sees Odysseus, her "much longed for" master, he reenacts the disappointment she surely experienced when Autolycus chose to name his grandson "odious"; otherwise put, Odysseus reveals himself to her as much by showing his hidden trouble-making essence as by inadvertently exposing his ugly scar. But it very well may be the case that the primal power necessary to bring about the restoration of his kingdom and household resides here; this could also mean that it is not simply love but a darker, more thumotic, love of his own that brings him back home. This forces us to ask if this love is entitled to own and dispose of that which it loves; in blunter words, does his love for an old Ithaca entitle him to take extreme measures against those who have turned his vault of pirated treasure into a den of thieves? Have they any rights? What claim does an ex-king have over the regime that has formed in his absence? Also, even if he has come to set the record straight about the truth of the war, bursting through the past's dead leaves or lives, does this give him any power over the next generation of youth, those who were left literally or at least culturally orphaned by his shameful failure to come home in a timely manner?

When Odysseus beds down in the courtyard of his own home—hidden somewhere between an ox hide, several fleeces of recently killed sheep, and a blanket—the image surely serves to remind us that the question about his identity also perplexes this polytropic man himself, as he literally twists and turns before the fire like the goat stomach he just consumed. In other words Odysseus does not have a fixed essence or identity that resides resiliently beneath his many disguises and lies; the secret of his amazing power to endure seems to be in the sheer energy of his being-for-itself. While Odysseus is truly an inverted Achilles: invulnerable and changeless in the heel only, insatiable in the belly, and perversely polymorphic from the scar upward, we also see that this odious pain-bringer takes in even more trouble than he gives out.

This is why co-extensive with the question of how he will appear to his subjects, is the problem of how far his revenge should extend. Odysseus is hidden in enemy territory as securely and tenuously as he was concealed within the Trojan Horse in the citadel of Ilium. Perhaps his famed fore-thought did not then extend far enough to foresee the hubris of the Greeks and its ruinous consequences. Homer's own audience would surely have included many who would have asked why Hellas was plunged into the Dark Ages by the great victory over the Trojans. In other words his justice cannot only secure his household, it must also found a city; his vengeance must not go so far as to ruin the future of the very people he has come home to save. Like a good forester he must burn dead wood in order that the new shoots of spring will have space to grow and rich soil to nourish them. Just as he promised the maids that he would take care of the fire in the hall, he must also supervise a greater blaze.

While the fire in Odysseus' shaggy heart is surely fueled by outrage at the wanton conduct of his maids, we cannot forget that to them—as beggar or king—he is but a Cyclopes. To the extent that he is blindly ignorant and angry about what happened in his home, he is a one-eyed monster from the dark past; this is also surely why his wife told him of her fondness for the twenty silly geese she had domesticated over as many years of his ab-sence; her maids' petty selfishness counts less than his guilt.

Nevertheless, our hero seems to have taken the place vacated by his dead dog as he growls within himself at the implicitly disrespectful behavior of his household staff towards their long-absent master. He checks the im-pulse to kill them then and there, which Homer suggestively likens to the anger of a bitch towards a man threatening her pups, and utters the famous words to himself "Endure my heart. You had worse to endure in the Cy-clopes' cave until intelligence rescued you from certain death." As the sig-nificance of the Homeric simile consists in Penelope's protectiveness towards the litter that Odysseus threatens, a fact underscored by the sleep-less queen's plea to Artemis, we see the sheer power of the bloody fury that almost takes him over. This terrible wave of jealous rage is only limited by pragmatic considerations, a far more cold-blooded desire for fuller revenge; this stormy state of continence is only strengthened, and not qualitatively enhanced, when Athena rescues him from this Ares-like state and promises him victory. When asked how he could escape after gaining revenge, Athena again assures him that they would defeat and rob the property of fifty battalions of men; the suggestion is that with her help he could rout *and* pillage even the forces of Achilles. While Odysseus' bloody-mindedness suffices for victory, this power soon warps into the mad rage of Ares. As was the case with Troy or the Cyclopes, Odysseus is his own worst enemy. This is why he needs Athena's guidance.

His wife says this in her own way when she asks Artemis to protect her maids and yet longs for what Odysseus was like before he left. She does not know if the beggar who so resembled her husband is real or illusory, she might fear that this man could talk like Odysseus the lover and yet display less attractive qualities when he acted; it could very well be that Penelope is already quite aware of her spouse's dual nature.

Awakened by Penelope's weeping, Odysseus emerges from his bedclothes and prays to Zeus. He seeks both a divine portent and a human sign. This suggests to us that Athena could be to him what the stranger was to his wife; in other words, they could both be phenomena that did not exist apart from a soul's deep longing. We must be attentive to the difference between divine inspiration and objective fact. It is also necessary to recall Penelope's distinction between the gates of ivory and horn; our desires cannot be divinized or regarded as being identical with the truth even if they come from Olympus. Neither Odysseus nor Penelope will let a god lead them to folly; in the polytheistic reality Homer describes, where deities are often at variance with each other, only Zeus can bridge the gap between personal god and divine destiny. In other words, the battle between the Scylla of object-orientated behavior and the Charybdis of self-doubting solipsism could go on forever. As in Aeschylus, Nike and Dike are only reconciled by a third element, introduced by Olympian Zeus himself. He must act against this cosmic horizon, beyond the vagaries of city or soul.

Zeus' thunder in answer to the prayer of Odysseus is only one half of the sign he sought; the other, more significant element of this response comes from a person placed so far beneath the hero as to place him equidistant between Zeus and her. This anonymous slave, the smallest and slowest of the twelve maids assigned to grind the wheat for the suitors' bread, speaks in such a way as to provide a *logos* to the otherwise random celestial event. The curse she places on the parasitic suitors immediately reminds us of the beggar's winged words to Eurymachus; any doubts we may entertain as to the motives behind the agent of divine nemesis are speedily removed by this reminder of what is really at stake here. The nameless woman has asked Zeus to hear her and grant that the suitors, who have condemned her to perform this arduous labor they are entirely oblivious to, will eat their last supper at the house. Though spoken to Zeus, her prayer did not escape the ears of her lord. Odysseus rejoices at her winged words; they strengthen him more than even divine Athena could. This hopeless maid is like Elpenor; she too stands at the very mouth of the Underworld. She and her kind may only be redeemed from their living Hades by Odysseus killing the vile suitors and establishing a more equitable political order. The suitors' fate is sealed by the union of the gods' will and the slaves' chthonic fury. It is not really Prince Telemachus who suffers the true burden of their dissipation; the suitors' swinish conduct has also turned the sheltering palace of Odysseus into a place where the kingdom's resources were callously culled, consumed, and cast off. As Eumaeus told the beggar, the suitors only wanted beautiful people around them; to this extent, they are typical consumers who do nothing to augment the stocks of scarce commodities they consume. We cannot forget that Homer's epics were not composed in a time of plenty; this made the suitors' profligacy all the more evil.

Odysseus' solidarity with the other nobodies is further indicated when Eurykleia tells an indignant Telemachus that the stranger refused the comforts of the house but chose to sleep on the floor, in the outer hall; this may signal that Odysseus' ultimate concern will be for good men who have been hitherto denied the respect and hospitality of his house. The sacker of cities must now build a new community.

This theme of merit continues when Odysseus, after another unpleasant meeting with Melanthius, makes the acquaintance of his cowherd Philoitios. In contrast to the goatherd, who judges men on the basis of present fortune, the cowherd greets the beggar with kindness and sympathy. He correctly identifies his king as a man of a noble nature fallen upon hard times, and laments the fickle ways of the gods. Even though the cowherd is wrong in his understanding of the subtle ways of Zeus and his daughter, he is the better man for refusing to flatter fortune or denounce the downtrodden. Philoitios tells the beggar about his own moral dilemma; although the herds entrusted to him by Odysseus have flourished, he feels no obligation to serve those who have overrun his lord's house, disrespect his son, and squander his goods. It seems that even though both the swineherd and cowherd do not mind serving in a relatively menial capacity in an orderly regime, they take strong exception to being part of an unjust order. Both men only continue to serve out of an old loyalty that no longer brings any tangible benefit; they serve a house that no longer protects them. It is again made evident that these are the ones, the deserving but downtrodden, in whose name Odysseus must act. Or better, Zeus and Athena have harnessed the rage of Odysseus to the service of a cause that transcends his murky personal interests. It should however be clear enough to Odysseus that the future of his hegemony and house rests on the support of this new class of people who have shown their virtue.

This contrast between the productivity of this moderate class and the decadence of the former guardian class is underscored a third time when the suitors' plotting against Telemachus is interrupted by an omen from Zeus. The evident significance of an eagle flying on their unlucky left side with a pigeon in its grasp is pointed out by Amphinomus. But even this decent man is seen to be clearly incapable of acting on the fullest implications of the divine message; he merely warns the suitors not to take measures against the young prince, and their attention is swiftly diverted by what they knew and did best, consumption. The best of the long absent king's flocks are sacrificed to the gods but consumed by these disgusting young men; reclining like the Olympians themselves, they are served and attended to by the three herdsmen.

Telemachus senses the suitors' contagious awareness of their own impotence and taunts them with it; just as they earlier believed they possessed a collective courage that none of them possessed personally, the thuggish suitors now individually and collectively sense their own pusillanimity. By seating the beggar beside him, the son of Odysseus takes it upon himself to avenge any insults his guest might receive. This was what he had feared when he first met the tramp at Eumaeus' hut. He fears the suitors no more. Now the boot is on the other foot. The stranger's presence is a bald reminder of their cowardice. Even when Antinous tries to provoke them by saying in mock seriousness that the young prince surely has authority from Zeus himself, for otherwise they would have killed him for all his eloquence, nobody rises to the bait.

Finally, after much drinking has ensued, one of the suitors, a rich lout called Ktesippos proposes to make the beggar a gift that he could in turn bestow on the woman who washed his feet. Apart from proving that the suitors did continue to receive intelligence from the maids, thus justifying Penelope's extreme caution, these words also suggest that the wastrels are now at the point of inebriation where rashness supersedes cowardice; in short, they were almost ready to be sacrificed.

When Ktesippos lobs a cow's hoof at the ducking Odysseus, Telemachus now takes hostilities to the next level. Secure in his knowledge of their cowardice, perhaps too secure, he challenges them to take him on like real men instead of being content to merely eat him out of house and home. He claims to prefer death in battle to seeing his guests insulted, his maids ravished, and his household overrun by drunken oafs.

At these fighting words the suitors are reduced to hushed silence. Finally Agelaos, conceding the justice of Telemachus' words, and asking his fellow-wooers to desist from gratuitously attacking the stranger or other servitors of the house, attempts to claim that they were there on account of Penelope rather than Telemachus. He urges mother and son to take his advice and accept the fact that Odysseus will never come home. This being the case, Telemachus should allow his mother to be married off, thus leaving him securely in possession of his father's house. In this way, Penelope can look after another while her son will be freed to eat and drink in his own house.

When Telemachus responds to this attempt to shift from tragedy to comedy by assuring the suitors that he would gladly consent to his mother's marriage were she to leave the house of her own free will but fears to expel her involuntarily, they are reduced to shrieks of uncontrollable laughter. Most of them are all too aware that, far from leaving Telemachus securely in possession of his inheritance, separation of mother from son would almost certainly lead to his despoilment and death. Just as the Greeks at Troy merely used Helen as the pretext for their invasion, the suitors of Helen's cousin Penelope were really after the fabled wealth of Odysseus. This shift from Aphrodite to Ares to Pluto once made every limp-speared Hellene a

Menelaus. Just like Sparta's King, they soon became living shades in Pluto's vaults; as we saw, rich Menelaus was just as dead as Agamemnon—only preserved better. Odysseus must now revisit Hades and feed the suitors' dead souls blood and knowledge. Yet we cannot forget that he too went via Ares and Aphrodite to Hades and got home; the suitors somehow better resemble his crew, the 600 men who never returned. It could be that his serial renunciations of Aphrodite (the Sirens), Ares (taking arms against Scylla) and (the temptation to stay in) Hades gave purgation from his sins.

We now see that ominous parallels are been drawn between the suitors and the remainder of Odysseus' last crew, those who consumed the cattle of the Sun. Both groups ignored strict warnings from Odysseus not to persist in their forbidden feasting, which began in his absence; both groups saw the flesh they consumed somehow come to life, while they lurched blindly towards their bloody deaths. The final warning given by Theoclymenos is every bit as terrible as the signs given on the island of Thriniakia; where then the meat being roasted by the sailors bellowed, the suitors themselves ate meat that oozed with red blood. Penelope's intrepid lovers somehow shed tears as they laughed at these warnings; it was as if their minds were already dead, even while their bodies wept in anticipation of their fate. Just as Odysseus' last shipmates were doomed to perform sacrilege even before they alighted on the isle of Helios, since the winds only died down after they had glutted themselves on the forbidden flesh, so too does it seem that the suitors were already destined to die once they invaded their king's home; the cautions given by Odysseus and Teoclymenos in this case were more ritual disclaimers than prudential counsel. Differently put, only the mind can leave the underworld. A thoughtless body cannot. In this context Theoclymenos is like Tiresias, the only man in Hades with his wits.

Meanwhile the doomed suitors, both victims and predators, continue to jest tipsily. They mock Telemachus' poor choice of guest-friends, refusing to recognize either the strength of the stranger or the powers of the prophet. They have failed to learn from the terrible beating given by the stranger to Irus or his winged response to Eurymachus' accusations. This invincible ignorance is proof that they are already in Hades. Meanwhile Telemachus within the hall and Penelope, sitting from where she could hear every word spoken, wait as vigilantly as Odysseus and his comrades once sat within the Trojan Horse, for the right moment to raise the dread aegis of Athen

Chapter 6
Rage, Revenge, Recognition, and Rehabilitation:
Books 21–24

Book 21

It is Athena, the goddess of war and wisdom, who sets her plan for the redemption of man in motion on the occasion of the feast of Apollo. It is only by the synthesis of Apollo and Athena that the blind fury of Ares, so necessary to the ultimate success of Odysseus, may be curbed. Among other things, Apollo is the divine defender of sacred limits. Once the bitter enemy of the Trojan War, which saw an old civilization violated by the greed and gluttony of a barbaric Greek army, he will now be invoked to punish that war's bastard imitation, the home invasion of Odysseus' palace. Just as Apollo made Paris the tool of his revenge on proud Achilles, he will now guide Odysseus' hand, as the same weapon will slay the hubristic suitors.

But though Odysseus will be guided by Apollo, Athena will merge with the prudence of Penelope and let the queen know that it is time to set her trap. As soon as the queen hears the prophet leave the hall, accompanied by the mad laughter of her suitors, she goes upstairs for the key to the secret chamber where the riches of the house are stored. We are not told the location of this teeming treasury; it suffices to find out that it, like Penelope's chastity, has been kept intact until Odysseus's return. It is good to know that the best resources of civilization were only hidden and not exhausted; we will soon see how this theme will be the key to decoding the truest purpose behind the bloody tsunami of terror that will soon be unleashed in the hall. While Apollo will be served up a massive hecatomb of a hundred bovine suitors, in deferred atonement for the cattle of the sun slain by Odysseus' last crewmates, it is Athena who will arrest the precipitous fall from brutish creature to brutal consumer that took place as the immediate consequence of the Trojan War and its savage end.

Ultimately, of course, everything depends on Odysseus. Even though Penelope and Athena give him much sage counsel and provide him with the only weapon that could be used to defeat the suitors, the key to the storehouse is only made of ivory. It only becomes transmuted into horn once words become deeds. Only then, by the heroic prowess of Odysseus, does a treasured keepsake become a lethal bow. In other words, whatever is brought up from Hades or down from the heavens still relies upon the virtuosity of man to realize its true essence. Otherwise these gifts of the gods could well become the very means by which wanton human cattle merely squander and consume their best potential. The human freedom to use or abuse all that it is given by the gods can never be taken away. But this power is all too easily squandered and made the instrument of its own degradation and destruction.

The material instrument chosen by Penelope has an interesting history of its own. The weapon that Odysseus will wield against the suitors was not originally his at all. It was the bow of Eurytos of Oichalia, the great archer who was so proficient in its use that he challenged Apollo and was killed by the god for his presumption. This tale, we recall, was told by Odysseus himself at the court of Alcinous. While there is a curious echo of Achilles' name in Oichalia, which is also preserved when we recall that the superhero's birthplace was also in Thessaly, our more immediate concern should be with Heracles being the other hero mentioned as having challenged the gods. Now Homer tells us that it was Heracles who slew Iphitos, the son of Eurytos, after he had gifted his father's bow to Odysseus. The bard also suggests that it was Heracles who first stole the twelve mares that Iphitos sought, and then killed the youth, even while he hosted the son of Eurytos in his own home. This terrible violation of the laws of hospitality seems to be connected to hubris; it fatally links the son of the violator with another who performed the same crime. Even though Iphitos has already given away the terrible bow of his father, he is yet robbed and then killed for this crime by one who had escaped sanction for the identical offense.

We note that though Odysseus did not take his awful weapon to Troy, Philoctetus, who inherited the bow of Heracles, did so and almost paid for it with his life. Just as Iphitos was slain by Heracles, Philoctetes was exiled on Lemnos by Odysseus. It is as though the two weapons vied with each other for victims, even when they were left unused or given away. While Philoctetes was exiled for ten years, before going on to emulate Heracles and using his bow to set in motion the chain of events leading to the taking of Troy, Odysseus spends an equal period of time away from other human beings after he brings the bow and its owner back to the Greek army. Now, twenty years later, he is reunited with his own bow. It seems to be Athena who desires the deadly weapon to be used in a way that that will bring honor to its patron, Apollo.

A final reference to Eurytos occurs later in Book 21 by a man soon to become his bow's next victim. Antinous, correctly anticipating the stranger will string the bow, not to emulate the drunken centaur Eurytos who, attempting to rape the bride at a wedding, ended up terribly mutilated for causing a terrible brawl. The implication here is that the stranger is trying to become Eurytus and abduct the object of the suitors' own marital desires, Penelope. It is clearly the case that the bow is primarily a hunter's weapon; it used to kill beasts rather than men. This is why it is fittingly used by Apollo and Artemis to slay humans who are to them as beasts are to men. It seems that the bow may only be used to kill men by the mortal agent of a god's will.

When Penelope brings the bow into the hall and offers her hand in marriage to the one who strings the bow and shoots an arrow through a row of twelve axes, thus emulating a feat once performed by Odysseus, the suitors seem intimidated by the challenge. While scolding the swineherd and cowherd for weeping at the sight of this relic of their lost master, Antinous admits that none of them is equal to what Odysseus was. The suitors are now gripped by awareness of their own impotence.

These words spur Telemachus to action. The young prince, while mocking himself for encouraging the suitors to try to win his mother, begins the contest by first neatly arranging the axes in the proper formation and then attempting to string the bow himself. The suitors somehow fail to see anything suspicious in Telemachus' ability to recreate the condition for a feat he had never seen before; their attention is instead taken up by the prince's determined attempts to string the bow himself. This is the first of many occasions where Telemachus will successfully distract any attention from the trap being set in motion by making himself conspicuous. His often rude behavior will make it far easier for Odysseus, Penelope, and their men to secure the house and allow the bow to be left in its master's hand at the right time.

After first making three mighty efforts to string the bow and win the respect of the suitors who had mocked and humiliated him throughout his extended adolescence, Telemachus performs an invisible action that shows the exponential extent to which he has grown as a man. Just when his fourth attempt at stringing the bow is about to meet with success, the young prince accedes to his sire's urgently telegraphed signal that he should feign failure. In doing so, he proves his adulthood to the one person he really needs to impress; this choice of self-knowledge over external admiration not only keeps their plan in place. It also gives new meaning to Odysseus' return. Now they are truly fighting for Ithaca's future. It's not just about getting revenge. By calling himself a weakling and asking those whose strength is greater to continue the test, Telemachus shows that he is stronger than himself and Odysseus' equal.

Antinous now proposes that the suitors proceed from left to right as they attempt to string the bow. In so doing, he ensures that Eurymachus and himself will be the last to test their strength. This proposal shows the extent of his cowardice. Not only wishing to avoid being tested, Antinous is even willing to run the risk that someone else will string the bow before him. Perhaps, once the bow is strung, he will gripe at not having received the opportunity himself; physical strength must not be his forte. This substitution of boldness in the place of courage is what separates the consumer from other men; even a menial creature would lead a life of purely physical exertion.

The bow now passes into the soft hands of Leodes. He always sat in a corner beside the wine-mixing bowl; despite being the suitors' soothsayer, he alone is said to have hated their excesses. We may infer that his fondness for wine prevented him from leaving their company. This pickled prophet now predicts that the bow will separate many of them from their souls. While these words are proved correct, they also bear out Socrates' insight that a prophet usually cannot explain his own winged words. In Leodes' mind, the bow will expose the pretensions of those like himself who share in the feasting despite having no real hope of winning Penelope. These men love the wine as much as they fear being shown up as frauds. Like the lukewarm in Dante's limbo, they can neither leave the endless party nor share fully in its dissipation; they are held in a Hades-like time-loop by this mixture of knowledge and incontinence.

Antinous responds, as Leodes feared, by mocking *his* weakness but promising that one of the real men would succeed. Thus despite the true words of the prophet, which voiced the hidden feelings of all the suitors, his prophecy only served to bind them together all the more firmly —to both false honor and dishonorable behavior. It is as if Amphinomus, literally trapped between two codes, voiced the stance of many when he urged non-violence towards Telemachus while refusing to leave his house. Just like those in Hades whose company they would shortly join, the suitors will be punished for freely joining an act of piracy they could not escape from as easily.

Now, confirming in deed what he denied in speech, Antinous calls for the bow to be heated and rubbed with fat, making it easier to grip. But the bow still refuses to be strung and soon only Eurymachus and Antinous have yet not tried and failed. It is as if even the greasing of hands can no longer sustain the suitors' corrupt pseudo-state. There is something visibly ludicrous about these young bravos trying desperately to string the bow while reposing in what could only be described as a "comfy chair"!

At this point, just as the social compact of the suitors is collapsing, Odysseus joining the swineherd and cowherd makes them an offer that could be viewed as the origin of the Greek city-state. Before getting to this point however, he asks them how they would respond to the return of Odysseus, through the hands of a god. He asks the slaves if their hearts and spirits would let them to fight for their king or the suitors. We note that he is setting aside the propriety of slaves fighting at all; we also see that he is not telling them that slaves are obliged to fight for their king and master. He addresses them as men who are free to think for themselves and fit to bear arms.

The cowherd, whose name means friendly spirit, makes a stirring response. We first met him right after Melanthius the goatherd, now busily supplying the suitors with tallow, accused the stranger of lacking any decency (cosmos). Philoitios responds to Odysseus in words that now bring the polis into existence, between the decency of his soul and the divine order of the cosmos. He prays to Zeus, promising to dedicate all the strength of his hands to serve the homecoming of his master. These heartfelt words also ring with irony, since they compare the mighty hands of the slave to the soft-handed suitors within the house. Despite his lowly birth, this slave has done nothing to separate his name from his soul. The cosmic order leans towards virtue.

It is one thing to mutter one's dissatisfaction with the suitors in the privacy of a hut but quite another matter for a slave to pledge himself to overthrow nobles by Zeus. This is why it is just as stirring when Eumaeus, despite his earlier skepticism about his master's fate, prays just as fervently to all the gods for Odysseus to come home. Just as Athena could only reveal herself to Odysseus, it is only before these honest men that their king can truly be seen as himself, rather than as a husband or father. Now revealing himself, Odysseus declares that it was only these two men who prayed for his return, as opposed to merely cursing the suitors. In recompense, he promises that they will be given wives, houses next to his, and always be regarded by him as if they were brothers of Telemachus. These words go well beyond arming or emancipating the slaves; they lay the foundation for a new political order based on merit rather than blood. After this, Odysseus physically identifies himself to them by revealing his scar. This sequence of events suggests that his identity as "much prayed for"—the sentiment that Eurykleia had in mind when she asked Autolycus to name him—had to precede the scar that marked Odysseus the odious troublemaker; simply put, his disruptive actions would be Zeus-mandated deeds for the good of all. The gods had to come before the new political order based on shared scars, stories, and sorrows: the hierarchy of cosmos, polis, and suffering soul had to be maintained.

The three men then return to the hall separately, but only after Odysseus has given his comrades their assignments for the impending action; Eumaeus is to bring him the bow before locking the inside of the house; meanwhile Philoitios will close the door connecting the hall and the courtyard. Between them they will seal off the hall. We see here that Odysseus is carrying out a king's most basic role; he is securing his home and protecting his people from the many pirates and thieves around them; his two herdsmen, fittingly, will be given arms to deal with these vicious human wolves. Only thus will the hitherto incompatible qualities of slave and outlaw be reconciled. The king must replace the *oikos* with a city, a place where the good can be their best.

Meanwhile the suitors have resumed their struggles with the bow and Eurymachus has become its latest victim. He laments, observing that while there are many other women in Ithaca and Greece, they will all know that he could not even string the bow of Odysseus. At this, Antinous, the final challenger, dissents. He suggests that it is not Odysseus they are striving against but Apollo, whose feast day must not be disrupted. He proposes that they set the bow aside and resume the next morning. The proposal pleases the suitors and they all drink their fill prior to their departure.

It is now that the stranger speaks. He humbly asks the suitors, especially Antinous and Eurymachus, that he be allowed to try his own strength against the bow. After this, the contest can resume the next day so the god will favor whomever he wants.

These words infuriate the already inebriated suitors. Antinous warns the stranger against emulating the aforementioned hubris of the centaur Eurytos, in a sense granting that the suitors are of a different breed from the men who went to Troy, and when Penelope counters that the stranger certainly cannot take her home with him and make her his wife, this being impossible since she is already his wife and he is home, Eurymachus voices their true concern; they would all be disgraced by the stranger being able to string the bow and shoot through the axes when none of them could. Penelope neatly counters him by pointing out that men who have invaded the house of an absent lord could hardly expect to be held in much honor. She is merely offering the stranger clothing, weapons, and transport to wherever his heart desires.

Telemachus now intervenes with rude decisiveness. He reminds his mother that the bow is his to dispose of and orders her to her quarters. We can safely assume that he does not want his mother to be around when the fighting breaks out. For one thing, she could easily be killed or taken hostage. There is also the risk that she would intervene to protect her son and add to the danger faced by Odysseus and himself. While we are not told that Odysseus and his son have been able to talk with each other since Penelope told the beggar of her plan to stage the contest, Telemachus would have suspected the direction of his father's thoughts from the time he was willed not to string the bow. Indeed, the very alacrity with which he arranged those axes suggests that Telemachus already saw the opportunity presented by the bow.

Eumaeus now takes the bow towards Odysseus, but deterred by the loud anger of the suitors, sets it down again. Telemachus now intervenes again and very violently orders his adopted father to give the stranger the weapon. He threatens to drive the swineherd from the house with a shower of stones and goes on to make public his wish that he could deal likewise with the suitors. This performance has the desired effect of directing the attention, anger, and amusement of the suitors towards the young prince; meanwhile the bow is safely placed in its rightful owner's hands. As soon as he delivers this weapon of mass destruction Eumaeus, as if shamed by the abuse he has received, leaves the hall to carry out his instructions. Eurykleia is told to lock the doors connecting the house to the hall. Then, simultaneously, Philoitios leaves the hall and bars its outside entrance using a ship's cable. The trap is set.

As Odysseus holds his bow in his hands and sits, checking it for any signs of damage, the suitors continue to unknowingly betray their fate whilst displaying the ugliness of their souls. One even goes so far as to wish that his good fortune were equal to his ability to string his bow. It is embarrassingly clear that they have never seen a real archer perform; neither do they appreciate the care that a true artist takes with his instrument, whether bow or lyre. Odysseus will now play them a tune that will send their souls hurtling to the underworld. The song begins when he effortlessly strings the bow and plays a sweet musical note that sounds as clear as a swallow's voice. At this point in the story, Homer and Odysseus are one. So too is Zeus. His thunderous response to the lyre is to the Greek what the dove from heaven meant at the time of Christ's baptism at the river Jordan. The import is the same. Zeus loves the stranger.

As the horrified suitors watch, Odysseus lets an arrow fly, unerringly, through the axes. He then triumphantly cries out to Telemachus that since his hands have not lost their cunning, they will now serve up to the suitors the full measure of their evening's festivities. At this Telemachus, clad in bronze, takes his stand beside him.

Book 22

Though all has so far gone according to plan, and Odysseus—armed with a weapon of mass destruction—is ready to kill his foes, this is the most dangerous predicament he has ever known. Now, just as in the tall tale he told of the Cyclopes, he will reveal himself to his enemies. With only an untested boy and two household slaves by his side, he must take on well over a hundred drunk, desperate, and depraved thugs who are about to discover his identity and murderous intent. They must kill or be killed.

His first target is Antinous. The nasty son of Eupeithes is not only the mastermind and ringleader of the suitors, as Eurymachus will admit; he is also the *alter ego* of Odysseus himself. In other words, if Odysseus is to retain his self-possession and not revert to his false Ares-identity, his nous must triumph over the ravenous and raging anti-nous that leads him astray. This battle is as psychic as it is physical. Although blind Demodokus (the opinion of the many) claimed that the fight with Deiphobus (fear of god) was the most terrible battle of Odysseus' career, the hero understood at that very moment that this was precisely when he went astray. Then he fought with Athena's aid for Helen but became Ares in the process and lost Ithaca. Now he must fight both the suitors and his baser self if he is to regain Penelope and Ithaca. While Athena will help him defeat his external enemies, his greatest struggle will be with himself. The final test will only await him after he has slain the suitors.

The other possibility is that Antinous was slain first because of opportunity. The co-leader of the suitors was fully occupied with draining a double-handed wine goblet. We cannot miss the irony in that the last words he spoke warned the beggar against drunken hubris. However since Odysseus' defeats—in Egypt or Ismaros—had much to do with this very vice, the godless Antinous' swan song could have been prophetic.

Pandemonium breaks out at this point. The drunken suitors cannot fully grasp what they have seen. They tell the beggar that he has killed the finest young man in Ithaca and promise that he will be eaten by vultures for this. It is only when Odysseus tears off his rags and proclaims his identity that they begin to see what lies ahead. They are accused by Odysseus of ravaging his household, corrupting his maids, and lusting after his wife; as they were deterred by neither the anger of the gods nor the fury of the men they oppressed, they must now pay the ultimate price of disgraceful death.

Opportunistic as ever, Eurymachus moves smoothly into the breach created by Antinous' death. If Antinous was Odysseus' alter ego, then

Eurymachus replaces his unreliable lieutenant, Eurylochus. Eurymachus is more sophist than realist; it was he who undermined Penelope's household by seducing her favorite maid. He does by stealth and guile what Antinous would accomplish through his violent charisma. Eurymachus now offers what seems to be a reasonable solution to what he must see as an impasse. He glibly offers the dead Antinous as scapegoat and offers monetary compensation for the material damage inflicted on the estate of Odysseus. Twenty oxen was the price Laertes paid for Eurykleia. This is what he proposes each of the suitors should pay by way of fine or ransom. There need not be any more bloodshed in a land already hard hit by the six hundred lost by Odysseus after the Trojan War.

While this offer seems reasonable, *prima facie*, we must see that there is no way it could be acceptable to Odysseus; neither does it seem to be congruent with the long-term designs of Athena. First, there are no guarantees. Odysseus has no way of enforcing this agreement. Once the suitors leave his hall everything reverts to the state of nature. The element of surprise was the only advantage Odysseus had over them. He has no way of ensuring that the suitors, or even half of them, would not reunite, perhaps under the leadership of Eurymachus himself, and overthrow him. The suitors have already colluded to kill Telemachus more than once and they had only recently refused to heed the earlier warnings given in good faith by Odysseus. We must also consider the criminal nature of their actions. Monetary sanctions are not adequate to cover the damage they had inflicted on his household and kingdom. We must also bear in mind the issue of incontinence. Can these drunken louts be trusted to keep their word? Also, could they ever be part of a new just regime? Men who feast on the cattle of the sun become cattle themselves and die accordingly. Odysseus knows that a part of his own soul was left behind on Circe's island; he saw his own men turned into swine and revert back to swinish ways before too long. His only allies are a swineherd and a cowherd. But can they deal with human swine? Can men who have known violence and dissipation return to a pre-fallen condition? Odysseus has learned the truth about Ares and Aphrodite the hard way. But could anyone of the ancient equivalent of the comic book generation ever learn from him?

This is why Odysseus must emphatically reject Eurymachus' brazen offer. While his explicit response takes the form of rage, it is undergirded with solid ironclad reason. Eurymachus has not taken any responsibility for the sinful and criminal actions of the suitors; a typical consumer, he speaks as if everything can be bought and sold. This is why Odysseus wrathfully says that not even all the property of Eurymachus and his father could compensate him for their crimes. His only recourse is to stand up to Odysseus and fight like a man. We recall his earlier response to the suitor's taunt that he had never done a hard day's work in his life. Once again, he challenges the entitled young drone to forsake idle sophistry and prove his right to bear arms.

Before these deadly words, falling like arrows, Eurymachus seeks desperately to rally the suitors. Drawing his sword for perhaps the only time in his life, he calls on the others to "remember their war-craft" and join him a mad rush against Odysseus, holding up the table as a shield and hoping only to push him away from the door so they could escape. Yet, when this man of words utters a loud war cry and charges, nobody follows him and Eurymachus, shot through heart and liver, dies painfully.

The next to fall is the best of the suitors, Amphinomus. His intent too was to drive Odysseus from the door so the others could escape. But now Telemachus saves his father from having to kill the only suitor who treated him with a trace of respect. But at least he is killed honorably in battle. Telemachus then dashes off to the storeroom to bring body armor for Odysseus and the two loyal slaves. This arming of the slaves suggests surely that the prince was privy to the plans that were made in his absence.

Now the killing takes its course. This, one of the older parts of the tale, is as famed as the equally ancient fantastical elements of Odysseus' tales at Scheria; it must also be read in the same skeptical spirit. Although the details here are more realistic, we must never forget that the suitors were drunk, inexperienced, and leaderless; one also runs the risk of being seduced by Ares into ignoring the moral core of this story.

At one point in the battle, when Melanthius has armed the suitors and the odds against Odysseus have measurably lengthened to the point of making him fearful, Athena appears disguised as Mentor. But when Odysseus welcomes his old friend, Agelaos—a hitherto unmentioned suitor who has assumed leadership over them—threatens to kill him, despoil his possessions, and exile his family. These words suggest to us that the suitors cannot be forgiven, dispersed, or rehabilitated merely by the slaying of one or two of them. Unlike Agelaos, who hoped they could still terrorize Ithaca after slaying Odysseus, the changes Athena and Odysseus must introduce have to uproot anarchy and terror. An armed citizenry must replace the old order where the decadent nobles supposedly protected the peasants and citizens in exchange for absolute political power over them. As we noted, the line between piracy and protection is more porous than any prince would pretend.

This idea is explicated when Mentor, whom Odysseus knows to be Athena, refuses to provide the kind of divine madness that he would receive from Ares but instead reminds him that instead of fighting for fickle Helen, as he did for nine wasted years, he is defending family and home. In this sense, although she takes no direct part in the combat, Athena lights a fire in his soul that is far stronger than Ares' toxic fury. Unlike rage, which transports one out of oneself, courage is built on love and honor. It is only after this, when Odysseus has successfully recollected what he is fighting for, that Athena raises her deadly aegis and spreads panic amidst the last suitors. As they stampede like cattle maddened by a gadfly, the deadly vultures swoop down. The suitors' total lack of military prowess is displayed in their inability to inflict any more than token injuries on Odysseus and his men, even when they were armed. We see here the obsolescence of the military caste. The hardworking hoplite, fighting primarily in defense, will replace a lazy noble class that is incapable even of piracy.

Only a few men remain alive and they beg for mercy. Leodes, the first to try the bow, is mercilessly cut down despite his claim to have been nothing but their diviner. Odysseus points out that as the suitors' priest and prophet he must have prayed that Penelope's husband would never return. On the other hand, mercy is requested for the minstrel, Phemios, by Telemachus. The singer has explained that as he sings to both the gods and men, presumably of the exploits of each to the other, Odysseus would regret killing him. When the hero relents, sparing both Medon the herald and the bard, he instructs them to always proclaim the superiority of good over evil. We may infer from this privileging of poetry over both priesthood and prophecy that the gods value virtue and its transmission above the offering of sacrifices. Indeed it may even follow that since the poets mediate between gods and men, even the very gods themselves are improved and pleased by the tales told about them by poets to men. Finally, the poets also mediate between the heroes and the masses. This is after all the task that Odysseus sets herald and bard while he turns towards darker matters.

Until recently, the fate visited on the twelve pretty maids all strung up in a row has received only slightly more press than the eleven ships lost to the Laestrygonians. Today the matter is viewed differently. The bad maids may even be viewed as proto-feminists, strong women who took charge of their own sex lives. This outrage is said to reveal the patriarchal agenda pursued by Odysseus under the flimsy pretext of obeying Pallas Athena, that bluestocking traitor to her sex! He even states explicitly that the maids are being killed for their loyalty to Aphrodite. What could be clearer?

The truth here, insofar as there is an objective moral value attached to the facts, has to steer a course between the Charybdis of anachronistic indignation and the Scylla of pseudo-ancient realism. There is evidently something brutal and vicious about the way the twelve unwise maids are treated but it is equally clear that there are hard political issues here that militate against regarding these young women's lives as sacred. Let us first try to state the case in favor of their slaying: though Odysseus raged inwardly at the sight of the maids leaving the household on their midnight assignations, the real issue was their betrayal of Penelope. As witnessed by their being killed in her absence and her own story of the geese, the queen had brought them up with genuine affection and solicitude; as such, they were given chances that others of their kind never had. Their ingratitude pertained to real favors received in a time of need and turmoil. Also, while the maids were no military threat, they were certainly well acquainted with the secrets of the house; they could have stirred up trouble with the families of the men they consorted with. The critical issue seems to be the integrity of the household. In times where piracy was a normal way of gaining wealth, the only line of defense was the *oikos*. Once this is breached, when those one is trying to protect turn traitor, all traces of civilization vanish. We see how well Penelope defended her household even in her lord's absence; but this only made the maids' treachery seem worse. They were betraying Ithaca itself. We recall how even the Greek raiders at Troy built a wall to protect their own ships. Otherwise put, the chastity at issue was not sexual but analogous with moral integrity. The freedom of the maids mattered little beside the organic integrity of the royal household.

Finally, we must note how Odysseus responded to Eurykleia's whoop of jubilation upon seeing the slaughtered suitors. He makes it clear to her that this must not be a second Troy, where hubris rendered the victors repugnant to the gods. Even though his nurse is allowed to name those twelve who disrespected Penelope and herself, he strongly suggests that—like the suitors—these maids condemned themselves by their own impiety and disloyalty. It is not pious to delight in their just punishment. Like Shakespeare's Henry V at Agincourt, god's justice has won. He is not the victor.

The ultimate proof of this reading of the episode of the maids must be found in the reception that the gory and begrimed Odysseus receives from the other women of his household. They greet him with tears of joy, bearing torches, and showering him with kisses. They treat him like a general who has relieved a long siege at the point when some people in the beleaguered city had been reduced to eating human flesh. Yet we cannot discount the possibility that their gratitude was also for his mercy. Simply put, he becomes their savior on account of his not having killed them as well.

Book 23

A chortling Eurykleia runs, faster than her aged limbs can carry her, to Penelope's bedside. Her dreams have come true. Odysseus has returned and killed the suitors who plagued *his* house, consumed *his* property, and humiliated *his* son. We note *en passant* that there is no mention made here of his queen's rights or interests; to his gloating nurse, all that matters is Odysseus' ascendancy; we recall Telemachus using her to keep the secret of his trip abroad from Penelope. She is still very much alone to the extent that this triumphant warlord, his nurse's avenger, has returned to ride roughshod over the quotidian realities that she lived amidst over his long absence. In other words, even if Eurykleia is the fury of the house and Telemachus is Orestes, Penelope is certainly no Clytemnestra. But Aeschylus does help us to read this book.

When we last saw Penelope she was being expelled, weeping, from the great hall by Telemachus; he had taken charge of the bow, thus apparently frustrating the artful plan she had hatched for the defeat of the suitors. She did not know that father and son were in collusion; this was why she argued so well for the stranger to be given the bow. Penelope must surely have been very frustrated by her son's petulance. By trying to assert himself, he had seemingly botched the springing of her strategem. It could not have been her expectation that Odysseus planned to kill all of the suitors; she must have supposed that once the stranger humbled them all, revealed himself and dispatched a few of the ringleaders, the rest would speedily disperse. The queen herself could have asked someone like Amphinomus to guide this withdrawal. Here we must recall Penelope's story of her dream about the eagle and her geese; while she subtly asked him to show mercy, he promised that Odysseus would kill all the suitors. We can imagine a similar difference of opinion over the best way to punish her disloyal maids; it is quite possible that the geese were the maids, not the suitors.

Surfacing abruptly from deep sleep, perhaps similar to that divine slumber known by Odysseus on his final voyage to Ithaca, the queen is now as discombobulated and suspicious as her husband was upon being told that he was finally home. Penelope responds to Eurykleia with irritation and disbelief. While her annoyance could have had to do with being awoken so rudely and may reveal her hidden dislike of the old harridan, the queen's disbelief pertains to the improbability of what she has just heard. Although she knows quite well that the stranger was Odysseus, she cannot see how he could have single-handedly slain all the suitors. It is far more likely that Eurykleia, having recognized Odysseus last night, is prematurely declaring victory. The situation still seems too dangerous for Penelope to disclose all that she knows; feigning total disbelief, the queen declares the nurse crazy and asks her to go away.

It is only after Eukyleia reveals that Telemachus had been operating in close collaboration with his father for a long time that Penelope lets her guard drop. She asks her how Odysseus accomplished the impossible task of fighting the collective body of suitors. Now the nurse admits that since the maids were locked out of the hall she neither saw nor heard how this triumph of the one over the many was achieved; she only saw the end result, battle-spattered Odysseus standing like a lion amidst piles of dead men. The jubilant nurse coveys his request that Penelope come down to share in his triumph; she congratulates them on the joy that has come after much sorrow.

The queen cautions the nurse, inadvertently echoing Odysseus' own warning against glorying overmuch in this victory. She refuses to believe the story as Eurykleia has told it, preferring to believe that one of the gods has punished the suitors for their hubris; further, as much she would love to welcome Odysseus, she fears that he lost himself long ago, far away from home. Just as Autolycus frustrated Eurykleia when she tried to feed him a name of her choice for his grandchild, now Penelope refuses to experience the emotion that her husband's nurse is asking her to feel. Even when the nurse chides her for her ever-mistrustful heart, citing as definitive proof his scar, Penelope still refuses to believe that Odysseus has returned, pointing out that the gods could work greater wonders than a clever nurse. Yet she does agree to go down to see her son, and so also observe her dead suitors and the man who killed them.

When Penelope enters the hall, her heart in turmoil as she ponders how to act, she finally sits by the hearth across the hall from where Odysseus sits by a pillar looking down. Each waits for the other to make the first move. Penelope looks for signs of the man she lost to the war twenty years ago and Odysseus, as is his wont, withholds disclosure of himself; he is very much in *outis* mode and she is as skeptical as ever. It is Telemachus who breaks the silence. He urges his hard-hearted mother to go up to Odysseus and ask him questions about all he suffered over those twenty long years. It does not occur to the youth that his mother endured equal difficulties, albeit not of her own choosing, over these very years. She responds to her son, declaring herself to be filled with wonder and quite unable to speak to this man or look him in the eye. Yet she assures her son that Odysseus and she, should this be he, have their own ways, their own secret signs of recognizing each other. By this very declaration Penelope is obviously challenging him to identify himself by revealing more than either his known physical qualities, or his being-for-itself, his uncanny *outis* aspect. Further, since Odysseus and Penelope both know that they have already recognized each other in private, the queen is demanding something else. She even refuses to take the bait when Odysseus mockingly accuses her of disliking him for his ragged clothing. What she seeks is neither elusive inner essence nor protean appearance; he can become Odysseus for glorious deeds but can he stay true to himself and her?

Penelope reiterates this point when Odysseus returns after his bath, after Eurynome has dressed him in fine clothing and Athena has enhanced his height, hair, and heft, to make him look like an immortal. When he then accuses her of being the most hard-hearted woman alive for refusing to receive him after twenty years of suffering and indignantly asks his nurse to make him up a bed, she resolutely contends that she knows very well how Odysseus looked when he left Ithaca, presumably the effect that Athena has created. This to her is but further evidence that he is not Odysseus. She calls for Eurykleia to bring out the bed that her master built with his own hands; in a sense that becomes clearer later, she suggests that he belongs more to Eurykleia than to herself. It was, after all, to his nurse that he first identified himself explicitly.

These words cause Odysseus to blink first. He indignantly asks her how it would be possible for this bed to be moved; only a god could move a bed that was part of the very structure of his palace. One of its four posts was a living olive tree that he had skillfully built their bedchamber around. This secret was not known to Eurykleia; only Penelope's old nursemaid knew it. It is now that Penelope finally gives in. Or perhaps it could be the other way around; in other words, the real question is not whether the stranger is not quantitatively identical to Odysseus. It is not sufficient to say to Penelope, as he did to Telemachus—who had never met his father—that this was the only Odysseus he would get. Penelope would not accept a polytropic man who would demand of her that she receive him in whatever mode he happened to assume; she wanted the man the gods took away from her when he went to evil-ium.

This means that she does not want Odysseus as Ares, or even as Ares beautified for Aphrodite; his insatiable wife is only appeased when he becomes truly himself, by winning the most difficult duel of his life to win his Helen from the house where she is being held. But this battle is not won by killing the suitors, as strange Penelope has just shown him; rather it is by knowing the secret of the bed in the proper way, by recollecting this fact in the very spirit of loving jealousy in which the bed was built, that Odysseus regains his wife. It is only now that he truly vanquishes his evil other, the anti-nous who would have possessed this knowledge and yet been unable to deploy it in the right manner. In other words, it is not the secret of the bed that wins the recognition of Penelope; Odysseus must perform something more difficult, a deed that even Athena herself could not bring about, any more than she could have brought him home from the underworld of Ares and Aphrodite; our hero must now abandon all masks and divine powers, just as Prospero drowned his book, and thus become himself.

He can no longer be anti-nous or nobody. It is not enough for him to slay all his enemies; he must resume full possession of his own soul. For this to occur he must do what he anticipated that day in the court of Alcinous; he must slay Ulysses. This is why he weeps; like those Trojan slaves who once shed tears for kind Patroclus but most truly mourned themselves, he cries bitterly over the identity he thereby renounces before his clear-eyed wife. In this sense they are really one mind; only Penelope understands the true reason behind these tears. Her iron heart has its own reasons for weeping. The lovers must struggle upstream against the flow of their own tears; worse, each must swim with recognition of why the other weeps.

When Penelope confessed her fear that another man would deceive her, she did not simply mean that someone else could have convinced her that he was Odysseus; this is made clearer when she claims that Helen would never have acted as she did were it not for a goddess introducing this awful passion into her heart. Penelope accepts the power of the gods but piously leaves unsaid her knowledge of their impotence; the gods cannot un-will what they have made of us, even though they can punish us for repudiating them in the sense that the after-effects of their terrible love cannot easily be overcome by a hubristic human soul. Well aware that the gods work by inflaming our passions rather than deceiving our mind, the queen fears being drawn to someone as artful and eloquent as Odysseus; we could call this phantasm what would simulate his intemperate aspect anti-nous. Indeed, worst of all, this could even be Odysseus himself! This is also why she is as anxious to ascertain that her Odysseus is not lost to himself as surely as her cousin was when she became Helen of Troy. Just as Helen is now held hostage by this role and is forced to play it as endlessly as the damned in Hades, the wife of Odysseus feared that he could not revert back from his alternate identity as *outis* or anti-nous. Although Athena could help him sustain his true identity, he must desire it for itself. This can only really come about through his love for Penelope; by playing hard to get, his queen reminds him of why he loved her. We recall the limited extent of the help Athena gave him during the fight with the suitors; rather than turning him into Bellona's bridegroom, she merely reminds Odysseus of what he is fighting for. His courage must be born of love. Its basis is proved by the riddle of the bed. He can still re-collect who he is. It is this show of potency that separates him from those shipwrecked by their hubris;

we must also not forget that this is how virgin Athena acts. She does not rape the mind.

The final act of Odysseus' reconciliation with Penelope occurs after they have wept in each other's arms. Homer compares them to survivors of a shipwreck, and we must appreciate the implied equation of Odysseus' adventures at sea and his wife's equally heroic exertions on land; while he struggled with himself and Eurylochus, she had to outwit Anti-nous and Eurymachus. Her struggle to hold his household together was just as desperate as those he faced in his many years abroad. This is why Penelope is quick to respond to Odysseus' claim that Tiresias required him to undertake another arduous labor; she demands disclosure of what the gods had put in *his* mind. Then, upon being told that Odysseus had to go on another long land journey and sacrifice to Poseidon before returning to a sleek old age, she contented herself with saying that at least the prophecy predicted an end to his troubles. Although the queen successfully deployed the image of an idealized Odysseus to hold his kingdom together, she knows full well that this figure is not real, In Nietzsche's terms, she has just seen her Apollonian Odysseus reveal his ugly Dionysian side; yet wise Penelope has not forgotten that his name isn't "much prayed for," it is trouble.

While any interpretation of Odysseus' exploits that denies their literal truth has to account for this divinely mandated mission, it is sufficient to assume that this trip has to do with making amends for some previous act of injustice; this perhaps was what was commanded by the oracle of Zeus at Dodona. It is not clear if the principal offended party is Poseidon or if some human victims are also involved. Perhaps he will commemorate the eleven ship's crews supposedly lost to the Laestrygonians. Further, just as his spared herald and minstrel were commanded to tell each other that the good is always to be chosen over evil, we may also infer that he, like Homer himself, will take this moral tale to landlocked areas that have never seen ships or known piracy. Eva Brann argues convincingly that this oar he will set up will be a monument to his former self; the Ulysses aspect we have separated from what came home. Thus, like the winnowing fan, the good and bad aspects of his psyche may finally be split and virtuous activity will be seen to triumph over hubristic vice; in other words, his poetic side will win out over his wanton appetite to be Ares. This triumph of the lyre over the bow marks the beginning of true civilization. The lyre must not be enslaved to the bow, doomed to sing only in praise of rage and death. It will defeat the sword and become the chief means by which men will be civilized. Homer will be the educator of Greece by singing of Athena rehabilitating Odysseus.

After Penelope has told him of her struggles against the suitors, Odysseus delights her with his tales of the sufferings he visited on others and the pain he brought on himself. We could hardly suppose that he would have told her of his many years as a mercenary or slave in Egypt or Cyprus, if this was the truth; the confession of his mad addiction to Ares and Aphrodite, a disease far worse than mere Lotus-eating, would only confirm Penelope's worst suspicions as to the past and misgivings about the future. His official story had to be that wife and son were "always on his mind"; that he was ceaselessly battling Poseidon and working his way back home to Ithaca. Only thus could an account of his sufferings also give his wife delight. Otherwise put, he is re-collecting the meaning of his Odyssey and not dredging up the literal truth. He also knows that his wife is well aware of this distinction; they have quite recently communicated by deciphering lying signs when honest speech would have suicidal. This is the only Odysseus, and the only confession, his wife can truly hope to receive; she is his equal in suspicion and prudence. While they both know the might of the gods, each is equally well aware of the other's powers of resilience and recollection.

We also note that Odysseus has owned up to his involuntary dalliance with Calypso. It is prudent to honor the gods as they accost us; by denying them we only run the risk of having our souls invaded. It was only in this way that Circe became Calypso. By contrast, Odysseus' incontinent shipmates were turned from pigs into cannibals; we can imagine them killing Circe's once-human beasts to slake their insatiate greed. It is noteworthy that the suitors underwent a similar metamorphosis; the beggar's reduction of Irus to a speechless beast entertained the suitors as much as the slaying of the great stag, once probably a human too, gave heart to Odysseus' craven crew. If this line of mythology is followed, Odysseus' crew slaughtered Circe's beasts, despite her explicit warnings, while he himself was enchanted by the goddess's siren songs of the dead; then, trying madly to escape, these guilty men were slain by Zeus while Odysseus was doomed to long exile in the no longer welcome arms of Circe/Calypso. Of course, the literal truth of these events is easily mapped onto the traumatized way the Ithacan veterans moved from desolated Ilium to raid Ismaros and/or Egypt before being led by drink, bloodlust, and folly to outstay their "welcome," perform unspeakable atrocities, and then inevitably meet up with defeat, disgrace, and death. It could even be the case that the curious Circe episode was Odysseus' channeling of Penelope's story instead of his own humiliating tenure as a slave in Egypt or Cyprus.

It is also possible that Odysseus told his wife the whole truth, a story as bald and ugly as his unadorned head and body. Although we are told what was supposed to have taken place in his bed, it cannot be denied that what happens in a bedroom is often best left there. Simply put, just as sex is where the surging dreams of the spirit are transposed into the body's lower key of necessity, it was here that Odysseus felt free to unburden himself of the dark truths his body had kept from his glib tongue. Only Penelope could truly have felt what he had undergone; only she would know why he could barely trust himself to speak his own name. Those who have had been loved by the gods know their true power. They share in the laconic fraternity of men cursed with double vision or second sight. They never finish each other's sentences.

This is why it is unlikely that Athena actually suspended the duration of the night so her hero could sing of his exploits; by drawing attention to the impossibility of this miracle before breakfast, Homer is making the truth clearer. As we have seen, there are few actual impossibilities left when Odysseus' treasures are brought ashore; the only real miracle is the storyteller. Simply put, Odysseus had all the time he needed to be debriefed by his wife; just as long sagas in dreamtime fit neatly, if impossibly, into a few minutes of clock time, so too does Penelope apprehend the whole truth.

When Odysseus awakens the next day, he draws distinctions between household, city, and kingdom that Telemachus could not have discerned, and indeed would not be made explicit until the time of Aristotle. First, after seeming to disparage the time she spent weeping for him while he battled Zeus and the gods to return home, he entrusts his household to her. Meanwhile he will set about replenishing his flocks, some by raiding and others by receiving gifts from the Achaeans. Though his words suggest that Odysseus is about to resume his old habits of piracy, it is also possible that he speaks metaphorically. We have already seen how easily men are turned into swine; it was indeed in this respect that Athena showed Odysseus that Eumaeus was his better. Now the new regime where Odysseus will treat swineherd and cowherd as brothers of his son could distinguish between natural slaves in need of mastery and those who show themselves to be "well born" by their self-mastery and power to rule beasts successfully. These natural rulers will govern those who, like the suitors, have a propensity to turn themselves into swine; the Achaeans who cannot follow his winged words must fill Eumaeus' pens. This will be the first school of Hellas. The initial self-ostracism of Odysseus allows a new order to be born within Ithaca—a mixed regime where Penelope, Telemachus, and Eumaeus have their distinct roles. While this regime does not have to reckon with his overwhelming presence in the city or household, he will serve as the formidable guardian of its limits. This gives Penelope the symbolic presence of Odysseus and the freedom to rule his homestead; he has given his wife her own space and granted himself the chance to fully regain her love.

But before all these things can come to pass, there is still the matter of the relatives of the suitors and their furious rage at Odysseus' latest exploit. Our hero accordingly takes his leave of Penelope, acknowledging her own wisdom but strongly urging her to stay still, keep silent, and take refuge in deniability until all is resolved. While he does not doubt her ability to handle the situation, especially now that the suitors have been slain, it is best that her complicity in their killing should never be known. Then, in the worst case, it would yet be possible for Penelope to use Circe's strategy.

Book 24

While Odysseus leaves the palace to meet his father and rescue him from the shady bower of depression Laertes had built for himself since the loss of his wife and son, the suitors' shades are taken down to Hades by Hermes. Here we find vindication of Odysseus' killing of the suitors and even anticipation of Aeschylus' famous dictum that man only learns by suffering. The story of this man of many sorrows shows us how the crooked lines of his fate bring great good to both Odysseus and his people when they are re-aligned by Athena and seen again from the right or just angle.

Laertes' name means "gatherer of the people" but it is Hermes whom we first see acting in this capacity when he collects the souls of the suitors and leads them into Hades. Their pathetic souls, which we have already glimpsed sight of through the prophetic eyes of Theoclymenos, are now delivered from the wine and dissipation that gave them a false belief in their seemingly grandiose collective identity. Filled now with awful but belated self-knowledge, they now swarm together like poor blind bats, indelibly imaged as they were in the hour of severance from their flesh.

Meanwhile, in Hades, Homer lets us listen in on a sad exchange between two shades, heroes who famously failed to achieve happy returns from the Trojan War. The one, Agamemnon, was rejected by his own wife and the other, Achilles, was immolated by his own rage after it made him betray the one he loved most. Though the quarrel between Achilles and Agamemnon was the central event of the *Iliad*, it is now long forgotten; they now converse with each other over their respective funerals. It is clear that the myth of Achilles' mortality in the heel most truly pertains to his own inability to "stick the landing" in the sense of returning to his own humanity. Now in death, falling after being elevated to divine heights by his mother's prayers and the plans of Zeus, he needs to be constantly told by others that he had the finest funeral. Strikingly, there is little talk of the glory they supposedly gained in the Trojan War. We recall Odysseus's report that Achilles now prefers life at any cost over *kleos*. But in spite of this, there is never any word of regret for the terrible bloodshed at Troy.

It would appear that both war heroes are trapped in time-loops, neverending AA meetings where they continually relive traumatic events from their last days alive. Their self-centeredness means that they can never really learn anything from their own stories or the lives of others; this is why these two great men from the *Iliad* are shockingly found to be much like the suitors of Penelope. Once the quest for lovely Helen is seen to be identical to the pursuit of rich Penelope, the Brazen Age is over. Just as the suitors do not express any true regret for invading Odysseus' home, the older generation of Trojan warriors hardly left them an example of virtue to follow.

When Agamemnon, echoing Nestor's earlier equation between raiding and trading, asks Amphimedon "two-thoughts" if this seemingly fine company of Achaeans was killed rustling cattle or besieging a city, he is clearly not making a value judgment. The inference that they did not die defending a citadel could be attributed to their all being men of fighting age; there are no elders, women, or children in their group. It is also noteworthy that the twelve disloyal maids did not go to Hades with them; even though there are many other women in Hades, their opportunism is seen differently. Bluntly put, like the Trojan warriors, the suitors may have acted more voluntarily. It is also noteworthy to recall Agamemnon's recollection that Odysseus resisted the demand that he join the Trojan expedition for over a month; in this sense he is quite unlike Achilles, who we found out from Agamemnon in the *Iliad* signed up because he actually loved strife, war, and battles. The high king was merely a war profiteer.

If the equation of the suitors with the rescuers of Helen exposes the hollowness of one pretext for war, the tone of Amphimedon removes another. Far from raging in fury and demanding that their killer be slain in turn, the spokesman for the suitors is pathetic even in death; all he wishes is what Odysseus has already allowed, that his body be properly washed and mourned. The Furies do not demand blood; as we saw, blood must be shed in Hades before the dead can even speak to us again. If Homer's two accounts are to be believed, they are self-contained in their self-pity; the gods have no power over their souls. Gods cannot see themselves reflected in dead souls.

As the hapless Amphimedon tells the tale, the suitors began courting Penelope once Odysseus had been absent over six years after the fall of Troy. He explains how she used the excuse of weaving a shroud for Laertes to delay them for three more years until one of her maids revealed the secret. Then they forced her to finish her work; this suggests that it was now that the conflict between the coy queen and the suitors became explicit. It is only when Penelope has exhausted her Circe-like wiles, that "some evil spirit" brings Odysseus home; in other words, this is when Athena is able to enter the picture. Just as the goddess needed Odysseus to cry out in prayer to the gods before she could help him, so too does she need Penelope to expressly reject her wooers. The very gifts that Penelope derived from Athena to finish her shroud, a awesome masterpiece of weaving "that shone like the sun or the moon," are now used against the suitors; the young fools find they are but flies caught in the terrible web jointly woven by gods and mortals. Amphimedon thought that Odysseus put the idea of the bow in Penelope's head; he also does not see that it was Athena who orchestrated Odysseus' restoration. Once Penelope and Odysseus gave up their dour existential autonomy and worked alongside her, the suitors' goose was cooked.

But we cannot entirely discount the possibility that Eumaeus could have played second fiddle in the overthrow of the suitors had Odysseus not cried out to Pallas Athena. In other words, the swineherd's banishment from the palace was an error; the gods are not ruled by human morality. Athena is only scandalized by lust or stupidity.

But Amphimedon is not alone in failing to recognize the hand of the goddess in this temporal symmetry. Agamemnon congratulates Odysseus and praises Penelope but fails to either honor the justice of the gods or grasp its necessary belatedness. Maybe this explains both his location and misery. Even Agamemnon's happiness at his old friend's triumph is short-lived; its deepest significance for him has to do with the untarnished virtue of Penelope. He soon falls back on the familiar refrain of cursing his wife. For him, all women, even the best, will be hated because of Clytemnestra. As long as he is trapped in his self-pity, whatever solace the dead have will never be available to him. He is too attached to his rage to drink the water of Lethe and forget. This could well be the punishment of all the other Trojan War veterans; they are too bound to divine rage to look beyond themselves for the grace to escape this trauma; as with Ajax, prideful resentment becomes its own punishment. No god needed here.

Meanwhile, in Ithaca, Odysseus is preparing for another journey into almost mythic space. He is preparing to meet another man, one who is bent on punishing himself for sins not unconnected to the Trojan War. This journey must be undertaken alone. While a god was needed to take Odysseus into the garden realm of Circe, the same Hermes is now with the dead suitors in Hades. While Hermes helped Priam to cross enemy lines and negotiate with Achilles, in the moving conclusion to the *Iliad* where Achilles saw that the Trojan king much resembled his old father, he must not come between Odysseus and his actual father. Here the great gods can do nothing. Laertes banished himself to his country estate shortly after the death of his wife and he has remained there ever since. The wretched old man divorced himself entirely from the desperate political situation of Ithaca and lives as poorly as a field slave, concerning himself solely with agricultural matters; indeed it is Eumaeus, and not Laertes, who even functions as Telemachus' surrogate father. If Odysseus is to be blamed for his long absence, surely his father must be held just as culpable for his internal exile?

Laertes' involuntary absence becomes even more inexplicable when we hear later, from his own lips, that he was a soldier and military leader; it is also not as though he was the opposite of his restless and curious son; indeed Laertes is said to have been one of the original Argonauts. It is more plausible to argue that the father feels guilt for those aspects of his own psyche that he passed on to his son; Laertes may have been the opposite of cautious Antikleia (against glory) and drawn to bold acts rather than the crafty way with words Odysseus inherited from his Sisyphean side. Freed from the restraining influence of his mother, which civilized Laertes and made him into a more bucolic figure, it is possible that Odysseus expressed his sire's vices; in this context it is relevant to recall that although it is said that Laertes was much drawn to Odysseus' nurse Eurykleia, and favored her as much as his wife, he did not lay hands on her for fear of Antikleia's anger. This opposition between Eury-kleia (wide glory) and Anti-kleia could be the key to the souls of both father and son. Eurykleia, who advocated the slaying of the maids, was the wet nurse of Odysseus. We recall also that it was Eurykleia to whom Telemachus confided the secret of his voyage abroad; by contrast, he blames Penelope for treating him like an adolescent. This could also be why Laertes does not live with Eurykleia; it is part of his penance. It was Eurykleia who fed Odysseus tales of glory that were as mother's milk to him; this also explains his being drawn to ageless mother figures like Circe and Calypso. In a sense, both father and son chose to hide (kalyptein) from reality in archetypes. Stranger yet, if the Cretan tales of the beggar are to be believed, both Odysseus and Laertes seem to have spent the last eight years or so doing the work of slaves. It is as though Laertes somehow sensed his son's plight and worked beside him in spirit. Yet, just as Menelaus cannot admit that he was unable to satisfy his wife, it would be just as fatal for Odysseus to acknowledge having been a slave; even the betrayal or surrender of his army would pale in comparison to this ultimate disgrace.

Further support for this claim comes when we recall Menelaus' tale about Odysseus, hidden in the Trojan Horse, stifling his comrade Anti-Clus when Helen is led to impersonate the voices of their loved ones. In other words, the voice of Antikleia has to be silenced for Odysseus to undertake his greatest feat, the sack of Troy. We recall again that it was this same Menelaus who then accompanies him to the house of the equally suggestively named Diophobos where Helen was held. Scripture famously tells us that the beginning of wisdom is the fear of God; here Odysseus slays the fear of God after subduing his mother's voice warning him away from paths of glory.

Laertes is the first freeborn Ithacan to whom Odysseus will introduce himself. Up to this point he has mostly had dealings with foreign-born slaves. This is significant because his father also seems to have passed into chthonic space; like Saturn, he has left human history and entered a pre-fallen agrarian realm of nature and life. It is for this reason that Odysseus relinquishes his weapons before meeting his father but, in a sense, it is also as if he is being reunited with the very spirit of Ithaca itself. None of the slaves, indeed not even Penelope herself, has this deep link to the soil; it is to the land itself that Odysseus must apologize for the many Ithacan men he lost at sea. This is distinct from the many political and familial issues he has dealt with so far.

We now have a better sense of the deep guilt and other associated emotions felt by Odysseus as he approaches his aged father. For this reason, it is no wonder that he decides to "test" Laertes, instead of giving in to the powerful impulse to embrace him. Just as Laertes is closely examining the roots of a plant he is moving, so too does Odysseus wish to avoid a superficially sentimental reunion and instead ascertain how the sad old man really feels about his prodigal child. He thus initiates speech by asking Laertes to explain his unkempt appearance amidst his well-cared orchard and then pointedly inquiring whether or not this was Ithaca. Apart from supporting our earlier claim about what Laertes represents, Odysseus' query also provides his father with two connected opportunities to link the questions by talking of his son.

Then, as if too impatient for a reply, Odysseus says he is seeking the son of Laertes of Ithaca. He claims to have given hospitality to this unnamed man and asks if his guest, whom he slyly claims to have loved more than any visitor, is back or in Hades. The old man breaks down in tears, telling his visitor that his destination is under the rule of violent reckless men he yet asks who he is and how long ago it was since he met his ill-fated son. When Odysseus, lying fluently, says that it has been five years, this causes Laertes to break down completely in grief; he ignores his visitor's claim that all the auguries were good when Odysseus left. It is only now, as his groaning father pours black dust over himself, that his wily guest sees fit to reveal himself.

Odysseus, still not voicing his name, but addressing Laertes as father, now identifies himself as the man he asked for; he's back to the land of his father, the very dark soil that Laertes has been pouring over himself, after twenty years. Telling Laertes that he killed the suitors and avenged their evils, Odysseus suggests they have little time to waste. But when his father, undeterred by this urgency, asks for an unmistakable sign, our hero first reveals his scar and then proceeds to number and name all the trees and vines his father gave him. Now Laertes believes that the man before him is his son. The combination of physical proof with the clear memory of a cherished moment from the past convinces him. Odysseus' way of testing before trusting was a further sign; long-suffering Laertes is freed to return his lost son's close embrace. As with Penelope, the right memory was chosen and recalled with the proper emotion. They are performative acts in that Odysseus becomes himself by these recollections.

Both Laertes and Odysseus are qualitatively transformed by their reconciliation. In effect, both recover their full identities; the father is no longer Anti-kleia and the son ceases to be ruled by the desire for Eury-kleia. We see the old king become aware of the risk that the suitors' kin would seek revenge against Odysseus, but even more importantly, he finds that he can believe in the Olympian gods again. His heartfelt words, "Father Zeus, there are gods indeed on high Olympus" indicate that Laertes is willing to leave the sanctuary of the nature deities and proclaim the goodness of the Olympian pantheon; he renounces the view that the gods are to blame for our woes.

Odysseus meanwhile, by being embraced by his earth-begrimed father, has regained his connection to Ithaca itself. This gives him the legitimacy to confront the suitors' relatives and speak authoritatively about their future and common good. The new regime that seems to be suggested by his actions will now be endorsed by tradition. It will be as though Laertes will be head of state, literally serving as "gatherer of the people" or the unifying principle when the virtuous slaves are brought into the polis. This structure will be stable enough to endure during the next absence of Odysseus; we can imagine how oligarchs like Telemachus could interact with decent freedmen. This community is shown in the republican "common meal" Odysseus, Telemachus, and Laertes enjoy with the cowherd, swineherd, and the remaining family of Dolios. It seems to matter little that two disloyal members of this family have just been put to death. This striking but unnoted fact seems to exemplify the true political spirit.

Meanwhile, in striking contrast to the healthy commonwealth that we have seen sitting down to dinner, rumor has convened an assembly of Ithacans dominated by relatives of the dead suitors. Eupeithes, father of Antinous, speaks on behalf of these "best and brightest" and demands revenge on Odysseus before he takes ship. Not content with losing his Trojan contingent, Odysseus then returned to kill the best of the next generation. Eupeithes, as persuasive as his child, claims that he would be disgraced if these crimes were not avenged. He would sooner die than live in shame.

The next speaker, Medon, warns the townspeople that Odysseus was acting with the support of the gods. He describes the events in the hall and tells how an immortal resembling Mentor helped rout the suitors. These words fill the people with raw fear but their effect is curiously dispelled when Halitherses, the old prophet, speaks. He reminds the many that they were to blame for the many wrongs of the suitors and urges them not to intervene further. But these words only cause more than half of those present to spring up and take arms. Homer reports that these words did not please them and we must surmise that mob assemblies of this kind are not moved by moral language. If anything, Halitherses' assertion that they too were guilty only leads them to defy the gods and prophets. As was the case when Telemachus came before the assembly, these Ithacans seem to be resentful towards the gods; ruled only by physical fear and family values, they refuse to believe in divine providence. The striking contrast between these two assemblies cannot be exaggerated. It sums up the vital distinction between politics, where men deliberate over what is just and beautiful, and human unions implicitly based on blood-ties, shamelessness, or greed. It cannot be the case that humans can only be ruled by the second set of criteria.

This, however, is the question Athena seems to ask Zeus, when the action of our tale shifts abruptly back to Olympus. She inquires if Zeus would first inflict fighting and strife or whether he would reconcile the two factions. In other words, do the bad old ways of the *Iliad* where the gods ruled evil through strife apply, or have the values of the beginning of the *Odyssey*, where Zeus mourns the ways men blame the gods for their self-inflicted wounds, superseded them? The king of the gods tells Athena that his mind is in accordance with hers; there is no hidden agenda behind his changed ways. He desires that the justice dealt by Odysseus be followed by reconciliation; it is also best that the son of Laertes should be king for life. No mention is made here of Telemachus; Odysseus will rule over a transitional regime that will be succeeded by one where merit and virtue will rule. Blind Homer foresees the rise of Athens.

These plans are put in motion when the palace party sets out to face the rebels. We see here anticipated the difference that marked the Greek from the Persians; though heavily outnumbered, Odysseus' men fight freely for the common good. Their foes are ruled by guilt and resentment. The battle itself is brief. Guided by Athena, that sturdy farm laborer Laertes sends a spear clean through the helm of vile Eupeithes; then Odysseus and Telemachus fall upon the ranks of the suitors' relatives. They would have finished them all off, we recall that father and son had just previously been goading each other to greater valor to Laertes' delight, had not Athena—clad once more as Mentor—commands the Ithacans to stop fighting in a terrifying voice.

Filled with great fear they drop their weapons. Many turn around and break for the city. Only Odysseus, unafraid, pounces down after them like the very eagle of Zeus he had previously been likened to. Now Zeus himself sends down a thunderbolt at Athena's feet and she then warns Odysseus against angering Zeus. It is as though she herself had become identical with her hero and needed Zeus to separate their souls. While we recall the previous thunderbolt that struck Odysseus' ship at Thrinacia, we also note ruefully that enraged Odysseus had regressed to his old ways, falling on his fleeing enemies—like Achilles or even Zeus—before the newer law of the gods restrains him. We also see that since these very gods only changed their ways and gained self-knowledge by seeing their images in man, human passion and divine order are inextricably connected. It seems that the very imperfection of a mortal hero serves as the means by which the gods gain their more secure self-knowledge; by this, they will then be able to inspire and evoke the fullest potential of our souls.

Our story ends with Athena/Mentor bringing the two sides together. As pledges of friendship override old grudges, peace and abundant prosperity is promised for all. Yet, far more importantly, we also detect the promise of reconciliation between men and gods. This joint denial of the closely linked concepts of divine arbitrariness and human incorrigibility is the most valuable lesson hidden in the *Odyssey*. This means that human virtue is possible. While refusing the siren's lure of divine perfection, we also see how humans can help one another, by love and friendship, and make a good life possible. Both politics and religion must advance this end of human flourishing. A positive view of the soul's erotic powers for wondering and wandering can free us from falsely divinized idols of cave, caste, or creed. Boldly put, only when men can trust themselves enough to accept grace, admit to imperfection, and seek friendship will they be freed to echo Laertes' cry, "There are gods indeed on high Olympus!"

This will not happen immediately; while Odysseus' account of his wanderings, as told to Penelope, will suffice for the moment, the other story that was related to Eumaeus will slowly percolate through the Antikleia-educated imagination of the noble swineherd. It is this tale, midwifed through the genius of Homer, that will ultimately albeit unconsciously animate the birth of Western Civilization in Athens.